EDUCATION IN A COMPETITIVE AND GLOBALIZING WORLD



# DISTANCE AND FLEXIBLE EDUCATION APPLYING ICT FOR AN INNOVATIVE AND OPEN LEARNING

# Education in a Competitive and Globalizing World

Additional books in this series can be found on Nova's website under the Series tab.

Additional E-books in this series can be found on Nova's website under the E-books tab.

EDUCATION IN A COMPETITIVE AND GLOBALIZING WORLD

# DISTANCE AND FLEXIBLE EDUCATION APPLYING ICT FOR AN INNOVATIVE AND OPEN LEARNING

BEATRIZ FAINHOLC

**Nova Science Publishers, Inc.**
*New York*

For permission to use material from this book please contact us:
Telephone 631-231-7269; Fax 631-231-8175
Web Site: http://www.novapublishers.com



**LIBRARY OF CONGRESS CATALOGING-IN-PUBLICATION DATA**

*Distance and flexible education applying ICT for an innovative and open learning / editor, Beatriz Fainholc.*
*p. cm.*
*Includes index.*
*ISBN 978-1-61761-852-9 (softcover)*
*1. Distance education--Computer-assisted instruction. 2. Distance education--Social aspects. 3. Information technology--Social aspects. 4. Communication technology--Social aspects. I. Fainholc, Beatriz.*
*LC5803.C65.D52 2010*
*371.3'58--dc22*

*2010033109*

*Published by Nova Science Publishers, Inc. + New York*

# CONTENTS

# INTRODUCTION

The chapters of this book explore and identify, from the perspective of distance education with the use of ICT, some theoretical-practical contributions for an educational, phenomenological, critical, and contextualized practice, in order to analyze and understand the new phenomena of the electronic online tele-educational modalities that have reached their peak in the twenty-first century.

Why is the practice of sociological thought of interest in distance education ?

Because it is adventurous to bet on a "real transparency" of the processes and factors involved in the educational programs we are dealing with in the information and knowledge society, since most of the time, they demand demystification.

What does the practice of sociological thought mean in distance education?

It involves realizing that these programs appear as "produced artifices" which require greater reflectivity to be truly understood, if the goal is to overcome the linear idea that states that in order to explain and to understand any sociocultural achievement of social institutions and organizations, in our case, of the above-mentioned projects, it would be enough to compare the stated intentions and objectives with the products obtained.

This idea is supported on functionalist lines of thought and common sense, which constitute simplifying, mechanical, and technocratic positions, when thinking that the constitution or change of institutions, occurs by decree or supported in the illusion of a spontaneous sociological evolutionism. The central focus of what is concrete and unpredictable of the multiple historical, -past and present -, and cultural determinations is yet unknown in the construction of social phenomena.

A sociology of distance education with ICT cannot ramble, - although, regrettably, it continues doing so- between the enunciation of social theory/ies without contrast, and empirical data without theoretical support and guidance, at the risk of resorting to poor and limited interpretations and images with regard to the socio-historical, educational, and cultural explanations and, therefore, without deepening knowledge, disciplinary research, and the improvement of practice.

Thus, Chapter 1- is dedicated to the sociological reflection of education and distance education with ICT and the sociocultural aspects of the information and knowledge society where education programs mediated by technology are inscribed.

In this framework of a new social and economic order, the expansion, generation, and circulation of digital information, based on global electronic telematics, show how technology drivesfar-reaching changes in the anthropological, epistemological, and educational dimensions of culture and society.

The practice of a sociological view of distance education requieres various inputs to explore the intimate relationship between technology and ideology, culture and society as inseparable facets of the same phenomenon, or to put it another way, the lack of neutrality of the technology with regard to the named variables.

Chapter 2- deals with the network society immersed in culture and its impact on the distance education programs within the information society.Thus, the interactive and communicational possibilities between individuals, groups, and organizations have been revolutionized,the conventional time-space coordinates have been modified, and the boundaries between the public and private spheres have been altered, which have an impact on the depths of subjectivity with positive and negative consequences.

The pressures of this type of society and culture, - closely related to innovation and creativity -, act in reciprocity with the global economy and need the emerging citizenry in general and knowledge workers that characterize it, to develop general and specific skills provided by life-long learning.

Chapter 3- explores the "sociocultural mediations", linked to technological-pedagogical aspectsof online distance education programs, a discussion that would allow us to surpass the previous instrumental analyses, which were focused on technological equipment or artifactual media. These are only used to store and transport large amounts of information quickly and to commercially monopolize the programs discussed, at the same time creating anarchy in the processes of social, conventional, and electronic communication.

These mediations encompass the set of material and symbolic actions or interventions facilitated by the devices and languages of ICT, which need to be studied from the sociocultural side of teaching and learning process.

This Task occupies a strategic place in the shaping of the information society, as it analyzes a comprehensive and demystifying approach of its ideas, actions, and impacts.

Thus, the various types of educational networks in international and intercultural contexts have sociocultural relevance, because of the practice of collaborative work that should take place within the above-mentioned educational programs in communities of learning and professional practice, as well as in communities of scientific-technological research or investigative evaluation.

It is also significant to consider and differentiate in these frameworks, the phenomena of social interaction and technological-educational interactivity, mediated by electronic technology in asynchronous and asynchronous way.

Chapter 4- discusses the possibilities, characteristics, and central criticisms of the process of sociocultural change and technological innovation in practice of distance education programs with ICT - in their various forms and formats (virtual education, e-learning, blended learning, etc) -, considering their counterpart in the subtle forms of social control and cultural disciplining, through the objectives and contents that appear in the interaction and interactivity mediated by the electronic technological systems.

The process of innovation, the management of technological change, and social change mediated by ICT in general, and for distance education, are considered, analyzing from a sociological point of view -, their resistance, contradictions, and conflicts, because if we learn to recognize the mechanisms that make (or do not) make innovations possible, a greater awareness will be achieved of individuals and groups, so they will be able to evaluate them as pertinent and thus, to plan them, direct them, carry them out, or discard them.

In Chapter 5- the sociological view looks at the organizations that drive distance education programs with ICT, which involves disassembling (deconstructing) their structures to understand the outcome of the process that forms consensuses and establishes negotiations within the proposals, besides conducting various prospectives or investing in technological infrastructure, within the information and knowledge society.

It also refers to the internationalization of distance education made possible by ICT, which leads the sociological view, with the hermeneutic[1] contribution given by the interrogation of the conditions of possibility and survival -, to investigate the prevailing social interests in order to interpret them, recognize the underlying motives, and see the disputes that destroy the obtained consensuses.

Conflicts within the network of multiple actors of such globalized virtual university organizations, - increasingly popular -, help to discover/deconstruct their underlying structure at the local, national, and transnational levels.

This is essential to not only find their meaning (or understand the not always conscious system of rules that underlie them) but to surpass them or overcome them, in order see that all meaning is interlaced with meaninglessness, if we adhere to the critical-analytical method for the study of the above-mentioned distance education programs.

Chapter 6- explores the sociocultural analysis of the student in distance education.

A proposal of descriptive and explanatory phenomenological reconstruction is presented, from the point of view of a critical sociology of distance education, considered from the student´s role in distance education programs.

The goal is to contribute some elements to this knowledge in order to overcome the usual interpretive reductionisms existing in the functionalist, Marxist, and empirist lines of thought.

The same have dissociated from the analysis of the interaction, teaching and learning, and telematic environments an explanation of the macrosocial mechanisms that gives meaning to the configuration of the role of the tele-student, within electronic programs. It is necessary to recognize their inscription in the social structure of the programs in question, and these within the configurations of delayed Capitalism, if the goal is to make the studied phenomenon, something which is not alien or alienated, as it has been interpreted in general.

For this reason, some revealing critical -structural considerations are presented and some journeys are described to the core of online educational programs, which students of this modality would adopt to obtain responses of satisfaction and dissatisfaction in terms of training needs. Also, the existing obstacles in the situations of social interaction and technological-educational interactivity mediated in these programs with ICT are described, in order to propose sociocultural alternatives that uncover and reveal greater pertinence.

The sociological analysis atempts to describe the zig-zags that the educational proposals with ICT organize as interesting or routine symbolic spaces so the student may train online at a distance, learn in a more comprehensive way, and interact with greater autonomy and social solidarity, great challenges of the educational processes in general, which are not always dealt with and faced.

Chapter 7- carries out a sociocultural analysis of tutorial actions in distance education with ICT.

The analysis is inscribed in the present society permeated by telematic networks, paradigm shifts in the configuration of mental maps and in the systems of expectations and

[1] Gadamer, H. 1975. Verdad y método. Edit Sígueme, Salamanca, España.

social roles of individuals and groups, as well as in the electronic educational organizations, all of them overwhelmed with contradictions and uncertainties, because if we can be certain of something,it is that societies, no longer are nor will they ever be as they were in times of the previous industrial society.

In the same way that conventional educators can no longer continue teaching the same content with the same methodology, tutors in distance education programs (now in connective onlinearticulation), will have to constantly re-adjust and re-create their roles within the new framework of mediated proposals.

This is not easy due to the existence of erroneous beliefs and myths that omit or fail to recognize the central characteristics of social practices; these are generally misleading and are later seen in actions in general and tutorials, in particular.

Identifying, defining, and comparing in practice theroles to be assumed by tutors in the exercise of their tutorial actions, is essential to decipher underlying conceptions, within the framework of the "new sociology of education".

Its theoretical-practical pillars are social phenomenology, ethnomethodology, and symbolic interactionism, among others, which emphasizes the idea that reality is constructed by subjects within processes of social interaction and negotiation, which makes us interpret reality in a way that is totally different from the traditional interpretation, linked to a "spontaneous epistemology", asserted in a simplified descriptive intuitionism within a linear sociological positivism (Bourdieu, Chamboredon, and Passeron, 1975).[2]

Chapter 8- proposes a discussion on which electronic distance education is required for an alternative knowledge society, by indicating some anticipations for the future.

This is a greatsocial, cultural, and ethical challenge for education in the society of the future in the context of a re-formulated globalization, that seems to lack an "ethical compass" to point to the lost notion of education in itself in our contemporary world!

We believe that some answers to the educational situation mediated by electronic technology within the above-mentioned global framework, must appear as a result of interpretive analyses seeking to understand and express the meaning and relevance of experiences, criteria, and phenomena of electronic education, categorized in light of the meaning that humanity needs to give it within globality[3] and which depend on the generation and development of sociopolitical settings of formative force, which propose creative syntheses.

Invigorating socially committed interaction and participation, - which defines the maturity of a society and its educational face-to-face and electronic programs -, will be the task to overcome unknown or never imagined difficulties.

The purpose of this contribution is to help professionals and students of the education sciences and disciplines summoned by virtual distance education deepen and improve their meaning and relevance.

---

[2]Bordieu, Chamboredon and Passeron (1975) El oficio del sociólogo. Siglo XXI, Bs.As.

[3] "Globalization" (Canclini, N, 1999. *La globalización imaginada*) refers to the concentration of the power and wealth linked to cultural and information flows, whereas "mundialization" refers to the deterritorialization of the market due to world strategies and "internationalization", the increase in economic activity beyond national borders.

*Chapter 1*

# DISTANCE EDUCATION WITH ICT, THE NEED FOR A SOCIOLOGICAL REFLECTION

## THE INFORMATION SOCIETY

Although there is no agreement on the definitive nomenclature of the current societal profile, through various notions supplied by social theory, it is without question that the development of technology in general and the new information and communication technologies – ICT- have brought about important changes in the social organization.

Among the multiple ways in which said social organization has been revealed, some of the notions that appear are of"self-poietic systems" and "polycontextuality" (Luhmann, 1998),[4] "hypersocialization" and "planetarization" (Melucci, 2001),[5] the"fluidification" of reality (García Selgas, 2001),[6] through the process of "individualization" (Lipovetsky, 1983)[7] and the concept ofthe "disembedding" of social action (Giddens, 1990),[8]"disinstitutionalization" (Beck, 1995; Touraine, 1997),[9] "hybridation" (Haraway, 1991),[10] (García Canclini, 1990),[11] "glocalization" (Beck, 1997; García Segura, 1998),[12]

---

[4] Luhmann, N. (1998). *Complejidad y modernidad: de la unidad a la diferencia* (edición y traducción de J. Beriain y J. M. García Blanco). Madrid, Trotta.

[5] Melucci, A. (2001). *Vivencia y convivencia. Teoría social para una era de la información*. Madrid, Trotta.

[6] García Selgas, F. J. (2001). "Preámbulo para una ontología política de la fluidez social", en *Athenea Digital,* Nº 1. http://antalya.uab.es/athenea/num1/selgas.pdf

[7] Lipovetsky, G. (1983). *La era del vacío. Ensayos sobre el individualismo contemporáneo*. Barcelona, Anagrama.

[8] Giddens, A. (1990). *Consecuencias de la modernidad*. Madrid, Alianza.

[9] Beck, U. (1995). "El conflicto de las dos modernidades". En U. BECK, *La democracia y sus enemigos. Textos escogidos* (pp. 13-31). Barcelona, Paidós.

[10] Haraway, D. (1991). "A cyborg manifesto: Science, technology, and socialist-feminism in the late twentieth century". En D. HARAWAY, *Simians, cyborgs and women: The reinvention of nature* (pp. 149-181). Nueva York, Routledge.

[11] García Canclini, N. (1990). *Culturas híbridas. Estrategias para entrar y salir de la modernidad.* Barcelona, Paidós.

[12] Beck, U. (1997). "En torno a la sociedad mundial: perspectivas concurrentes". En U. BECK, *¿Qué es la globalización? Falacias del globalismo, respuestas a la globalización* (pp. 127-155). Barcelona, Paidós. 1998.

García Segura, C. (1998). "La globalización en la sociedad internacional contemporánea: dimensiones y problemas desde la perspectiva de las relaciones internacionales".

En *Cursos de derecho internacional de Vitoria-Gazteiz* (pp. 315-350). Madrid, UPV/EHU y Tecnos.

(Pérez-Agote, 2000),[13] "estetization" and the "desubstantification" of reality (Jameson, 1991; Baudrillard, 1983),[14] and already since the mid 1970´s, "information society" (Nora and Minc, 1980; Negroponte, 1995; Miège, 1998);[15] "informationalism" (Manuel Castells 2000),[16] among others, all coinciding with the dawn of neoliberalism.

Towards the middle of the 20th century, technology and ICT in particular acquired a central role as input and revolutionized the production and communication processes of the time.This has not only reconfigured the whole of human relations predominantly in the States, social organizations and markets – all of these of global inscription- but has also unsuspectedly restructured the bonds between individuals and groups which are now considered "glocal": a reciprocal articulation and tight interdependence between global and local cultures is seen.

Known in general as the "information society", with a conceptualization that originated from the central countries (represented by the European Union and the United States), it refers to a polysemic process that, although it brings with it previous symbolic and material inheritance, constantly reconstructs its own precisions and orientations in general.It appears, not without difficulty, in countries where the engine –the technological development of new materials par excellence-, is pronounced and socially unequal.In the so-called emerging countries, or peripheral of the south of the world, said societary configuration and movement are not presented in the same way since they are difficult, in light of the contradictions and crisis that characterize them, which therefore require an *alternative formulation.*

There have already been statements on this, although it little affects the nomenclature, such as "the communication society" (Vattimo, 1996),[17] "the post-information era" (Negroponte, 1995),[18] "the third environment" (Echeverría, 1999),[19] "the knowledge society" (Drucker, 1993; Levy, 2000),[20] "the liquid society" (Bauman, 1999),[21] etc.

In general, the information society describes a new social and economic order rooted in expansion, generation and circulation of digital information, based on the electronic global telematic.It is characterized by interconnected information as its raw material and by the technologies of growing electronic convergence and integration, present in all processes of individual and collective existence.

The information society presents important structural changes produced by the speedy development of the treatment, storage and distribution of information, which with the systems of microelectronics, telecommunications, and computer technology penetrate and impact on

[13] Pérez-Agote, A. (2000). "La crisis de la homogeneidad cultural". En *Estudios de la Facultad de Ciencias Sociales y de la Comunicación en homenaje al Profesor Iñaki DomínguezVázquez. El bienestar en la cultura* (pp. 439 – 459). Bilbao, UPV/EHU.

[14] Jameson, F. (1991). *Teoría de la postmodernidad*. Madrid, Trotta.Baudrillard, J. (1983). *Las estrategias fatales*. Barcelona, Anagrama.

[15] Nora, S. y Minc, A. (1980). *Informatización de la sociedad.* México, FCE.Negroponte, N. (1995). *Ser digital.* Buenos Aires, Atlántida.

Miège, B. (1995). "Las etapas del pensamiento comunicacional", en *Signo y Pensamiento*,N° 26, Universidad Javeriana de Bogotá.

[16] Castells, M. (2000). "Paraísos comunales: identidad y sentido en la sociedad real". En M. Castells, *La era de la información. Economía, sociedad y cultura*, vol. II (pp. 27-90). Madrid, Alianza.

[17] Vattimo, G. (1996). *La sociedad transparente*. Barcelona, Paidós.

[18] *Op. cit.*

[19] Echeverría, J. (1999). *Los señores del aire: Telepolis y el Tercer entorno*. Barcelona, Destino.

[20] Drucker, P. (1993). *Postcapitalist society.* Nueva York, Harper Collins. LEVY, P. (2000, noviembre). ''Cyberespace et cyberculture'', p.2. www.uoc.es/esp/perasabermes/canals/societat

[21] Bauman, Z. (1999). *La globalización. Consecuencias humanas*. México, FCE

all the communicational processes.In this way, an intense and unstoppable reorganization of the economy, society, and culture put pressure on the education sector in all its manifestations.

Although some sectors consider that the changes in the current information society, supported on international deregulation and competitivity (Becerra, 2003),[22] will lead to the improvement of the population's quality of life, there are serious misgivings about this promotional speech due to the strong regressive consequences it shows.

The "informational revolution" developed by this society in a continuous way deserves a sociological reflection in general and for the education sector in particular.It is an unavoidable task if we consider such a society as the "web society" due to the incidence of ICT and among them, the *web of webs ofInternet,* have in people's education.

In the information society, the greatest accent departs from and arrives at the economy, which allows a flexible and interconnected production of information in horizontal and vertical processes.By contrast. and at the same time as a complement, it is necessary to highlight the *sociocultural dimension* which presents an increasingly central role.In reference to this, Castells[23] points out that the "Internet is not only nor mainly a technology, but a cultural production" because it presents itself as a social practice of cultural –and even artistic-creation in the society in question; it is part of the sociocultural code in effect since it is legitimized by the system of values, beliefs and forms of human interrelation.The logic of the telematic power, globally present in the form of Internet, is the one that producestoday identities as the reflection of said sociocultural practices.

We stand before an epochal change and, therefore, a sociocultural mutation in form and content, which is seen in the convergent networks, of accelerated activity and transportation and without distance, mediated by ICT.

It would seem, that the idea and concept of "society" today corresponds to the transitory and open globalization, made possible by the constant fluidity of human constructions (Bauman, 2004)[24].

However, the above mentioned characteristics are not linear, but report zigzags, pressures and contradictions –not without various neoconservationist resistances.With dizzying impulse the application of ICT is promoted in the educational programs in general and specially in distance programs, for the "new" online electronic learning.

The education sector is not represented by its true protagonists, planners, managers and direct professionals, but by computer professionals, systems engineers and by the global marketing referred to the sector, which support the height of the supply of information and above all the exponential increment of the capacity to produce, process, encode, store, distribute, search for, and send bigger and bigger volumes of information, claiming that the education sector "cannot be" out of the loop.They are tendencies of all types, which impact on all socio-economic areas, structurally change processes and products, and fire enthusiasm through a fast articulation of these services in the educational structures and processes.Nevertheless, there are few serious reflective analysis due to the delays with which this sector has approached a technological inclusion.

---

[22] Becerra, M. (2003). *Sociedad de la información: proyecto, convergencia, divergencia.* Buenos Aires, Grupo Editorial Norma.

[23]*Op. cit.*

[24] Bauman, Z. (2004). *La sociedad sitiada.* México, FCE.

The introduction of ICT, therefore, rushes the education and training of the work force necessary in general, for the elaboration of fundamental goods and services in a liberalized, deregulated economy on an international level, known as "the knowledge economy".

## THE KNOWLEDGE SOCIETY

The "knowledge society" appears directly linked to, although with differences and going beyond the nomenclature before mentioned for the information society, as a necessary construct to link the information society with the new dimension of knowledge.Knowledge is today a strategic factor of management, production, and communication of the concrete social historical units and coherently impulse the above mentioned economic progress.However this does not imply the production of the usualreflection with the aim of planting and activating another awareness beyond the desired pragmatic use (Drucker, P. 1993).

Actually, it was Bell (1976) [25] who coined the expression "knowledge society" as he verified the shift from a society concerned with the industrial production of objects towards a post-industrial society whose work force is more concentrated towards services, ideas, and communication.This is why it is imperative in this type of society to encourage the production of knowledge in science, technology, investigation, and development with innovation.

In the early 90´s, Peter Drucker introduced the notion of a "knowledge society", which in his opinion would allow a fast adaptation to the changes as a way of solving the new emerging economic needs.Drucker suggests that it is possible to apply knowledge to knowledge, with the purpose of reaching a superior or broader knowledge.He observes the development factor or economic trigger that is attributed to the production and circulation of knowledge.

Information is subsumed, therefore, in a significant resignified way to the notion of knowledge to become a part of the communicative processes and those of symbolic exchange, and so underline some of the most outstanding characteristics of the knowledge society.

**Epistemological aspects**

| Industrial society | Knowledge society |
|---|---|
| Linear structure (book). | Recursive hypertextual structure in electronic supports |
| Simplistic, fragmenting | Complexity – Flow *continuum* |
| Knowledge with guidelines | Non-structured knowledge |
| Ontology of individual and general emphasis | Ontology of situated, collective, and distributed construction |
| Management of stagnant content | Management of independent processes, products and services |

[25] Bell, D. (1976). *The coming of postindustrial society*. Boulder (Colorado), Basic Books.

**Social aspects**

| | |
|---|---|
| Industrial society | Knowledge society |
| Restricted access and distribution of information | Unrestricted access and distribution |
| Fixed space-time coordinates | Delocalization |
| Person-group dialectic | Person-virtual collaborative environment dialectic |
| Institution centered | Digital environment centered |

**Educational methodological aspects**

| | |
|---|---|
| Industrial society | Knowledge society |
| Knowledge and experience acquired in stable times. | Lack of stability and certainty.Life-long learning. |
| Teacher centered education. | Education centered on the student, process and interaction with the environment. |
| Evaluation- control. | Evaluation- improvement. |
| Instructionism. | Interactive socioconnectivism. |

In this way, its *sociocognitivecomponent* values intelligence in general and above all the collective one, as a result of the interactive work of the ICT user in networks.Great importance is given to technological and organizational knowledge highlighting the processes as well as the products, which tilts the educational scales towards the consolidation of another type of competencies and skills.In this way, in this type of society central leading roles are attributed to education and reflective practice in comparison to earlier socioeducational stages.

The transformation of the industrial society into the knowledge society recognizes several aspects referred to the act of knowing.

## The Sociological Studies of Distance Education: The Social Phenomenon as Object of Study and the Sociological as Area of Thought

A. Comte is usually mentioned as the founder of sociology in the middle of the 19th century: this author perceives it as an autonomous discipline, which arose from the study of multicausal historical human interaction –disconnected from metaphysics, ethics or theology- and committed to a scientific-theoretical search. Comte is the first to pick up the torch of the tradition of positivism and the subjection to the scientific method originated in the Renaissance with Galileo: the spectacular development of Physics, with the empirical observation and verification of facts, shifts towards the analysis of society.

E. Durkheim (1864-1920) is attributed the authentic paternity of sociology as a positive science, stating that its object of study – in other words what configures and defines it-, are the social facts as non-physical, nor organic nor mental phenomena: he considers the empirical reality of the organization of human groups beyond individualities.In this sense, social facts are defined as the substrate of the objective ways of acting, thinking, and feeling external to the person, which hold a power of domination over the person from the multiple and simultaneous action of other individuals that impose themselves as collective preexisting models, elaborated by past generations.These models are transmitted through education (through values, beliefs, moral and judicial laws, prejudice, etc.) which are fixed in the collective conscience and in objective products (cultural goods, life styles, works of art, technology, fashion, etc.) which, although they are partly modifiable by new social interaction, they offer the resistance to change as a defining characteristic.

Apparently, all sociological knowledge is related to education, which is why we could state that *all sociology is constituted by some sociology of education.*This could be conceived as such because the world is known not in itself but through the practice of social interaction.The image of the world we have elaborated acquires, therefore, through the representation that was provided by all the existing symbolic languages: from the verbal oral language, written texts, fixed and moving images of video, music, digital sounds and effects, up to new technologies and other electronic resources.These languages constitute a part of early socialization and consolidate the education received and re-created in a concrete historical cultural context.

Nevertheless, the construction of the object of study of sociology cannot be reduced to the naivete of the empirists who take as scientific object the concrete "real" object, without keeping in mind that in this procedure abstractions of common sense are assumed, without considering it a historical and socially constituted set of problems (Bourdieu; Chamboredon and Passeron (2002).[26] It is worth remembering that what is concrete is concrete because it is the synthesis of multiple determinations and appears in thought as a result, not as a point of departure, where intuition and representation also carry considerable weight. Both should be considered in the interpretation of *everyday*[27] *as well as scientific*[28] *knowledge.*

Continuing with the object of study of sociology, in other words, society and social interaction, we may observe that today it faces several *paradoxes*: it would seem that, for different reasons, its natural object of study has been *naturalized.* As the identification of "society" with the Nation State- was reframed, the same lost the manifest character it possessed in the past. The same has happened with the identification of "society" with the set of existing social “structures” within it, to which, today, virtual reality is added. Although the "social reality" continues being managed by tangible agencies or "of bricks”, these possess in general and in an interdependent way their replicas in cyberspace. As a consequence, another "*ethos* of culture" is constituted, still without consolidation. Nevertheless, this does not mean

[26] Bourdieu, P., Chamboredon, J. y Passeron, J. (2002). *El oficio del sociólogo*. Buenos Aires, Siglo XXI.

[27] *Everydayknowledge* -nonsystematic and acritical- is acquired without organization in common experience, where sometimes superficial knowledge appear unconnected to each other and/or juxtaposed. It is the customary and spontaneous way a person has of knowing; it is produced in the direct relationship with things and phenomena that fill everyday life, on which in general there is no reflection. Nevertheless, and although it is heterogeneous, it is the knowledge that is used in an effective way as a guide for social action and anticipation. It varies according to the times and social levels, which contributes to the change in its content and extension.

[28] Scientific knowledge –which may penetrate the previous one- appears when the person, when perceptively facing various problems of common sense without a solution, must overcome the immediacy of this sensory certainty of superficial knowledge to produce an explanation with regard to what before was understood. Through the practice of meticulous and systematic observation, hypothetical formulation and empirical contrast as alternatives of problem solving, the person arrives at new knowledge: the scientific or disciplinary.

that the fragile, fluid, uncertain and provisional instances have been surpassed, which characterize (Bauman, 2004)[29] the profiles of the new society.

The technological society of information tied up in the globalization of communication and finances, and as a product of the virtualization of the world economy, is accompanied by a political fragmentation and a loss of the socioeconomic sovereignty that the Nations-States possessed. This statement does not mean that sociology has arrived at the end of its existence, on the contrary. This discipline tied its destiny to the possibility of a self-affirmation of humanity, which is the truly human way ofbeing-in-the-world, today full of questions and obstacles in its "liquid" phase (Bauman, 2004).[30] We believe in a revival of sociological preoccupations or in a recovery of its interest in the explanatory, anticipatory, or ofintegrating reconstruction, contributions that can be assumed in facing the risky and uncertain stages presented by contemporary society.

## What does it Mean to Consider Something from a Sociological Point of View and Distance Education in Particular?

Since the beginnings of sociology, it is considered that its task corresponds to the present need "to sociologically think" phenomena. Therefore, sociology as an activity of continuous reflective preoccupation (Bauman, 1994)[31] tries to contrast the inherited knowledge with new experiences, in order to deepen, increase and modify said knowledge. It is represented by a body of knowledge, as well as by practices of production and use, in close contact with culture, political sciences, history, anthropology, economy, since it takes care of the practical aspects or those which possess an impression referred to the human actions that change at a different pace and through time from one society to another.

We emphasize in sociology that which seeks to identify what is put in practice, whatis known and learned of the world to interact in practice; and to recognize that what is put in practice originates from the image of the world that is possessed, which is a constructed and internalized model of the same, existing as a mental map in each one of us and which unfolds in acts that were modeled during the socialization and education mediated by language.

Therefore, the distinguishing characteristic of sociology is to consider human interactions as non-random dispositions of the actors which are inscribed within a network of broader mutual interdependence, in various settings, and to ask itself what consequences it would have for the possible behavior of the human actors organized in groups and other social forms (real and virtual).

Stated thus, the sociological way of thinking is related to *common sense* as it considers the life of common people where everyday knowledge appears. Before sociology undertook its study, it was the subject matter of those who were strangers to sociological reflection. Thus, also, the social plane is differentiated from the individual, to arrive at the general from the individual.This makes us think about the meaning that arises from the comparison of private experience to that of others, where both originate from and return to the everyday experience named by common language.This is conjugated with the concept of *habitus,* as the

[29]*Op. cit.*

[30]*Op. cit.*

[31] Bauman, Z. (1994). *Pensando sociológicamente.* Buenos Aires, Nueva Visión.

system of dispositions, generating principles and organizers of practice, and collectively orchestrated representations (Bourdieu, 1991),[32]the socialized body of knowledge, that is incorporated by individuals and which structures its perception and action.

The central role of socialization and education is therefore understood, because it is a system of internalized structures of perception, thought, and action to interact in life, with a relatively autonomous permanence: in other words, that changes, although in a slower way in comparison to other structures, such as the economic ones.

The work of the sociological analyst (or investigator) would seek to make evident certain actions that are repeatedly manifested while who is carrying out these actions, and what type of rules are being implemented in the game remains hidden, and from there deduce what type of game is being practiced.In this way, the social analysis considers and involves the set of possible actions, the immanent rules, the bets, the players, their knowledge and their habitual dispositions, the benefits obtained, the strategies to reach them, the characteristics of the field, among other elements.

We believe this framework of sociological analysis is comprehensible and easily transferable to the global proposals of electronic learning as the format of distance education which is today at its peak with the use of ICT in the information society.

To deepen the study, it is necessary to add the category of sociocultural *conflict*as the opposition or characteristic antagonism existing between individuals and groups, a product of the set of structured social relations, from the differences in the various socioeconomic, sociopolitical, sociocultural and sociojuridical orders.The conflict appears due to the tacit agreement to leave the essential hidden; that is, the structure of the objective antagonistic positions, where the power –as will be seen here- plays a central role.

In other words, sociology shows and studies the general sociocultural aspects of how the individual biographies are woven into the general shared history and how conflicts are (or aren't) solved.

For the practice of these scientific analysis – which must go beyond common sense-, it is advisable to consider (Bauman, 1994) the following:

- what has been publicly and unlimitedly verified by the scientific authority as a responsible and believable discourse;
- a broader level of understanding in relation to everyday experience that goes beyond the partial and unilateral aspects of interaction to inscribe it within a complex network of interdependence, which ensures a difference in the quality and the use of sociological knowledge, and does not characterize everyday knowledge;
- the overcoming of the self-evidence of the familiar that distances critical perplexity and reflection."To defamiliarize the familiar" according to Bauman, which corresponds to the deconstruction according to Derrida, with the aim to confront the everyday world of habits and beliefs to ask questions and to cast doubt on the habitual ways of life, in other words, to question and disrupt routine with freedom and self-control.

In this way, sociology attempts to overcome the limitations of common sense, that are "naturally" explored and imposed on human condition.The sociological analysis seeks to destabilize said anachronous structures and remove stereotypes or fixations to combatthe manipulation and disciplining given to individuals and groups, due to the establishment of

[32] Bourdieu, P. (1991). *El sentido de la práctica.* Madrid, Taurus.

heteronomous rules in the revision of all the existing repressive "isms".Apparently, education in all its manifestations (formal, non-formal and informal) and in all its formats (face-to face, at a distance with social mass media mediators, and mediations with ICT and online) should strive to deepen the reflective process and therefore anticipate future removals and innovations, with which it would strike up another dialogue with sociological thought in general and the educational in particular.

On the other hand, training in sociology and/or practicing sociology does not a involve a linear task, but a recursive activity, of contradictory practice due to the fact that it does not present itself as mathematics does in a defined multiplicity or with some continuity, or by an instrumental rationality, or means to ends, or technical, as it happens, for example, with medicine or jurisprudence, if we tackle them within a reduced paradigm.

Society, education, and human relations are characterized by the existence of *paradoxes*[33] and *constituentcontradictions*.The task of sociology is to discover below the surface of the facts, and even of the apparently coincidental theories, the forces that contradict and face each other.For these reasons, the science of society could still be accused of lacking absolute reliability, total transparency, and univocal fundaments (Adorno, 1968).[34]

Moreover, due to the above mentioned, it is possible to maintain that there are no closed truths in sociology, but that everything is pluridetermined by interests, social mediations and preexisting forces.This establishes the fact that what should be considered relevant as social knowledge cannot be determined *a priori.*

In some way, these reflections are refreshing because they propose the characteristic dichotomy of sociology that becomes sociopolitical confrontation, between the beginning of the order and the change, or between the beginning of the static and social dynamic.In reference to these principles, today the dynamic pole is found primarily through technology, considered as the key category of innovation in the relations of socioeconomic-cultural production, as we'll continue seeing in the following pages.

Although these reflections do not necessarily lead to the proposal of construction of a better society, they allow the exercise and predominance of free thought, independent and critical, essential to examine and deconstruct a society, or in our case, the microcosm of a system or program of distance education, an auspicious invitation since it points in the same way, although on a smaller scale, to all the possibilities of transformation that characterize a social unit.

## THE SOCIOLOGICAL STUDIES OF DISTANCE EDUCATION

The contribution of the sociology of education to the understanding of the components that intervene in electronic distance education programs (with their conceptions of planning, design, and evaluation of materials, training of tutors, among others) results from the ability this discipline possesses to analyze in a developmental, dynamic, and historical way the sociocultural context where said mediated formative processes are developed.

---

[33]Logical principle and of the idealistic philosophy of Hegel and materialist of Marx that establishes the existence of the union of opposites, the contradictory unit of the one and the multiple, the harmony bound to disharmony. Therefore, a *paradox* is a declaration, true in appearance, that entails a logical self-contradiction or a situation that contradicts common sense.

[34] Adorno, T. (1968). *Introducción a la sociología.* Madrid, Gedisa.

The sociology of distance education, as an instrument of critical analysis of the mediated and connected training, inscribed within a sociohistorical perspective, shows a lack of sociological tradition in this sense.The few or non-existent sociological studies on the particular must overcome the accustomed descriptive stage that characterizes said format so the later may be palliated with the conduction of explicative studies, even considering the first distance education programs by correspondence to the current electronified ones.

It is necessary to search for the origin, explanation, and interpretation of the development of the distance education processes in social institutions, when considering the multicausal factors of social reality, with the use of various sociological concepts, among others, class inequalities, ethnic migrations, and gender differences in the context of different programs and, in a broader sense, in educational policies related to said modality.In general, the progressive forces of educational technology, identified as appropriate and critical (Fainholc, 2001),[35] have mainly been concerned with introducing various concepts of sociocultural theory, at the same time achieving the professionality of the frameworks that operate in said modality.It is time to dedicate our efforts to other things, since sociology has a practical meaning of huge concrete implications for education, mediated interaction, and the citizenry in general, in helping to understand social and cultural differences between institutions and organizations in various social situations.This is why,it should be a useful instrument for the increase of social self-knowledge of the educational modality starting from the construction of its identity in relation to the factual and virtual environments.

With an approximation of a sociology of distance education, the neutrality of any educational mediation is questioned (Fainholc, 2004)[36] in order to center the attention on the educational program as a place for interaction between the academic and everyday culture in all of its components.This makes it so sociology changes direction towards a critical study of these components to recognize that knowledge and failure are socially constructed in the interdependence of the interior with the exterior of the programs: there stems the need for a *situated conscience* in relation to all the intervening variables in the above mentioned programs.

The sociology of education is also essential to give a critical look at the educational innovations, giving them theoretical interpretations and practical analysis which allow us to understand and act on the social context where they are inscribed.We would thus overcome the common sense knowledge –which forms the majority of the stereotypes found- in encouraging the study of mutual conditioning between education and society, reconstructing common places, criticizing the irrational myths that those recently arrived to the area harbor without the use of a collective memory, among other elements.Said sociology is presented as a way of knowledge that helps to know the social and cultural context where projects are installed, to show that education varies depending on the social class, to visualize that education embodies content that individuals later resignify, depending on the means and ends used.

One of the most interesting critical contributions to the sociology of education in general and the sociology of distance education in particular, is the *criticism of formalism*that is

---

[35] Fainholc, B. (2001, September). "La tecnología educativa apropiada: Una revisita.
a su campo a comienzos de siglo", in *Revista RUEDA Nº 4*, Red Universitaria de Educación a Distancia, Universidad Nacional de Luján.

[36] Fainholc, B. (2004). "El concepto de mediación en la tecnología educativa apropiaday crítica". http://weblog.educ.ar/educacion-TIC/archives/002461

carried out with regard to pedagogical conceptions and practices –as it rescues the initial contribution from Saint-Simon, and Comte, later-, which present education as a factor of inculcation and unification of society.Some time later, Marx states the need to unify the education/school with the work/factory, criticizing elitism and idealism as formats of pedagogical formalism that contribute to social reproduction.From a positive point of view, Marx attributes an important role to education in the process of social emancipation, stating the need for a new *praxis* to play a significant part in the process of solution of class conflicts, fundamentally through the articulation of manual labor and intellectual work. To achieve this, he proposes a curriculum that encompasses an intellectual, physical, and technological instruction.

Veblen´s [37] contribution to the sociology of education is also relevant when recognizing educational institutions as a meeting place for the social pressures and interests in conflict, where educational proposals act as transmitters of culturalguidelines and ideological forms belonging to some groups (the upper classes) in relation to others.

Antonio Gramsci,[38] in turn, contributes valuable elements with a powerful criticism of the traditional school as well as the different progressive models.He opts for a curriculum of humanistic values, which allows knowledge to be discovered by itself, defends the substantive knowledge facing formalism and discourse, affirms the need for intellectual self-discipline and moral autonomy inscribed within group work and advocates the active methods with which we learn through discovery.

In this same line, Mannheim (1941)[39] places himself between the so-called method of authority and method of freedom, criticizes the pedagogical formalism and calls attention to the sociocultural perspective for the understanding of educational problems, mostly of a social kind.

The sociological alert facing the illusion of transparency, that common sense gives to ICT, originates from the idea that, to explain and understand electronic educational programs, it would suffice to find again the intentions of which they are a product.This idea of common sense owes in part its strength to the commonly existing attitudes that lead to a kind of technocratic illusion.This is why, the position that conceives technology only from the artefactual point of view should be revised in light of reflectivity.[40]

In consequence, the whole field of educational technology should be revisited where the chapter on distance education is inscribed or inserted.For the same reason (Giddens),[41] it is necessary, instead of searching for a synthesis between thc conceptualization of the agent and the theorization of the social institutionalization, to direct our attention to a dynamic reality, situated and recurrent, through which the reality of social practice is constituted.This praxis, as an antecedent, can explain the subject (cognoscente), the object (virtual structure) and the relationship between both.Here, we not only consider human beings but all social events, both in their face-to-face acts and distance acts given by their social relations of copresence at a distance.

---

[37] Espinosa, E. de Lamo, González García, J. y Torres Albero, C. (1994). "La sociología del conocimiento nortemericana", en La sociología del conocimiento norteamericana. Madrid, Alianza.

[38] GRAMSCI, A. (1981). *Cuadernos de la cárcel*. México, Era.

[39] MANNHEIM, K. (1941). *Ideología y utopía. Introducción a la sociología del conocimiento*. México, FCE.

[40] We use reflectivity according to GARCÍA SELGAS, F. J. (1994*). Teoría social y metateoríahoy. El caso de Anthony Giddens*. Madrid, Siglo XXI.

[41] *Op. cit.*

The notion of "human action or intervention of agents" (Giddens, 1982)[42] takes place in the structuring (production and reproduction through space and time) of social practices known as the "structuration theory"(Giddens,1991).[43]The same considers the recursive and reflective quality of life and social practices –re-created by the actors-, useful in explaining how said structures are constituted through action, and how action is structurally constituted.

Independently of the enormous relevance to educational technology of the fact that actions may install a difference in the world –due to the possibility of doing things differently and/or transforming them through the exercise of power-, what we are trying to emphasize now is the center of said recursivity.The same appears in the competition of agents, with their cognitive ability and reflectivity which allows them to control (*reflective monitoring*) as much what they are doing as the other's reactions and the circumstances in which it all happens.To this articulation of recursivity and reflectivity is added the fact that action occurs as a continuous current of conduct, with its linguistic-conceptual capacity, which allows it to reflect on its knowledge and at the same time be imbued in a continuous process of rationalization and justification of its course of action.

In this way, the action presupposes a factic motor, that organizes or designs the activity you want; for example, an educational program in various ways (Giddens, 1986).[44]

Everything above mentioned occurs in distance education, if we conduct the analysis from a sociological perspective, which overcomes a spontaneist sociology, which owes its coherence to the systematic character of the illusions it creates.[45]Contrary to these illusions, it is necessary to remember the complexity of the pluridеterminations that a socioeducational program or institution owes to its past and that are reedited in the current sociocultural context (Bourdieu, Chamboredon y Passeron, 2002).

It is necessary, once more, to resort to voices from the past.There are positions such as Plato's, who defended the statement that all artifacts (including works of art) are imitations of something natural, genuine, or original.He maintained that something is "artificial" when something seems to be, but is not really that which it imitates.Aristotle thought that nature and art (the natural and the artificial, respectively) have nothing in common, constituting two different spheres of reality (López Cerezo, Luján and others, 1998).[46] The world of art was a product of human ingenuity in believing that man's creations were very inferior to the functioning and the products of nature considered as something alive and autonomous, while the "artificial" was something dead and inferior to natural things.There are thus conformed two ontologically different realities, as the first forms face the secondary forms, as in the same way, from the epistemological point of view, we refer to the theoretical knowledge *versus* the productive one.

With Aristotle, for the first time, the "know how" (or the type of knowledge held by the artisan and the engineer) is distinguished from the "know why" or search for a demonstrative understanding (what characterizes the work of a scientist).This turns out to be important for the educational-technological field of work, considering that education is permeated by technologies, such as is currently manifest in distance proposals.

---

[42] Giddens, A. (1982). *Profiles and critiques in social theory*. Londres, McMillan.
[43] Giddens, A. (1991). *Sociología*. Madrid, Alianza.
[44] Giddens, A. (1984). *The constitution of society*. Cambridge, Polity Press.
[45] Durkheim, E. (1973). *Las reglas del método sociológico*. Buenos Aires, Schapire.
[46] López Cerezo, J., Luján, L. y otros (1998). "Filosofía de la tecnología". *Revista Temas de Iberoamérica*. Madrid, OEI.

The Aristotelian dichotomy of "natural-artificial" was overcome and replaced by the dichotomy of "real-unreal" in the 17th century, through the work of Bacon and Descartes.Technology, according to Bacon,[47] may contribute to the development of natural science, because we learn more from nature when it is subjected to the trials and interventions where it suffers transformations, on the hands of an intelligent being with intentions of practice.

If we try to relate this understanding of the artificial to distance education proposals and we were to ask which should be the ideal conception – as an abstraction of all condition of time and place-, we could implicitly admit that an educational system is not real in itself.We only perceive from it a set of institutional practices that have been slowly organized, with the passage of time, solidary of the rest of the institutions and social values that express them.This is why, we could recognize that this or that online electronic educational organization is not the same everywhere.In fact, every society, considered at a specific time in its development, has a system of education, that although it transports and encodes content in specific media and technological resources, depending on its cultural time, goes beyond said equipment, and appears to individuals in a preestablished way.

Although ICT still meet some resistance in education proposals and electronic programs, their presence and penetration are greater and greater.They are a product of the current sociocultural time where computer telecommunications rule, as in other historical stages where the education systems were formed and developed depending on religion, on the type of political organization chosen, the degree of development of the sciences, the state of the industry, etc.

The sociologist, therefore, faces the exteriority of the social phenomena named in the extension and opacity of the past where they came from, as well as the multiplicity of actions that these phenomena involve.The rhizomatic ambiguity of this social universe must be postulated, which supposes, besides the epistemological recognition of the illusion of the prenotions seen, the intellectual and ethical conviction that the scientific-technological discoveries are not easily grasped directly, nor are they likely to be accepted as a block.

With the aim of building a sociological reflection of distance education in the online modality, although in everyday life there is interaction with ICT, many times they are not accepted due to the representations that were conceived of them in general, far from a serious scientific-technological interpretation.The awareness we have of these does not reveal their internal nature nor their sociotechnical genesis.We only have confusing and pragmatic, subjective impressions, unfinished explicative concepts.

## What Makes the Significant Difference in the Comprehension of a Sociology of Distance Education

The practice of a sociological reflection of distance education in the online modality allows us to overcome the reductionism and dogmatism represented, in the current cultural times, due to spontaneisms, functionalism, scientificisms, or various positivisms.Except for exceptions in the history of ideas, until the 60´s or 70´s there ruled frameworks such as the ones mentioned with an educational theory supported on a vision of social reality, whose

[47] Bacon, F. (1963). *De argumentis scientiarum*. Londres, Spedding Works.

explanations were believed to be exempt from value judgments.Moreover, the positivist orientation sustained itself in a functionalist image of human behavior conceived as determined by impersonal laws that would work far from people's control (Carr y Kemmis, 1988).[48]

Once these beliefs were broken, the sociology of education adopted a different direction, presented by M. Young (*Knowledge and control)[49]*, through the "interpretive" approach, essentially derived from Schutz's (1967)[50] social phenomenology and Berger's and Luckmann's(1967)[51] sociology of knowledge.

According to this "new sociology", society is not an "independent system" of external relations, but the central characteristic of social reality is its intrinsically significant structure, formed and sustained by the routine interpretive activities of its individual members.The "objective" character of society points to a reality independent of that which is tied to the people.Society possesses a certain degree of objectivity thanks to the social actors who, in the process of interpretation of the social world, exteriorize it and objectify it.Society is only "real" and "objective" as its members define it as such and guide their conduct toward said reality, such as they have defined it.

This way, the "interpretive" sociological investigation should concern itself more with revealing the network of meanings from which the social actors constitute and reconstitute any social order (or in our case, an educational program). It is the preoccupation with an investigation to understand social processes by means of which the social life of a social unit, organization, or educational program is produced, prolonged, and re-created. In other words, it contributes to thinking that since education is the product of everyday understandings, the social sciences that study it in general should seek to reach an "interpretation" of the phenomena it includes, and not to adhere linearly to scientific explanation *per se*.

The "interpretive" approach of meanings, such as the one we are dealing with, received the name of "hermeneutics", which in social sciences has a long tradition. From the protestant theologians of the 17th century, and already in the 18th century, it is used as a methodology to interpret Biblical texts, literature, works of art, and music. Also, jurisprudence and philology appealed to hermeneutics.[52] During the 19th century the "interpretive understanding" was the

[48] Carr, W. y Kemmis, S. (1988). *Teoría crítica de la enseñanza*. Barcelona, Edit. MartínezRoca.

[49] Young, M.D.F. (1971). *Knowledge and control: New directions for the sociology of education*.Londres, Collier MacMillan.

[50] Schutz, A. (1967). *The phenomenology of the social world.* Evanston, North-western University Press.

[51] Berger, P. y Luckmann, T. (1967). *The social construction of reality.* Londres, The Penguin Press.

[52]Hermeneutics: theory and philosophical method for the interpretation of the human actions and messages of the mediators and mediations, as practice that tries to understand the authentic version of the carried out accomplishment. Dilthey used the term for the method of "cultural sciences or of the spirit", understood as sharing the meaning that occurs between the creator and the interpreter.

Gadamer tried to validate a surrounding phenomenological hermeneutic of the notion of "hermeneutic circle" maintaining its power of recognition and generalization from a particular way only because it can be interpreted, since the validation processes are always opened and provisional and that the truth is partial and is subject to revisions.

Paul Ricoeur (1981) also develops this position focusing insights or sudden glances that fit into the critical theory and maintains that the text has a mediating key position between tradition and unicity, which leads to a potential critical position about the world and himself. Similar positions occur with Habermas, with his "hermeneutic criticism", an attempt to illustrate that any interpretation is subject to communication, which is distorted by capitalist relationships of power. Frequently, hermeneutics is criticized for its characteristics of "relativism" and "subjectivity", but it is a stimulating proposal of sociological, useful debates for educational technology and distance education, mainly because it remains as a science of problems that rise from the symbolic.

great methodological discussion between historians and social theoreticians of German speech like Dilthey, Rickert, Simmel and Weber, in the eagerness to obtain an alternative epistemological foundation for scientific sociological studies.

Aspositivism faced harsh criticism as the dominant model for sociological investigation, it started being replaced by the "interpretive" and "illuminative tradition" (analytical neowittgensteinian philosophy of action, language and social life), whichundermines positivism as it offers another logical support to the interpretive approach on how to explain and understand social phenomena, among them the educational, conventional and non-conventional ones.

By adopting into this framework the definition of sociology of Max Weber, we could paraphrase it towards a sociology of electronic distance education as the area that tries to achieve the interpretive understanding of the socioeducational action mediated by ICT. The -manifest or subjective- "action" includes any process that the individuals implicated in these projects grant them when resemantifying various meanings, within the context shared with others to, consequently, guide their intention and direction.[53]

## Why Is "Interpretive Understanding" Important to the Sciences in General, the Social Sciences in Particular, and, therefore, to Education?

Making something intelligible is only achieved by reference to the sense that the actors give it. In other words, an interpretation of the meaning that the actor confers to a phenomenon, process, or conduct is required.Another way to explain it would be to maintain that all the descriptions of actions must contain an interpretive element. So that any behavior can be interpreted, some identification of its "subjective meanings" or particulars of the reason of those who carry out those actions is needed. The actions, unlike the behavior, incorporate the interpretations of the actor and for this reason may be understood. One of the missions of the "interpretive" social science consists of discovering those meanings to make the action within a social context intelligible where it acquires sense. Therefore, when describing an action of an educational program or material, of electronic distance education that "teaches", we would implicitly appeal to a background of operative rules within a determined society, which in turn includes the specifications of what will be understood in this context to be taught.

The social character of these actions arises from the networks of meaning that the individuals grant to the context in their past and present history through the "forms of life" of the social organization in question, those which in turn structure in a certain way some interpretation of "reality".

From the perspective of the interpretive investigator, the meaning of the actions depends on the understanding, the purpose, and the intention of the agent and on how the latter interprets the meaning in the context of an electronic teleeducational action. The interpretive approach of the social sciences tries to discover the sense and meaning of the actions in a rational and authentic way to generalize understandings and to extend the reach and the precision of the language used in the description of this action, so as to coordinate it with other actions and thus produce knowledge in such field.

[53] Weber, M. (1964). *The theory of social and economic organization.* Nueva York,The Free Press.

To this, what is "practical" and the "the practical deliberation" (Schwab, 1969)[54] must be added, which seeks to consider different possible options of action in a determined situation, the intentions and the commitments of the actor involved, given the specific circumstances with its possible limitations. In other words, the interpretive social science attempts to deepen intuitions and vitalize commitment as ittransforms consciences, differentiates the ways of apprehension, and illuminates the respective action. It thus feeds, the interior of an online distance education system, the practical deliberation that deepens the meaning in action in an indirect way, that is, through the reflective mediations of the social actors involved.

## The ICT Defy the Various Distance Education EFFORTS. Characteristics and Risks of the Information Society and the Knowledge Society

Understanding the "knowledge society" as a process of gestation of phenomena, more than a destination of accomplishments, as it considers the set of socioeconomic and cultural transformations that are generated within its social network, not only seeks to emphasize the raw material of this process –the processed and resemantified information- but characterizes its transformation into "knowledge".

For this reason, it is said that "knowledge is the production center of new wealth" (Drucker, 1993), [55] or in sociology it is considered the central opportunity for the achievement of a "social mobility". It is knowledge that grows and multiplies supported in permanent learning and training when shared with others. This involves transformations, not only epistemological, but in the same structure of social relations within a social organization and, therefore, of the proposals of learning that include new sociocognitive models of collaborative work in the use of virtual environments of telematic communication.

Associated to the knowledge society, some theoreticians (OCDE, 1997)[56] consider this the " network society " (or of *networking*), where the new sociotechnological logic establishes organizational forms based on interactive connections between different levels and positions within a network-organization. The operation of the network made possible by ICT contributes to the flexible conformation of the current globalization, as an entity in constant interdependence and interaction within a changing, although contradictory, environment. The network should not be conceived as a pure phenomenon of technological connections but as the systemic disjunction of global and local relations (or "glocal"), of the public-formal and the private-real, represented by the elite that inhabits the timeless space of global flows. In reference to the logic of global power, the majority of the countries of the south of the world inhabit the fractured localspace/time of their cultures, and they take refuge in the logic of a *hybrid identity*. We are facing new phenomena of a social mutation, or the beginnings of a true change of time.

There stems the need to not only think of conditions to favor the shift to a type of still nonexistent society, towards another more current and of greater social pertinence, but also to

---

[54] Schwab, J. (1969). "The practical: a language for curriculum". *School Review*, vol. 78, p. 124.

[55] Drucker, P. (1993). *La sociedad postcapitalista*. Barcelona, Apóstrofe.

[56] Ocde (1997). *Sustainable flexibility. A prospective study on work, family and society in the information age.* París. Citado por MARCELO, C. (2002). "Aprender a enseñar para la sociedad del conocimiento", en Education Policy Analysis Archives, Vol. 10, N° 35. http://epaa.asu.edu/epaa/v10n35

form an alternative (or counterhegemonic) proposalto the knowledge society, as will be mentioned further ahead.

The concept of knowledge that little by little was added to the one of information[57] was originated bound to the new ways of operating imposed by ICT and by the change of political-economic model with the new above-mentioned way of working in relation to the handling of information. This gave as nomenclature the appearance of the "knowledge society " that although it is different from the characterization of the information society, it acts in interdependence and complementariness with the same, as mentioned in previous pages.

This way, elaborating knowledge means relating concepts in a systemic and innovating way. Consequently, this production of knowledge as process and product of the action of knowing takes place through the applicative exercise of higher cognitive functions when understanding a situation, a relationship, a phenomenon. The novelty that the "knowledge society" contributes is not the constructive activity on the part of the user with the use of language (Ceberio and Watzlawick, 1998; Watzlawick and others, 1991; Derrida, 1972),[58] but the greater number of social instances that take part in that construction.

We are claiming the need for a new ontology or a new look at the social phenomenon,described now in not only collective terms but of "flows": capital flows, informational flows, of nomad and migrant groups, fluid forms of construction of identity, etc., which means that everything becomes labile, malleable, adaptable, difficult to manage under the same form: they are weak, liquid or ephemeral forms.

With the listed characteristics, information as well as knowledge penetrate all the dimensions of socioeconomic and cultural life. Their greater emphasis lies in the economy with the transit of mechanical execution of repetitive tasks - of the massive industrial type with manual labor and standardized physical force-towards the performance of work that involve greater re-creation given by the higher thought functions.

New ways of thinking, solving, and doing mediate, which demands a know-how that unfolds competencies related to innovation and creativity.

Consequently, a new mapping of professions with a new configuration of sociocultural and labor roles emerges, among others, increasingly professionalized, which establish unheard of ways of producing, communicating, and managing. In turn, the new professional who appears is a person committed to his permanent reconversion since his information and knowledge become unstable at the same time as his job (in the hiring, duration, wages, health benefits, education, etc.). He also makes a cult of individualism, not only due to the exacerbation of the conditions (called flexible) of competitivity, but to palliate the given fragmentation with regard to the previous "communities of office" and the collapse of many of the supportive institutions like family, the State, conventional companies, etc., and above all life styles, values and beliefs (Barbero, 2000).[59]

---

[57] Information needs *fact* as a necessary antecedent to arrive at the same,and thus reach, by processing, the knowledge of something. Nevertheless, although it is a necessary condition to establish common codes and to store them in a neuronal and/or computer science network, is not sufficient to produce knowledge and to take part in a learning process.

[58] Ceberio, M. y Watzlawick, P. (1998). *La construcción del universo*. Barcelona, Herder.
Watzlawick, P. y otros (1991). *Teoría de la comunicación humana*. Buenos Aires, Tiempos Contemporáneos.
Derrida, J. (1972). *De la gramatología*. Buenos Aires, Siglo XXI.

[59] Barbero, J. (2000). "Tecnicidades, identidades, alteridades: des-ubicaciones de la comunicación en el nuevo siglo". *Diálogos de la Comunicación*, México.

Many authors refer to the knowledge society (Castells, 2002)[60] visualizing a special sociotechnological transformation, since, in fact, all the historically known societies have been and are "knowledge societies". Information and knowledge are elements – like mortar for social cohesion and integration-necessary in a decisive way for the generation, exercise, and distribution of power, prestige, and wealth within a society. We ask ourselves if we would have to think ofalternatives to propose to other tighter knowledge societies, as we'll see further ahead, to other realities beyond the existing ones in central or hegemonic countries.

What defines the present society, like the information society and knowledge society, (incarnating different although complementary characterizations) are the conditions and intentions that generate and invigorate them, which were modified by a revolution of ideas and ICT. These material - andsymbolic – technologies penetrate all social, institutional, economic, and cultural contexts, not only of a social unit, but of blocks or regions of countries to exploit their limitless and speedy possibilities of communication and expansion.

The specific aspect of this model of societal development is the *action ofknowledge in and for knowledge itself as the main engine of productivity and creativity* impelled by the telematic interaction of the scientific-technological revolution, as it offers opportunities of all types, although centralized in the economic.

Consequently, when we name the knowledge society, we point to the launch and expansion of the energy of thought, innovation, and creation. Therefore, it is remarkable how the knowledge society *surpasses* the information society concerned with reducing every operation to the set of information given by data processing. Although technology makes this processing possible in its more generic application, it does not guarantee the generation, potentiation, re-creation and transfer of knowledge per se. It is worth mentioning that innovation requires intelligence and anticipation, extremely important motives that change the profile of the society in question.

"In the knowledge society the wealth is in the ideas" (Cornella, 2000),[61] in other words, on the stage ofthe intangible, which demands greater reflectivity fromindividuals and groups (Giddens, 1997)[62] to act with greater awareness and responsibility. We are dealing with a society guided by the autonomous and mature learning of permanent revision, due to the situated and shared construction of knowledge; therefore, by the evaluative and critical analysis the information. In this society the invisible technologies incarnated in thought strategies (or mindware) have a central role, without which all *hardware and software* cannot produce nor operate. *All of it*is improved with the great relevance of telecommunication, which is why, conceptually, this society is tied to the paradigm of the "network society " (Castells, 2002).

This way, the challenge of the future, which has just begun, is in the *design of the knowledge that involves a sociocognitive revolution*. Its substrate is the technological knowledge (Fainholc, 2005)[63] that expands throughout all ofthe social reality: from politics,

---

[60] Castells, M. (2002). "La sociedad del conocimiento: un nuevo paradigma tecnológico",en *La dimensión cultural de Internet*. Barcelona, UOC.http://www.uoc.edu/culturaxxi/esp/articles/castells0502.html

[61] Cornella, A. (2000). *Infonomía.com: la gestión inteligente de la información en las organizaciones*. Bilbao, Deusto.

[62] Giddens, A. (1997). "Vivir en una sociedad postradicional", en U. BECK, A. GIDDENS y S. Lash (eds.), *Modernización reflexiva*. Madrid, Alianza.

[63] Fainholc, B. (2005). *Enseñanza y aprendizaje en la sociedad del conocimiento*. Buenos Aires, Publicación CEDIPROE.

economy to epistemology, ecology, biotechnology, ethics, etc., and imposes a deep challenge to education in all its manifestations and modalities, among them the electronic remote or distance ones.

For the same reason, the sociocultural impact of the incorporation of ICT in education in general and specially at a distance should be studied, through not only the sources of information and their processing, but through the appearance of new environments of virtual learning in courses of electronic learning (pure e-learning or blended learning when appealing to a combination of media). This deserves a sociological analysis due to the particular characteristics that they give to the mediated pedagogical relationship, visualized in the tutorial, the creation of contents, the use of social communication channels and/or technological platforms, the organization, administration, and management of the information within the interactive proposal for learning and teaching, among other elements.

The knowledge society is the society of continuous trainingand learning throughout life, which cannot be separated from the formation of a whole citizenship, a culture of dialogue, a democratization with equality in the distribution of possibilities andcommunicative ethics, which absorbs the various cultural multimediations and facilitates its symbolic and material appropriation.

Learning to learn, or arriving at the knowledge of knowledge from the mature personal introspection passing by what is group shared, should be considered in the discussion about the complexity of what is real, which is now articulated with the virtual-global. Moreover, the holistic systemicism and recursivity (Morin, 1999)[64] should necessarily find themselves inscribed in the multidiscipline,in order to allow us"to think sociologically" – as said by Z. Bauman (1994)[65]- the everyday experience, the sources of power, and their need to transform/overcome. It is also important to allow us to think that the new type of structural change that is being analyzed fragments and gives fragility to, with concurrent transformations, individual and social identities (Barbero, 2000)[66], the cultural landscapes of class, gender, ethnic group, race, and nationality, which in the past had provided solid locations in countries, groups, and individuals. It is important to recognize, also, that the tension between identity and difference, unit and plurality, the antagonisms, the contradictions, and the most various exclusions that this setting produces are elements of sociological reflection, impossible to delay, in the analyses of this society.

## Characteristics: Between the Democratization and the Technological Manipulation of Meaning

The information society and the knowledge society will be understood, then, as they are inscribed within the paradigm of *complexity*, which involves (Morin, 1995)[67] a weave of heterogeneous components inseparably associated to present the paradox of the one and the multiple. The unit is the whole and the whole is the unit. Within this system, the complexity

---

[64] Morin, E. (1999). *La cabeza bien puesta*. Buenos Aires, Nueva Visión.
[65] *Op. cit.*
[66] *Op. cit.*
[67] MORIN, E. (1995). *Introducción al pensamiento complejo*. Barcelona, Gedisa.

is fed on multiple entrances (or *inputs*) and exits (or *outputs*), infinite in terms of flows, not always eliminating uncertainty, ambiguity and imprecision.

In addition to the mentioned characteristics of the information society, there are others like prosumption (Drucker, 1993)[68] given by personal and group protagonism in the production of knowledge through technologies in general and ICT. Also, the impulse of developing self-use of individuals and groups in projects, where the demand and the use of ICT and Internet is perceived with more intensity, along with the necessary socialization and development of sociocognitive and communicational capacities through technology. Thus, autonomy projects are developed, which must be understood as social practices to build meaning of the greatest density and diversity, from personal objectives defined and shared in a group, which forms a network-community.

To think of this society from complexity does not mean to think of it from difficulty or how complicated it appears to us for its analysis, but that we opt to understand it from the multidimensionality and multiplicity supportive of the objective and subjective variables that compose it. It involves conceiving, in turn, the cyberculture of the information society and the knowledge society as a communicative practice or way of life mediated by technology, that modifies the types of communication in the transformation of space and time, of real to virtual of simulation.

Nevertheless, when creating a socio-phenomenological description of the globalizing process, beyond considering the internationalization of information and finances via telematic virtualization of its processes and results, it is important to recognize not only the transformations originated by ICT but also the existence of imbalances and delays that take place due to political fragmentation and the loss of several sovereignties. Simultaneously, *globalization* is seen as the characteristic marked by different expansions, in addition to the territorial ones given in the past, and which involves a strange experience of a "world that exhausts itself" (Bauman, 1999)[69] unlike other historical experiences.

According to Virilio (1995), [70] globalization is based on a temporary distance that diminishes as the capacities of transportation, transmission, and teleactions increase. The new global space is speed, instantaneity, momentaneity, simultaneous disappearance and appearance of actors, given by quick changes in human communications and actions at a distance, with unlimited vulnerability of objects, impossible to predict. It is a space where the borders are erased with speed, agility and cleverness, where unstable coalitions prevail or the temporary coexistence that responds to the convenience of obtaining benefits because, otherwise, the same vanish or are suspended. The social relationships are not lasting and solid, but liquid (Bauman, 2006)[71], fragile and brittle although useful, because otherwise they would not be materialized.

Globalization, resulting process of the capacity of certain activities to work in real time and on a planetary scale, constitutes the content of the network society (Castells, 1998)[72],fluid and open, where connectingto "surf", typifies the new mentality or continent. When we "surf", we proceed faster than swimming and without submerging into depths, in other words, there is a more superficial contact with the substance where a person moves. Sartre (1943)

---

[68] *Op. cit.*
[69] *Op. cit.*
[70] Virilio, P. (1995). "Speed and information: Cyberspace Alarm".http://www.ctheory.net/text_file.asp?pick=72.
[71] Bauman, Z. (2006). *Modernidad líquida*. Buenos Aires, FCE.
[72] *Op. cit.*

referred to this sensation as "swamp-like"; it is avoided so as not to sink in it. On this matter, it will be illustrative to consider some deductions made by students about electronic programs, as we shall see later.

Some metaphors also help to perceive the "sociality or exposed relations" allowed by the connections of ICT. Although these are useful to connect (and build social bonds), they are also easily disassembled (because they are ephemeral); among other sociological characteristics, this will mark the difference between those who are "connected" and those who are "disconnected" within an unequal social frame of "endless" time.

It is interesting to analyze and decipher the semantic content of the word "globalization" in its reference to culture, in order to show its possible ideological loads. It is also interesting to analyze, from the perspective of the present economy and ICT, the impact it produces in the economic-social-technological and educational inequalities, due to the concentrations of power and wealth given by the production, consumption, the differential quality, and the direction of the global flows of information.

García Canclini (1996)[73] typifies globalization as the hybridization not only given by the mix of heterogeneous elements, but mainly by the suppression of old repertoires and collections of characteristics, and by the erosion of old identities and values. This is pronounced within globalization with the deterritorialization, dematerialization, and despatialization (Castells, 1998)[74] that accompany the phenomena of migrations, uprooting, and disintegrations: all challenges for the educational task.

Some relate these processes to the sociological appearance of new social movements that fight against the double disappropiation produced by delayed hypercapitalism: the one related to work and the one related to one's own meaning of life. The first one given in economic and symbolic terms since the work is separated from the worker, therefore nobody can recognize his work. The second, because as there is more information, there is greater misinformation or of less sense and meaning in the face of events, which shows a certain perverse logic.

No deconstructive and rupturist sociological analysis, in other words, reflective, explanatory, and interpretive, resists consideringglobalization only as an economic, financial, and administrative business, supported by telematics, if it does not include a philosophy also directed to favoring social inclusion, mental openness, and the respect for interculturalism in the world time and space: another challenge for the formative task in all its modalities.

Globalization shows its weakness in respecting the distinction between the internal and external world due to the height of the transnationalization of symbolic flows, the appearance of new regimes of sovereignty, and the redefinition of the obligations of the nation-state, the multiplication of the conflicts of values and traditions between civilizations and communities that defy the legitimacy of a genuine world governance.

The question of the legitimacy of governments - associated to the above mentioned- is gradually displaced by the concern about world governability and this is evident in several dominions. In the *dominion of economy* it involves a transformation of the relations between the states and the markets, an intensification and reorganization of multilateral commerce, an increasing emphasis on the comparative competitiveness of nations, and the multiplication of

---

[73] García Canclini, N. (1996). *Culturas en globalización*. Caracas, Nueva Sociedad.

[74] Castells, M. (1998). *La ciudad informacional. Tecnologías de la información, estructuracióneconómica y el proceso urbano-regional*. Madrid, Alianza Editorial.

"systemic risks", like the destruction of the environment or the transmission of crises by contagion, specially financial.

It entails, in the *social dominion*, the arising of a transnational civil society that includes the increasing recognition of spheres of public action in private organizations and the emergence of anti-establishment movements as a response to threats to the integrity of its identity, which communicate with each other and seek to counteract the homogenizing effects of globalization and its impact on the local communities. In the *cultural dominion,* it promotes the appearance of multiethnic and multicultural societies, the formation of world cultural industries, the transnationalization of the symbolic flows, and the multiplication of conflicts between civilizations and communities surrounding values and traditions.

Another characteristic is evident by virtualization. A phenomenon based on the virtual (Queau, 1993), it arises articulated to the globalization of ICT; in other words, as the basic technological support of the information society and the knowledge society. This nomenclature is applied to various phenomena and social organizations, like the virtual company, virtual democracy, virtual hospital, virtual university, virtual classroom, etc., which adopt this modality of existence and operation. Such phenomena occur in "cyberspace", concept coined by Gibson (1995)[75] to refer to the delocalized place where there are virtual objects and phenomena, nonphysical but created thanks to digital logical-mathematical operations carried out at enormous speeds by sophisticated computers in connection to networks as the result of ever more popular computer and telematic transactions in order to designate the correlation of real places. It gives as aresult, spaces where a high percentage of the social interaction of the 21$^{st}$ century takes place, through cybercafés, cybermarkets, cyberbanks, cybermuseums, etc., which form the cybersociety and cyberculture.

It is epistemologically considered that what is virtual is opposed to what is real – although it really isn't - because what is virtual is imaginary when forming a type of different reality, formed by material and tangible objects, in other words, made up of atoms. Negroponte (1995)[76], Levy (1998)[77] and De Kerckhove (1999)[78], among others, study virtuality and cyberculture as what ranges from what is real to what is virtual including what is possible and what is present. It is worth remembering, here, the category of "the potential" enunciated by Aristotle.

What is virtual (Levy, 1998)[79] is not opposed to what is real but it can have its own reality being more *the opposite of what is current*. For example it would be, according to the author, the existing language but that nevertheless possesses a virtual(or possible)existence and is updated – goes from possible to current- when it is named or written about. Let us remember that in these contexts language appears as a numerical and logical representation of reality or any convention today represented by the electronic form, production, and storage in the memory of a computer of telematic distribution.

This way, the ICT allow us to surpass narrow and localist visions of reality, increase knowledge and cultural contact of different social groups around the globe to facilitate the participation in global communities and, therefore, to remodel the efforts of electronic education programs.

---

[75] Gibson, W. (1995). *Neuromancer*. Nueva York, Ace Books.
[76] *Op. cit.*
[77] Levy, P. (1998). *Qu'est-ce que le virtuel?* París, Editions La Découverte.
[78] De Kerckhove, D. (1999). *Inteligencias en conexión. Hacia una sociedad de la Web*. Barcelona, Gedisa.
[79] *Op. cit.*

Certainly, this process of telematic networks plays a key role in the phenomenon of creation of an awareness and world perspective, where it is possible to experience new ways of citizen organization and participation beyond the scope of the traditional states when rescuing other spaces given by associations, institutes, nongovernmental organizations, etc. Nevertheless, this is not foreign to the commercial interests of the multinational companies or many governments in general and/or in particular, of other centers of power like universities and institutions of postgraduate investigation, with damage like the appearance of certain cultural uniformism in world views and practices to the detriment of cultural diversity and wealth represented by the set of existing organizational proposals.

In short, the telematic networks encourage new forms of social participation beyond the local territorial limits. The performance of the individual, generally limited the scope of the community or specific territory where he/she lives, is opened now, through the digital technologies of communication, to their intervention in globalized spaces. It also reaches political action, the organization of the so-called antiglobalization movements and even the violent fundamentalisms, of no acceptance in mature and responsible communities.

Nevertheless, when recognizing other facets of the issue at hand, we also point to those who are segregated and do not have access to the new developments and virtual activities of ICT, because they do not have electricity and connections, or lack the minimum technological literacy with the required competencies to move in the new society and economy based on information and knowledge. For this reason, we mentionwhat is held by Castells: "The new technologies neither create nor destroy employment: they transform it ". It seems logical that education must contribute to oil these gears training individuals with flexible minds to share this ideology and pertinent abilities but in a reflective way, even more so if they receive the influence and global pressures in conception and canned products of programs and materials, specially of distance education programs through electronic learning (*e-learning*), the main contributor of a global electronic economy.

We are dealing with an important sociological concern given by the dissolution of the bonds of the so-called "organic solidarity" (Durkheim, 1973)[80],where the interaction and social interdependence in groups and institutions (like family, community, and local company) were emphasized in the first industrial stages of society and which today are reduced to being "contacts" in the network, made possible - with or without risks- by the existence of ICT.

Therefore, fissures, paradoxes, and contradictions are evident due to the strong presence of values, beliefs, uses, and new habits in the society in question, which cannot be lodged or contained, if it were not with unfruitful processes of regulations and adjustments. These issues are studied by a "sociology of order" which in a sly way hides the search for a "perfect society" disguised by homogenizing elements extracted from the global context where the network society named is registered.

On the contrary, as we face this new "civilizatorial" paradigm, it is convenientto produce and organize information without disregarding, on the one hand, the facts from the past nor, on the other hand, those that are exchanged today to arrive at knowledge, understanding, and wisdom in the future. Therefore, it is necessary to help and to help ourselves for a future of more self-control, of a human face and respect, useful in reconstructing mental

---

[80] *Op. cit.*

representations and objective sociocultural realities appropriate to the new historical times and, in turn, to demystify false panaceas and illusions.

There are other characteristics of the information society and the knowledge society related to the appearance and use of ICT and which concern direct, indirect and mediated communication, interesting from the sociological point of view of a distance education, such as the one which is being built:

- *Openness,* because concentration and a fixed geographic residence is not demanded; users can be dispersed; also, because there is amultiplicity of cultural contexts, levels, and social needs like learning styles presented by the users of ICT in various programs
- *Flexibility*, because it is not tied to rigid requirements of space, attendance, time, and pace but there are possibilities of combining and harmonizing different formative resources in the presence of demands from family, work, and learning/study.
- *Economic optimization*, as it saves travel expenses; change of workplace; facilitation of selection and edition of information and updates of materials; etc.
- *Lifelong learning*, because it allows the education and training of adults in service, the acquisition of new abilities and values, like continuous updating.
- *Personalization*, because it favors the possibility of studying in private and without the pressure of a group; the individual work of the users according to its demands is encouraged since each one can look for and consult whatever interests them according to experiences and previous knowledge.
- *Interactivity*, because it makes possible the synchronous and asynchronous multidirectional communication, makes the remoterelationship close and immediate; and it allows tele-ubiquitous interaction because the participants can be virtually present in many distant places at the same time.
- *Active learning*, because the user/student is the protagonist and symmetrical subject of self-learning; it demands activity, personal effort, processing, and a high degree of implication in the workon a greater scale.
- *Collaborative learning*, because the work in groups and the cultivation of social attitudes is encouraged; learning with others, from others, and for others through the exchange of ideas and tasks.
- *Democratization of information from various multiformats* - multimedia and hypermedia -, because with Internet we have at our disposal the greatest media library or cosmic documentation center, in comparison with other centers like colleges and those of investigation.
- *Intelligent recovery of information*, because it encourages the user to change from being a mere receiver of information to a producer of the same demonstrating his/her capacity to look for, value, select, and recover data as a protagonist.
- *Multidirectional democratization oftraining*, because in having access and connectivity we canbegin to surpass various limitations and barriers in reference to education.
- *Diversity and dynamism of information*, because it is presented in an attractive and engaging way.

- *Immediacy*, because any information/material can be present in the network ("to be posted") and be available from that moment on within the margin of the hour and place.
- *Permanence*, because information is not fleeting like that of face-to-face encounters or those of radio or television since the documents are registered.
- *Interdisciplinariety*, because all the angles, dimensions, and perspectives of varied disciplines, facing any issue, problem, idea, or concept, can be boarded from different disciplinary areas through hypertextual links and search engines presented in an immediate way.

## RISKS. THE DIGITAL TECHNOLOGIES ALSO HAVE A DARK SIDE

The new technologies improve the effectiveness and quality of almost all services with the creation of accessible data bases from any geographic point at any time, along with computerized management of volumes of information, to allow the remarkable increase of the speed and effectiveness of access to infinite areas of the information society.However, this civilization is dependent on technology in progressively increasing levels, since without digital machines there is no processing of information and, therefore, this society would not work. In this sense, the fear of possible faults, robberies or deficits in computers caused by computer virus, attacks of cyberterrorists, or flaws in the servers is extended, with which we've had someexperience – the "mythical" Y2K - of possible computer error, or the repeated attacks to Internet servers with their great multinational companies that alert us about this.

The analyses from the sociocultural perspective of technology, ICT and their application to distance education, online programs, given within the framework of globalization, delocalization, dematerialization, and the logic of flows, demonstrate that fragmentation, uprooting, and exclusion, among other characteristics, is produced on the part of those who do not access, do not interact, nor apply ICT and Internet in their everyday life and work due to a lack of literacy in general and specific technological competencies. This excessively impacts on the configuration of their identities: in some cases in a positive way, preparing higher thought functions with powerful *cognitive residue* as a result of the interaction with technology, that otherwise would perhaps not exist; and others in a negative way, when not being able to share with theircontemporaries, due to various segregations, the new cultural and communicational habits mediated by technology.

Therefore, a moral void and a cultural indifference within the local techno-socio-cultural world is created, a reflection of the international world that exports images and merchandise from the center to the periphery, from north to south, to millions ofusers as "migrant consuming clients". A cultural disciplining in the life styles and consumption of merchandise through symbolic and material objects takes place. Such cultural disciplining that involves social control emphasizes the existing contradictions within the phenomenon of globalization and ICT.

This way, globalization equals and homogenizes profiles, standards of life and consumption preferences, at the same time exacerbating the cultural and ethnic differences that lead to intolerance and violence facing varied issues. It is possible to observe this from the countries of the north to those of the south of the world, as well as some bordering countries - for example, in the south, from Bolivia and Argentina to Eastern European countries –just to name to some of the conspicuously excluded.

The ICT impose a uniform and standardized cultural model as part of the process of globalization supported in the control of mass media, that lead to the cultural hegemony of western civilization on the rest of the cultures of the planet. A great part of the youth in different geographic points consumes the same clothes, music, foods, games, films, communication routines by text messages, etc.; in other words, has the same cultural experiences mediatedby the same technological mediators. We move towards the cultural uniformism in detriment to the local cultures, and this increases the cultural confrontations that in many cases lead to violence.

As Barbero (2000)[81] says, the technoeconomic logic and migratory pressure discover contradictions within the universal speech of Western modernity, to which now are added the above mentioned risks of ICT, varied violence and threats due to the proximity of someone or some who are different, which leads to ostracism, the practice of unique thought, impositions, exclusions, and persecutions. This inaugurates other social and cultural distances, challenges for the existence of coexistence and the respect for difference, which education - conventional and distance- cannot always solve. Why? Because the problem is not only formative but, beforehand, ideological, sociological, and cultural. And thus it arrives and impacts on education in general and specially on distance education.

Associated to the listed phenomena, it is not easy to visualize the existence of respect when faced with the varied existing diversities but, on the contrary, the appearance of prejudice shown by segregation which occur within the factual and virtual social interactions. This is manifested in the relationship of opposition given by the "we and they" (Bauman, 1999)[82] with the usual "social distance" described by the school of phenomenology in sociology[83] (Schutz, 1977)[84] as opposed to the mental and moral proximity, that aspires to seize the "subjective significant structures" through an intuition that allows us to carry out an immediate and respectful seizure of the processes and products.

The ethics and political philosophy of the referred socio-phenomenological approach frame respect and are obvious as they involve not only the macrosocial dimension of the social bonds but also micro relationships; for example, within educational programs, the subject of our interest. Through virtual and telematic bonds, as it is the case of distance education, we appeal (or not) to the human capacity of empathy and acceptance (or not) of individuals and groups in everyday interaction.

For this reason, it is worth focusing on the study of the "we and they" who represent not only two separate groups of individuals, but two attitudes supported in different social values, given, on one hand, by emotional articulation and empathy, collaboration and confidence, and

---

[81] *Op. cit.*

[82] *Op. cit.*

[83] *Phenomenologicalsociology*: Phenomenological sociology (Schutz, 1932, Berger and Luckmann, 1967) is the child of the subjectivist philosophy of Husserl, who understood to phenomenology as the subjective study of the self. It is the preserving counterpart of the so- called critical theory, which appears in spiritualism (or antimaterialism) and subjectivism, through the ontological and methodological individualism that impregnates it, as well as the conservatism, as much ethical as political.

A consequence of phenomenology is to understand that social reality is a construction of the subject: all the facts are "significant" and therefore they must be "interpreted" by somebody to make them such. Therefore, according to this line, everything that is social is subjective, intersubjective at the most, instead of material and objective.

[84] Schutz, A. (1977). *Estudios sobre teoría social.* Buenos Aires, Amorrortu.

on the other hand, by suspicion, insecurity and fear, respectively (Bauman, 1999)[85], which in sociology refer to the recognition of the distinction between being "inside or outside a group", in other words, to the possibility of "belonging or exclusion". Understanding that "what is outside" is the imaginary opposition that the group needs to have identity, cohesion, emotional security and internal solidarity, and would necessarily help intercultural understanding, coexistence and respectful dialogues, which now increasingly appear in ICT and Internet. But we are still far from it. In the presence of the phenomenon of globalization mentioned with the consequent migrations as a constant of the dynamics of the global knowledge society, understanding the complex relationship between the "established and the foreign" would explain many underlying conflicts in social interrelationships and the widespread and unsolved prejudices, even by Internet, that cross the globe. The same would occur in the interaction of individuals in virtual forums: the most equal gather together with regard to the less equal.

It is not about if there are or aren't online educational programs of equal reach but *before that,* it's about culturally denied or unrecognized identities, in other words, characterized by old social, cultural, political, linguistic, etc. exclusions, as injustices accumulated in time to which various nationalisms, xenophobias or religious fundamentalisms are added, which as it is well known,cannot be overcome and least of all solved by education alone. Education acts like an intervening variable in any macrosocial analysis that is practiced, in the style of the one carried out here with regard to the modality of mediated education, here, at a distance with ICT. It may help, cooperate, and even maintain the genesis, configuration, and consolidation of the sociocultural, productive, and formative changes that are being called for in general, but it can hardly inaugurate them in anindependent way because these inequalities are not exhausted; they do not begin nor end, only in the sphere of education.

The times of social fragmentation and identity crises are mixed with the contradictions that appear within the hegemony of instrumental reason (or the application of any means to obtain the ends) which affect them. Identity (Barbero, 2000)[86] is not what is attributed to someone by merely being agglutinated in a group, but the expression of which gives sense and value to the life of said individual. The identity that is expressed depends on and, therefore, lives on the recognition of others. Identity, subjectivity, and citizenship are constructed in the dialogue and exchange with others within a climate of respect and peace, since it is there where individuals and groups feel recognized or accepted.

Multi and interculturalism increasingly show that the multiple figures of cultural diversity which create tension in the present information society can only be overcome by a policy of extension and practice of human rights and universal values towards all sectors of the population: women, young people, nomad, ethnic, and religious minorities.

In the present sociological analyses (Castells, Cornella, Virilio, Bauman, among others) we are shown, and alerted simultaneously, about the phenomenon of *infointoxication* and/or *overinformation* of the structures of the information society within the new equations of an "informational economy" and/or "culture of information",where it seems that the greater the amount of information, the greater the misinformation. Consequently, when facing infointoxication due to the indiscriminate and unethical access to information, there is a need to generate new "informational skills " (*literacy skills*), to counteract the nonexistent

[85] *Op. cit.*

[86] *Op. cit.*

competencies in individuals and groups, to palliate the "functional illiteracies" (technological-computer science, language and informational) like the nonexistent capacity of comprehensive and critical reading in electronic support in a computer screen with connectivity.

A new approach is therefore proposed in order to understand the formative task of the electronic educational programs that many call "informational pedagogy". This approach reframes the meaning of "human and technological mediations" given between human experience and the information distributed in the present society, to recognize information as a point of departure and arrival of the sociocultural, and education and learning processes.

Another one of the risks articulated to the already mentioned, is the result of informational exclusion. In everyday life, in the information society, the true yield is demonstrated when responding to the demands to learn to recognize what information involves in all its dimensions: access, analysis, evaluation, production, use, application, etc.

In this new paradigm, the generation, processing, and transmission/distribution of information become the main sources of productivity and power (Cornella, 1999)[87]. In the labor field, the " knowledge workers " must possess and apply intangible tools to which they must not only access but also operate and manage a mediated interaction and, at the same time, re-create them through the generation of new knowledge.

Another risk as a result of the use of ICT, leads to the loss of privacy and the increase of control over individuals and social groups, an impact essentially of a sociopolitical kind, since it is related to the nondefense of the rights to freedom and choice that each individual carried out through his/her actions.

Technology, like it or not, makes privacy disappear, in other words, it does not allow intimate spaces or actions, hidden to someone's knowledge. An individual that pays with a credit card registers numerous signals of this economic activity (whom he/she pays, the amount paid, the date and time, the place). Whenever a telephone call takes place, on a fixed or mobile phone, it is registered, with the possibility of identifying the number the call was made to, the time and duration of the conversation. A person who surfs the Web must know that the visited sites are stored and anyone, by means of this information, may have knowledge of his/her tastes, interests or leisure activities. There are, thus, computers that have access to numerous data on human existence, located in different services of public administration in their various jurisdictions (city councils, local, national, and international governments). All the governments have the temptation, almost inevitable, to seize the technological capacity to find out all and each one of the movements of their citizens. There are also different companies whose commercial goal consists indeed of tracking and storing computer data on each individual, to later sell it to other companies with advertising aims. Thus, a cyberspace terrorism begins to emerge,from which politicians, industrialists and citizens would have to defend themselves.

The ICT with their impact on modernization and globalization generates new types of social inequalities and distances which, besides producing populations of emigrants, refugees, and declassed as "outcasts" (Bauman, 2006)[88], have enormous consequences and apply pressurewith regard to the responsibilities tied to education. There is ample evidence to affirm that the access to the new technologies is not within reach of the totality of the planet's

[87] *Op. cit.*

[88] Bauman, Z. (2006). *Vidas desperdiciadas*. Barcelona, Paidós.

population, not even of the great majority of the citizenry of the economically developed countries. Therefore, the access to culture and education articulated with the use of these technologies will only be a reality for those whose economic level allows them to acquire them and who have the required and suitable skills to understand them and use them.

If what we want is that the technological mediations in general of the information society, and specially those through which electronic educational programs pass, not serve a social disciplining, but rather the transformation, creation, and promotion of equality, it will be necessary to grant predominance to the education of the various symbolic codes of media and mediators as one of the steps to lead to a democratic participation and with respect towards the multiple cultures conceived as open spaces. But this is not enough if we do not choose "principles of procedures" (Carr, 1993)[89] that propose an ethical, expressive, equitable, and supportive character, in its conception and execution, in other words, alternative to the current instrumental rationality, not only for technology but for all social relationships.

As it is easily seen, there are no processes and products of technologies that guarantee *per se* understanding, discernment, and ethics in the application (or transfer) of knowledge. The appearance of ICT and other new technologies is not innocuous: many risks are foundinwhat is known as the "second derivative" produced by the impact of technology on social life, when perceiving the complementariness of the mentioned factors and their consequences. The "second derivative" oftechnology, or unanticipated consequences, amongits various elements, is exemplified with the exhaust fumes released by the combustion engines, which are changing the planet's climate. For many years people assumed that the solution would be in the alternative fuels, although there is no evidence of their useon a large scale. Another findings states that, although a surface of the planet covered with millions ofwind mills would have a great positive effect on the reduction of carbon dioxide emissions, it could also have unidentifiable consequences on the climate on a continental scale. In other words, any problem in excess has negative effects on a global scale -which seem to be the majority-, next to the existing positive effects, although in a smaller quantity. Another example is the toxicity that would be generated in the planet in the medium term from extending nano-things (or very small things) until they become something normal in our everyday experience; not to mention Spam, the "second derivative" of the technology of electronic mail, which floods and contaminates us on a daily basis, makes us spend more on telecommunications, and makes us lose useful hours of work, and which still does not have an effective antidote.

## PALLIATIVES AS CHALLENGES

In the information society and the knowledge society, factors and phenomena more complex than those merely represented by the appearance and omnipresence of digital technologies appear and cross each other. They include varied sociological, economic, political, cultural, and educational processes such as those that have been succinctly described. The analysis of the relationship between technology and its sociocultural implications, with the configuration and development of an awareness and systemic-holistic vision that understands technology and scientific-technological development within an interdisciplinary space, is represented in the concerns which today characterize the emergence

[89] Carr, W. (1993). *Calidad de la enseñanza e investigación-acción*. Sevilla, Díada.

of a sociological perspective of reflection and action, referred to the modality of electronic distance education.

The so-called Science, Technology, and Society (STS) movement is sensitive towards this in order to overcome the traditional dichotomy between science and culture, the individual and social, the natural and the artificial-technological, dichotomies formulated from Greek thought and that continue in western modernity. In this framework, we propose considering the role of ICT, not from a descriptive perspective of their physical characteristics or scientific advance, but as far as their role in the construction of culture and social relationships with their sociocultural and educational, positive and negative effects. Different contributions in this sense constitute the before mentioned works of Echevarría (1999)[90], Wolton (2000)[91], among others.

In the present time, the integration, implantation, and generalization of TIC in our everyday life are carried out under the parameter of market logic, which means that economic factors are determinant in the access, use, and meaning of the same. For this reason, cultural distances as one more factor of social inequality, now relative to ICT, demand from the public and educational policies a fundamental role in the avoidance or, at least, in the compensation of these inequalities in the access and interaction with information and knowledge. Distance education is not left out of this. The new technologies of information and communication can separate more than unite. They narrow communication between those who use them, but exclude those who don't.

What is being suggested? That in an immediate future those citizens who do not know how to manage in the digital culture and technology in an intelligent way – to know how to connect to and surf networks, to look for useful information, to analyze it and reconstruct it, to communicate it and share it in order to re-create it with other users-, will not be able to access the current digital culture, the labor market, nor the reality of the information society, which leads to a state of vulnerability due to the incapacity of demystified use of the present resources of communication.

In the same way as the Industrial Revolution required the literacy of the manual workers so that they could use the machines in the factories, the telematic revolution also requires a new type of literacy linked to the reflective use of digital technologies. The public and private companies and administrations are aware of this, since without education there are nopossibilities of competitiveness nor growth of wealth in a society, nor social awareness. In conclusion, the technological education for a whole citizenry and of the productive agents in particular, is a strategic element for the equitable and supportive development of the information society, when generating pertinent knowledge.

---

[90] *Op. cit.*

[91] Wolton, D. (2000). *Internet, ¿y después?* Barcelona, Gedisa.

*Chapter 2*

# THE SOCIETY OF NETWORK FLOWS AND DIGITAL CULTURE: ITS INCIDENCE IN DISTANCE EDUCATION PROGRAMS

## TOWARDS A SOCIOLOGY OF DISTANCE EDUCATION, INFORMATION FLOWS, AND NETWORKS OF KNOWLEDGE PRODUCTION

Sociology shows, as one of the present scientific characteristics, the concern for studying phenomena and processes from the sociocultural perspective: for example, how the individual biographies in interaction are interwoven with others, forming interdependent and complex networks within a shared social history. This way, these mechanisms that are put into practice are those that are known about the world itself, through the practical interaction of everyday life. They are a product of the image of the world that people possess (or *habitus*, according to Bourdieu) as models built during socialization through language, which unfold like mental maps in everyday acts.

While all educational efforts - more or less conscious-throughout the history of humanity have relevance for a sociological interpretation – such asthe one that is being outlined -, we will only consider, in this contribution, the perspective of educational technology (Fainholc, 1990, 2001) represented by the modality of distance education, with special emphasis on online programs and those mediated by ICT. Therefore, to begin, we will seek to justify the possibility and the need for a systematization of positions, observations, reflections, and contrasts made from these references.

We refer to the sociology of education as a discipline that uses concepts, models and theories of sociology to understand education in its social dimension. Related to this, we speak of "social pedagogy" as a pedagogical discipline that takes into account the social education of a subject as he/she integrates him/herself into the environment and/or when he/she actively and responsibly participates (or not) to improve it. It is also recognized as "educational sociology", where the analyses begin with the social aspects. Its intention has been primarily in training, because its goal was to study the learned behavior of the person as a social being and, therefore, to better understand society.

Thus, it could be argued that the sociology of education is a "special sociology", like other sociological sciences (such as the sociology of family, of work, of religion, etc.), which deals with a specific aspect of the social sphere: the formative social forces. It also constitutes a "science of education", as it possesses the educational phenomenon as study object from the social perspective. Which does not mean that it is a pedagogical science or that it belongs to pedagogy: it is a sociological science that belongs to sociology. Therefore, it is an explanatory and descriptive discipline, that possesses a provocative and critical character as it explores and creates awareness about the possible revisions, social changes, and transformations that exist in relation to the current interpretations onthe educational phenomena.

As we shall see further ahead, and in view of what has already been said about the development of distance education programs in general (Fainholc, 1999), and in particular in the knowledge society of the end of the 20th century and beginnings of the 21st- with the educational projects mounted on the Internet and/or online -, we will consider the modality of interaction mediated by technology/ies, and the sociocultural aspects of these phenomena and processes.

## THE ICT FOR A KNOWLEDGE SOCIETY

The knowledge society arises from society and the digital cultures, inscribed within the line of constant socio-historical-cultural change. For this reason, it demands overcoming the Cartesian and linear mentalities, and requires the development of competencies to transform the accumulation of information into knowledge, intervening variables in the production of material and symbolic goods. In this great technological convergence and innovating power, these competencies are process and product of the individual and collective creativity and productivity.

For this reason, the development and articulation of national policies that promote and sustain ICT in the general and professional education and training, in public and private educational programs (formal, nonformal and informal), will strengthen the training of competencies – with technological literacy involved-, to achieve, with sustainability, the referred societal transition.

Society, with this emerging citizenship, as well as the economy, with knowledge workers, needs to re-create/learn new competencies to adapt to the times. It is necessary to reason, process, and evaluate the volume of electronic information that arrives, applying processes and tools for a comprehensive and critical reading, in conventional and combined support with ICT. While it is still not easy and equal for all social layers and groups, considering the historically specific possibilities of inequity, it is a reality that knowledge today is constructed in a situated way and distributed in intercultural and multilingual networks.

Difficulties and problems, contradictions and paradoxes are not lacking in this social or group dynamic inscribed within this 21st century where the costs of telecommunication are still expensive for many regions of the world, because a competitive connectivity or a consensus does not exist with regard to the use of democratic *open software* (or open source). The non-existence or unequal existence of connectivity by satellite or technological infrastructure of broadband in rural, remote, marginal areas, with no continuous technical support (in schools and other base organizations) does not facilitate socialization with ICT, a climate that would have to impregnate the transition to an alternative knowledge society, with a critical change of mentalities.

A commitment from the community will not be promoted without the democratization of the referred possibilities, through a training in ICT, if we seek to close the digital gap between urban and rural areas, between the north and the south of the world, within an interpretation that is conceived beyond cost analysis. Training, enabling, updating professionals, showing the pedagogical and ethical benefits of reflectively integrating ICT into the everyday life of the citizenry and into their work, will help people move from being passive consumers to being re-creators/producers of information, and develop and exercise their media and communicational competencies (Fainholc and Ferres, 2006) in real and virtual "communities", as we shall see further ahead. If there is no experience in making, interacting, verifying, and sharing information with its impact on accomplishments, change in attitudes and mentalities for less hierarchical organizations, there will be no production but an imposition of knowledge. Production involves the appropriation and intelligent use of technology in order to extract all the benefit possible to improve processes, results and opportunities, as well as promoting creativity within a society that learns throughout life.

## The Networks

The electronic communication originates new forms of social networks known as virtual communities. They share with the traditional physical networks all of their basic aspects – a community of interests, limited objectives, periodic interaction, emotional intensity, etc. (Dabas and Najmanovich, 1995)-, to which they add new specific properties offered by electronic distance communication, like intense relationships of absent body, the transcendence of geographic barriers, among other aspects. However, the networks of social models are not the only important thing in the information society. Some of the most important, if not the most important, are those that form the new economy in networks. This not only involves the rapid processing and transnational bringing together of local and regional economic-financial data articulated into the global economy - to such extent that they are confused in the international and global commercialization -, but that such information is the key factor when adding value and generating economic productivity. The new economy points to the network-company that works thanks to the ICT and which, due to their interactive interdependence, mobilizes all of the factors of production, minimizes costs, maximizes resources, increases production, and satisfies users with processes and products through greater technological benefits.

In other words, a new "field" (Bourdieu, 1990) of forces (and antagonisms) is outlined in the virtual cultural socio-economic space, where millions of people are connected daily from their terminals in the five continents and use computers for tasks as diverse as looking for information on any subject, selling services and products, living romance, studying at a distance, sharing work or research experiences, etc. It is a structured space of positions - which involves a system of status-roles -, whose properties depend on said positions in such a space and which, sociologically, can be analyzed independently of the characteristics of its occupants (although they are often partly determined by them). Here, as in any field, we will find a struggle (Bourdieu, 1990) of power and for the power, whose specific forms are recognized in a comparison between the newcomer to cyberspace, in our case, who will defend his/her right of entry, and the dominant one, who will try to defend his/her monopoly and exclude the other. Thus are established the most important qualities of the fields: the properties of the positions vary since they are often predetermined; and in all of the cases there is a struggle between the dominant and the dominated ones, in other words, relationships of power in which the actors are inserted according to their condition (veteran or acclaimed, and others, like the newcomers or novices). This concept seems to be extremely appropriate and useful for the sociophilosophical analysis (Bourdieu, 1993) of the subject at hand, because it indicates the notion of field as instrument for the scientific study of new virtual realities in the society of the 21st century, from a reflective rationality and of its typical values, if we are attempting to sociologically study the global industrial production and distribution of homogenizing materials supported in networks.

The network society does not constitute a simple phenomenon of technological connections, but it is a sample of the relationship (that includes systemic fractures) between what is global and local, public and private, through the penetration of the power of the elite in all of the orders of everyday experience, which inhabit the virtual and timeless space of global networks and flows (Barbero, 2002). This means that the asynchronies of paces and acceptances of the changes must be considered, which are not always accompanied by an interpretation with regard to the role of the financial capitals in their integration into the new way of generating economic projects. Fragmentation, lack of several representativities, and pseudo participation show how far countries and regions are from a march towards global interpretation of the economic world and the creation of oportunities for advancing economic organizations and others, alternative or nonconventional.

This paradigmatic model of a type of technological capitalist society, which has a bearing on politics, economy, culture, and education, and even on biology and wars, to name the most outstanding, is process and product of its fluid capacity to process and distribute information as its ubiquitous energy, that flows through networks of various kinds, towards the set of all human activities and lives of individuals and groups.

This extraterritorial "network", free of physical ties, provides, in addition, a "provisional" character to objects, which are not nor can be durable in this ephemeral logic used while it is useful and satisfactory, thereby eliminating the possibility of establishing a permanent bond between object and user. The figure that appears par excellence, as a result, is the consumer. Therefore, the life experience of individuals and groups is understood through the consumer choices that are carried out from the attraction to purchases in shopping centers, television channels, and Web sites, of ubiquitous competition. The objects have no lasting value. They must be used while their capacity to satisfy is not yet consumed or has not been fully consumed yet, and no more than that: every object carries with it from the beginning an expiration date (Bauman, 1993).

So, the network society is defined by a model of sociotechnological, economic, and cultural development within the globalized world, where ICT influence all of the cultural dynamic: from the most basic economic social activities to the scientific, as theyallow the expression of social movements to the formation of identity, production, distribution, and consumption of material and symbolic products and services; which are delocalized, by the information flows, to absorb cheaper manual labor and more easily accessible resources, within a market stimulated by *mass media* and telematics. Today, this is organized and optimized through world strategies thanks to the Internet, the network of networks, with the enormous role of communicating and propagating vessel as it becomes the new social, economic, and cultural space within globality.

Professionals do not always operate, nor surf, with the general, specific, and cross-sectional technological competencies that they should possess and implement in the referred context. In fact, it will take light years for these performances to become habitual in all of the users, the majority of whom is excluded and marginalized, and whose lives become increasingly segmented and "disposable". Their actions no longer refer essentially to a long term insertion in required tasks, but to designing, leading, and acting in situations as part of a fluid and unstable culture of networks, with teams, coalitions (or alliances), and malleable forms of organization that can be assembled, disassembled, and reassembled in minimum time limits on demand. The interactions are of fluid, plastic, fast, ambiguous assembly, in a society increasingly less solid. To what extent is this not contradictory in training people through education, in all of its manifestations?

## THE VALUES OF THE NETWORK SOCIETY

The frameworks, life projects,and images of a social organization as a solid and lasting totality are no longer relevant, but fragile despite having demonstrated the use for which they were conceived (Bauman, 2004). The values that prevail in the delayed capitalism of globality interwoven into the "network society/city" are flexibility, versatility, and transitoriness, which apply to all of the interpersonal, social, and labor relationships. Jointly, rationality and the concept of "the space of flows" (Castells, 1998) prevail with the supremacy of the circulation of information in the global market, in the belief that technology (artifactual) is the solution for all of society´s problems.

In this context of the function of technology, the same effect of uncertainty occurs as within globalization, in which individuals and groups do not have a shred of certainty with regard to their lives, work, projects. The highly trained professionals - and also people in general- undergo maladjustment, social descents, and sudden unemployment, due to the appearance of a new global and extraterritorial technology. In turn, among the cultural components of their lives, the language, now, of Internet carries a special weight, as shaper of subjectivity and as mortar of relationships.

Thus, the vocabulary is intersected by the new communication habits mediated by ICT (Fainholc, 2004), which in the vast majority is not only altered (deformed and shrunk) by the technology that is its vehicle, but also downgrade knowledge established by the accumulated historical experience. The everyday vocabulary used by children and young people refers to and includes exclusively the world of connectivity and the weight of the "influences" in social relationships, rather than recognize the controlling forces of a multiple, complex, and fast administration. Therefore, it carries the values of ambiguity, uncertainty, and the paradox of the informational contexts, most of the time confused and chaotic, although present in an implicit, invisible, and centralized (monopolistic) way.

Being and knowingin this societal context involves being able to communicate easily, having a wide circle of connected individuals, building a communication network (noties) in expansion, where each subject is an interface of the reticular multitude. In other words, this new bonding possibility processes the social reality through the networks and is identified/named as a network (perhaps without a prolonged life expectancy) rather than as a society. This way, it begins to manifest itself in online electronic educational programs with ICT.

## Characteristics that Begin to Exert Pressure on the Educational Distance Programs

Within the reticular framework of non-physical spaces and new communicative-cultural habits, we increasingly see a greater pressure to transfer the mentioned characteristics to educational processes. Mobile and wireless Internet (Rheingold, 2004), with other artifactual communicational additions (I-pod, Podcast, Youtube, Web.2, MP3 and more to come...) exert pressure for their incorporation into distance,remote, and online education. In distance courses some of the named supports are already included because the students rely on them for their interactions, which does not mean that they are being incorporated, combined, and exploited with caution, criticality, and precision in the new formative and communicational contexts.

## What Makes a Significant Difference in the Practice of a Sociology of Distance Education?

We could answer this question by paraphrasing the suggestive assertion about the existence of "the reform of the sociological understanding by epistemological criticism" belonging to Pierre Bourdieu and his colleagues (2002), to indicate that the different interpretations as well as the possible conceptual and methodological errors that may appear, are not originated by being a little or very stuck to a formed theory, but refer to an intellectual "disposition". The same is indebted, in its explanations/interpretations, to the current social characteristics in the present cultural and intellectual world, which often appears in an anachronistic way, or in a totalitarian way, or closed by its ideology in the transforming future of the historical times.

It could be argued that the existing compartmentation in the explanation of social phenomena is not based on a theoretical reflection that affirms the autonomy of the studied field, but on a mechanical adhesion to the tradition that established isolated disciplines, as watertight or separated fields for study and research. Thus, we face epistemological misinterpretation, which as erroneous and prejudiced beliefs, ancestral suggestions or affirmations, within social relationships, discard the search for holistic relationships and various remeasurements.

The result of this is preventing the practice of " reading between the lines", rectifying and expanding the reflective optics of the investigator in his/her scientific work, as it makes it impossible to articulate an epistemological criticism of the work that should include a sociological analysis of the sociocultural conditions of his/her production, as well as considering data as a hypothesis to verify, to conduct a criticism of the sociocultural results and impacts and others.

In other words, the monopoly of an explanation of universal, deterministic or hegemonic pretension still prevails, concealing reductionism of various kinds, such aspetty attitudes and practices in the face of existing controversies, which require a revision with negotiation of the interpretations about the realities that must accept questions from the less evident.

As can be expected, any social and cultural reality surpasses any explanation, which is why it is expected that the unilateral and excluding determinism crumble, along with the indiscriminate extrapolations, the watertight compartments, and other frameworks which do not consider the systemic-holistic and the " knowledge frontiers" as more encompassing input for the scientific-technological explanations necessary today, which rescue the specialization within a contest of disciplines in cross-sectional and organic solidarity.

## DEFINING DISTANCE EDUCATION TO ESTABLISH A SPECIAL SOCIOLOGY FOR ITS STUDY

We are dealing with an alternative educational modality that mediatizes the sociopedagogical relationship with the use of different technological supports/media which today include telematic networks, virtual classrooms, videoconference, etc., with mediated teaching strategies and learning materials of different types, from the most conventional and artisan, like print material, video and audio cassettes, posters, theater, marionettes, etc., to the most electronically sophisticated, like CD-ROM, telematic networks and ICT, with the corresponding didactic processing of the content to be dealt with, to constitute formal, nonformal, and informal training proposals, according to an anticipated training, in discontinuous and/or remote time sequences.

This modality requires the design, management, and practice of educationally-technologically mediated learning and teaching, which involves an educational innovation of real weight in the socio-political agendas of governments and countries (today organized in blocks), groups and organizations, as well as of institutions of higher education and colleges (of graduate and postgraduate degrees) which show a special interest in their reflection, investigation, investigation and application thinking about a possible cost reduction.

Distance education does not necessarily mean "open education", since many educational distance programs adopt the same face-to-face criteria - some restrictive of conventional institutions -, which do not adhere to the philosophy of democratization and overcoming of inequity that open education has set out to accomplish, as a global trend, for people over 25 years-old. Distance education has adopted, with the articulationof ICT, the denomination of "connected education", as itrecognizes that connectivity is established today as the space and goal in order to create new environments and nonconventional learning opportunities, within the widest possible sociocultural frameworks and pedagogical contributions. We must remember that although distance education includes online education,not all online education is distance education, and less so, open education. (Fainholc, 1999).

Of course, the appearance of the modalities of distance education, in general, and electronic in particular, has implied a change of frameworks within the shifts of paradigms (Tapscott, 1997), that show the passage from linear learning to interactive learning with ICT; of instruction towards discovery in the construction of knowledge; from learning centered on the expert (or professor) to the one centeredonthe learner (or student); from a position where he/she absorbs contents passively, in a transmissive way, to moving towards the active learning of how to learn (metacognition by means of a reflective navigation) with other people connected to the network in a synchronous or asynchronous way; from massive and indiscriminate learning to customized learning; etc.

We adhere to a point of view of *alternative* interpretation of distance education, where it is perceived and understood that *knowledge occurs in action*, to formalize *socioculturaltheories of practical aims*, developed from the critical reflection on mediations, mediators, and media. This way, we enter another conceptual and practical weave that articulates the participation and interaction of everyone involved. Itis the communicative, expressive, imaginative, metaphorical rationality, according to which actions are guided by the ethical-socio-political, the reflective cultural practice, and the autonomous free accomplishment of the individual and groups. The new *ethos* underlying of above-named rationality of reflective and critical practice thus guides the interrelationships of individuals in their mediated contexts as spaces of interest and action with the global world, rather than just focusing on the interconnected supports.

The difference that is added and concerns us, apart from including the sociological approach to a distance education mediated by ICT, would appear in overcoming the instrumental rationality through the practice of a holistic, historical-prospective, and comprehensive vision. The same would seek a multiple synthesis and interrelationships in order to understand the educational modality referred to in a situated way and, thus, construct transdisciplinary and cross-sectional frameworks for its cognitive-conceptual-perceptual, and axiological deepening, specific to each context and program.

Overcoming the instrumental rationality as an ethical concern – a challenge of formative achievement - aims to review human alienation. It does not mean that the person has lost control over him/herself (a worrisome fact considering the technological consumption that often includes the symbolic violence of the present penetration of media) but it would seem that the exerted self-control has not been enough.

This way, a look from the critical sociology of distance education, such as the one being presented, marks an analysis anchored in the sociocultural interdisciplinary aspect, supported in critical science and situated discernment with regard to the existence of electronic online educational projects of cultural hegemony, as evidenced by the enormous expansion of these programs, often in an indiscriminate or nonpertinent way, in other words, mercantilist, with the use of ICT.

The underlying conception of "cultural hegemony" (Broccoli, 1979) is based on the relationship between the strategies of the organizations and/or consolidated blocks of groups and countries, that operate with certain privileges with regard to the subordinated groups, within a setting in conflict, in any organizational field. In order to understand the issue of the present hegemony and digital culture, we would have to bear in mind that behind the culture there are powerful groups that immobilize people's capacity of re-creation and their values, which make a social order or organization resist change and reject the changes in honor of various ideological fundamentalisms, in other words, perpetuating (Habermas, 1981).

In addition, the subject of the present hegemony and digital culture refers to the necessary contextualization of the operations of information processing, process that is carried out, in general, in a centralized way to facilitate its commercialization. The networks with connectivity to Internet possess extremely varied systems of collection of information, conduct analysis with investigation goals (supervision of all types) where the virtual habits of all of the people connected to the network are controlled, to not only more finely delimit the consumption segments, but also to collect numerous data. For the development of thesefunctions of social control, academic scholars, economists, and investigators of outstanding reputation, who work in global organizations dedicated to telematics and its various applications, are employed.

In the same way, electronic online distance education, should also have to be located within the framework of an existing virtual globalization that extends the control of a privileged minority (educational designers, content experts, and supraterritorial suppliers of technological platforms of management of contents and tutorial actions of international courses (Local Multipoint Communication Systems - LMCS -, wireless broadband systems) using and thickening an "academic capitalism" (Slaughter and Rhoades, 2004). It serves a majority of the universities, with global students who - in general, due to market pressures- continue training programs (which often hide curricula inspired by unique and deregulated thought) within the framework of a hegemonic cultural project that today spans virtually the entire planet.

The difference that interests us refers to the stage ofwhat is intangible, since we need and demand from individuals and groups greater "reflectivity" (Giddens, 1998) so they may act as much in the public sphere as in the private one, with greater commitment, awareness, and responsibility if we desire a society guided by autonomous and mature learning of permanent revision, caused by the situated and shared construction of knowledge within social life.

Reflectivity is understood as the way in which institutions, groups, and individuals examine in a permanent way, and without time lag, their activities and practices. It is the continuous revision of the social practices in light of the new transformations referred to the same, which inevitably alters their constituent character. In modern societies, this socio-psychological-cultural revision, as an epistemological monitoring, would take place in a "taking charge of its destiny" with regard to all aspects of life, to return to the practice and reflect on past and present actions, rectify them (or not) taking into account the motivations, ways of performance, use of various knowledge in everyday life, etc.

In general, there would be two levels of reflectivity that do not seek to oppose each other in the spheres of public and private life. On the one hand, the function of revelation produced by a quantitative analysis of the appropriation of cultural practices, personal and group paths, inequalities, adverse effects, which concludes in an analysis of the argumentative logic used in actions; and, on the other hand, the level of support, given by a serious and comprehensive analysis of people'slives through the stories where they describe their lives and present their experiences.

Reflectivity as an individual and collective socioanalysis should be configured as"cross-checks" of the disciplinary debates in the style of a critical sociology of reflective scientific approach (Passeron, 1991). The axiological issues are not ignored here, to which scientific statements are linked, but we indicate the need to assume them in a reflective way, individually and collectively. Moreover, we should remember the historical contribution of W. Mills (1959), who opposes the aseptic technician of an applied sociology to the "intellectual craftsman" who clarifies hypotheses and their moral and political implications in the society where he/she is developed. Hewould, thus, serve two main functions: of research, to define the rigor and range of validity; and from the standpoint of the commitment to reality, of clarification of the supports of the interventions made and orientation in relation to socio-political uses, in our case of the formative nonconventional processes and products and with ICT for a more suitable and desirable application, depending on the cases, contents and needs.

In the information society, consequently, the tool heritage of the "invisible technologies" (Fainholc, 1997) embodied in the strategies of thought or *mindware* play a central role, for the intelligent accomplishment of the named analyses and the characterization of the knowledge society. Unfortunately, said *mindware* is not yet extended with equity, unlike the *hardware* and *software* that have invaded wide areas of the planet.

It is also important to note a certain illusion of informative transparency, that originates in the idea that, in order to explain and understand programs, it suffices to rediscover the intentions of which they are a product. This is a weak idea, or of common sense, which searches for isomorphisms among objectives and products, carries out superficial readings of the phenomena and owes, partly, its strength to common and everyday attitudes present in a society or organization. The same lead to an ethnocentrism or moralism; to the artificialist illusion of technocratism; to the belief that we are able to build or transform institutions by decree; or to the illusion of the evolutionist, for whom the past can only provide the example of forms superior or inferior to the present ones. This serves to illustrate the main means of the spontaneous sociology, which owes its sociopsychological coherence to the systematic character of the illusions it arouses. Against these illusions, Durkheim noticed that, we cannot avoid , in no social analysis, the complexity of the determinations that a social institution owes to its past and to the system of institutions in which it is inserted at the present time.

We should ask: which could or should be the ideal distance education, as an abstraction of all condition of time and place? From this perspective, we would admit that implicitly an educational system does not have anything real of itself. We would only be able to see a set of institutional practices that have slowly been produced and organized, through time, in a supportive way with other social and training institutions, and which are expressed in general today, emphasizing the economic and technological aspects.

Perhaps it is permissible to carry out investigations in these ways, because every society, considered at a specific moment in its development, has a system of education beyond the existing means, which is chosen and used to carry out its tasks, which are imposed upon individuals and groups with a generally irresistible force. This happens with ICT – which are conflicting and not always easily accepted- incorporated into education and for online programs, which are increasingly imposed. They are a product of the cultural times, the coexistence, and express the needs of the society. They are a product, to a great extent, of goods and services historically existing as vestiges of the accomplishments of previous generations. The whole of the past of humanity has contributed to producing the set of practices that form the present education in general and the "supported" technological-educational mediations in various mediators.

This is why, when studying in a comprehensive way how the electronic systems of pure or mixed distance education were formed and today are developed, we may see their dependence of cultural factors (even of religion), political organizations, the degree of scientific development reached, the progress of industries, among many other variables.

The sociological analyses of distance education are indebted to pre-existing realities that were not created out of nothing, cannot be destroyed arbitrarily, nor transformed by sheer will. Only through this understanding, we'll be able to comprehend the various existing electronic educational programs to the extent in which we have learned to know them, to recognize their nature and the conditions they depend on.

The educational sociologist faces the exteriority of social phenomena within the extension and opacity of the cultural past from which the multiplicity of actors and telematic agencies have emerged, applied today to virtual educational programs.

In order to construct a sociological reflection on distance education with the use of ICT and in the online modality, it is recommended to start with the everyday aspects, which interact with unknown elements, with the mental representations that the subjects have been able to construct about them throughout life. We should remember that in facing this, in general, people have been trained without method or criticism, which is why what they perceive as important turns out to be confusing, fleeting, subjective impressions, and not explanatory concepts. For the same reason, they could lack scientific value and should be complemented by more contrasted approaches in reality. In order to be willing to carry out these analyses of sociology, it is necessary to have reached a certain degree of intellectual maturity that recognizes and includes turbulence and rizomatic chance. The sociologist will not move among issues and phenomena that are immediately transparent to the spirit or the mind,because dark doubts, contradictions and problems face their attempts at explanation. The interaction in groups and social institutions today includes situations of crisis and passage/redefinition of various paradigms with regard to the State, genders, family, contractual and labor relations, ethnic minorities, etc., in which the feeling of ambiguity, ignorance, and difficulties is enormous.

The task of the sociologist of distance education, electronic, in our case, is just beginning to approach the development of a critical interpretation of the technological formative mediations that take part in the construction of subjectivity with the use of mediators - various artifactual, human and symbolic ones-, through the contemporary training proposals.

It is enough to review various productions in virtual books or documents on e-learning, virtual education, collaborative work, and other adjacent subjects to observe that in general in these studies the instrumental perspective, which refers to the environments and their design, production of connective materials, and training in tutorial functions is emphasized. Little is considered the invisible, in other words, investigating the double meanings in virtual interactions and texts, demystifying legitimized or consensual meanings in Web sites and Internet pages, deconstructing the quick acceptance of preconceptions. They deserve deliberate and planned studies, that cannot be exhausted quickly and without specifying the previous assumptions and notions from which they depart, which every investigator should take into account when undertaking a serious study.

## Place and Impacts of Technologies and ICT

Some theoreticians refer to the place of technology as the one formed by the abilities, procedures, and re-creations made possible by the information it involves; other sides consider it as the tools, machinery, and materials used to complete tasks in a situation, organization, etc. In other words, they point to the nature of the processes and the results obtained. These conceptualizations imply that technology incorporates the idea of how the resources to produce processes, products, and services are conceived, used, and applied. In other words, the technology deals with the transformation processes, by means of the application and the re-creation of knowledge and skills combined with tools in order to approach and solve problems or specific tasks.

The technology also deals with the way in which the individuals of an organization carry out their tasks (know-how) to produce products and services. Nevertheless, technology goes beyond the tasks directly included in the process of transformation, because it refersto the way in which the production and the distribution of products and services, with their activities of support are executed. For this reason, it is possible to argue that, from the sociological point of view, technology is the articulated set of all of the knowledge used in the production, storage, distribution, and use of goods and services, when extending the possibilities of transforming and modeling the world, and satisfying needs with diverse materials. In this task, the knowledge that allows us to do things appealing to different alternatives is included, with input like scientific knowledge, creativity, intuition, everyday techniques and even those used by our ancestors. Therefore, technology does not consist of the hard devices - based only on knowledge from sciences like physics or chemistry, or those referred to computer science, microelectronics, laser or space activities -, but rather we visualize above all the knowledge that has been incorporated into these and the way in which groups and society apply or use them.

Nevertheless, most of the definitions refer to other input that point to the procedural, which is usually called "know how", given by the implementation of soft technologies. These are not tangible objects, but they anticipate sociocognitive strategies, never complete, that allow individuals and groups to handle, integrate, evaluate, and create possible information - by means of different degrees of skill and practice- to be able to work agilely in the information society.

It will be necessary to recognize that these technological resources - in an explicit way- "make decisions", in an automated and mainly foreseeable way,once people have granted them a meaning and "permission" to act, after issuing a corresponding order for a greater trajectory (referred to a higher thought function such as analyzing, comparing, evaluating, and others). This type of decisions of superior order affects - within a sociotechnological pair- the training processes. We collect the imprinting that characterizes the mediating code of each technology, which influences the skills/competencies of each person and makes them evolve, in a line of change and permanent, transforming movement of knowledge.

The internal tools we refer to, of the person, allow him/her to apply various methods and obtain products. It deals with the design of technological projects and the evaluative analysis of their results, which, applied to the subject of distance education, points to the "design and management of electronic online distance education programs" and the "evaluation of products" corresponding to such proposals as the design of graphics and navigation of the educational sites in Internet, the technological platforms or systems that manage and process teaching content with their respective interactivity, the selection and combination of media and mediations carried out for pure electronic learning (or e-learning) or mixed (or blended learning), among other components.

These executions, which involve infinite interdependent variables, attempt to reflect, like a photograph, the structural elements and those of dynamic operation that are presented by social institutions or organizations (industrial, commercial companies or services providers, or institutions) which contain various programs and specifically, those that are online distance education programs, for the most suitable and pertinent fulfillment of the training objectives that characterize them.

Therefore, there are many contributions to these soft technologies, like sociology, the psychology of organizations, economics, design or management, and telecommunications, accounting and management operations, the logistics of production, marketing and statistics, the sociopsychology of human and labor relationships, systems engineering, the development of software and robotics, for programs of education of distant coverage or remote reach.

For this interpretation of technology, which conceives it as formed by designs and instructions that allow us to operate with procedures and a re-creation of information, as well as the second side, that considers technology as formed by the tools and machinery we require, so that "they work", more tacit technologies, referred to an implicit and invisible know-how given by mindware.

This way, we point to reflective knowledge, represented by the thought and execution strategies that allow the field application and evaluation of any technological proposal, as well as those of distance education, in general, and online, in particular. This statement supposes the association within an organization, which incorporates online educational programs, the adoption of technologies dependent of technological systems or platforms, used today for programs/courses of online distance education that supply the user-student with all the components to facilitate their learning.

The place of technology, thus, is shown with the new technologies and the ICT, which from the substantial point of view appeared little more than 50 years ago and which are perfected in an increasingly faster way with the contribution of transdisciplinary scientific research and practical confrontation.

Nevertheless, from the sociocultural perspective it is of interest to emphasize the technology (Barbero, 1987) embodied in the mediations where it is no longer merely instrumental, but becomes thicker, denser, something substantive or structural.Therefore, technology today does not refer to apparatuses, but to new ways of perception and language, to new sensitivities and writings, where the weave ofhypertexts/hypermedia reigns profusely, inscribed within the context of globalization and telematically oiled by ICT. Thus, technology delocalizes knowledge, modifying the cognitive statute, as well asthe social and organizational aspects within its conditions of production and circulation of material and symbolic goods and services. This produces two consequences: on the one hand, it erases the borders between reason and imagination, knowledge and information, nature and artifice, art and science, expert knowledge and everyday experience (common or lay); and, on the other hand, it distorts the meaning of the sociocultural demands that are expressed in the social mass media and ICT - as mediators -, and delegitimizes any questioning of the social order, which only the market and technologies shape, as social control, with the lack of privacy of individuals and groups.

In other words, besides the fact that it is an hegemonic conception, it submerges the citizenry in an increasingly compulsive consumption of a technological fatalistic kind, although attributing "panacean" characteristics. Therefore, the ICT possess an epistemological and politically strategic role in the tension within the sociohistorical mediations that grant them meaning, consensus and social scope. Regrettably the quota of critical thinking that they promote is reduced, if we do not intentionally and systematically intervene with spirit and educational actions that create awareness.

The convergence of mediations, media, and mediators through digital language inscribed within the globalization of ICT also forms a new ecosystem of languages that, in addition, forms new temporarinesses linked to the compression of information, to the emergence of new figures that digitalization provokes. The emergence of "the between- the-lines of the imaginary" written in virtuality, where the present is written with amazing speed and shapes, although in a blurred way, all reality, predisposes towards an unpredictable and uncertain future.

This way, the technologies are produced by devices thought and generated from a place; they are situated, not only socioculturally but as answer to the ways of thinking, values, beliefs, and ideology that their creator/s and designer/s have granted them and that the users resignify.

In light of the above-mentioned, a series of questions arises (Montagu, Pimentel and others, 2004). Is there an ideology of the technological world of ICT? As an idea and deterritorialized product, how is it resemantified by each user/interpreter at a specific moment? And also, by each student in a distance education program, who belong to a group/subculture? Which is and how is the ideological dimension defined to approach and understand ICT and Internet in each electronic training proposal that includes them?

For this reason, it is important to remember (Marcuse, 1972) that the conception and development of the technique depends on the relationships of power existing within a social unit, where from a certain place, a group decides various directions when holding some type of power. This means understanding the present digital technology, which has been developed from mentalities, life styles, and Anglo-Saxon capitalist cultural parameters. The conceptions and modalities of technological development are closely related to the cultural configurations of different societies (Lopez Cerezo, Luján and others, 1998), which is why it is possible to observe a certain coherence between the technologies that a society creates, or is able to create or assimilate, and the rest of the cultural features that characterize it.

Ortega y Gasset (1939) already indicated it in his *Meditación de la técnica*, as heattempted to explain the different technological styles of the East and the West, or as he opposed the cultural models of the nobleman and the gentleman. More recently, the debates over the "appropriated technologies" for the so-called emerging countries, of the south of the world, and the controversies on alternative models of economic development, have also highlighted the importance of cultural factors to explain or guide technical change. It is evident not only in the implication of language, but fundamentally in the beliefs and uses that emphasize the private over the public sphere, the individual utilitarian over the socioemotional and collective aspects of the users. Consequently, a certain pragmatic worldview tied to the slogan of the "American dream" has been formed for the ICT, which reappears even with the present "information highways" and the globally assumed development of telematics.

Consequently, in the information society and the knowledge society, shaped by the advance of scientific knowledge and investigation, it is necessary once again to define and disassemble what constitutes technology and the central sociocultural role of great penetration in all of the aspects of life and therefore in human interaction, production and distribution of all kinds of goods and services. The point of greater incidence points here to the enormous speed and great density of ICT and networks of telecommunication and Internet, which with audio-visual, multimedia, and hypertextual convergent formats have devastated social consumption and communicational habits - the same as before with social mass media (SMM) -, towards a saturation or infointoxication of the consciences (Gramsci, 1976), more than driving re-creation or expression, as an unheard of opportunity in the history of humanity.

In distance education, technology (Broncano, 2000) presents several characteristics of relevance that grant enormous influence and power to the programs mediated by it and, therefore, to the contexts that lodge it. Among the infinite input that form the distance education proposals, to name the less conventional, there is the fundamental relationship with *creativity* (which involves innovation and the functional specialization of the intuition of the right cerebral hemisphere), considered a central contribution for all sociocultural elaboration (industrialist, enterprise, formative, re-creational, etc.). Moreover, its characteristic of *functionality*, when articulating different functions or elements from various scientific and practical origins in the programs in question; and its *intentionality*, since it cannot be separated from objectives, expectations, and interests of individuals modifiable throughout the life of individuals and groups.

The new technologies inaugurate and/or deepen contradictions and paradoxes of different magnitude and importance. They are not transparent, but, on the contrary, quite opaque and not entirely friendly yet, thus, they appear a little threatening (Burbules and Callister, 2001). Nevertheless, opinions vary. Some argue (Bates, 1999) that technology and ICT are not good nor bad in themselves, but it depends mainly on the way in which they are used and for what aims, above all in distance education. From this view, it would be necessary to understand the strengths and weaknesses of the different technologies, contextualized in a specific training project, and this within the above-mentioned sociocultural setting with specific actors (students, faculty, citizens, etc.), in order to satisfy requirements for a pertinent use. This involves operating for social inclusion in a flexible way and taking precautions against the temptations of the marketing of devices, in order to adapt and not adopt ICT that arrive from other latitudes and are not always adapted to the local requirements.

We believe that the local processes of appropriation of technology finally reflect the adaptations that emerging countries make or can make with the devices and materials that reflect the dominant culture.

Addressing the controversies about the sociological issues of equity, accessibility, credibility, critical reading in Internet, censorship, lack of privacy and confidentiality, high marketing, etc. that characterize ICT, are not only problems of teaching and learning, but must drive the social and political critical reflection on the assumptions in which the socioeducational practices are supported mediated by these technologies. Therefore, it is important to raise awareness and to work on the introduction and articulation of ICT in social and educational practices and institutions. It is a technological change as aconstellation of multiple interdependent elements covering both what is chosen consciously and what is not chosen, what is anticipated as much as what cannot be anticipated (Burbules and Callister, 2001), which demonstrates how complex and conflicting this process is, fraught with diverse ambivalence.

Only a relational (and not instrumental) rationality of technology towards the search for a "post or meta technical" stage, applied in the area of formative public policies as well as of social norms and customs, should be a starting point to reflect on the organizational, group, and personal conditions, possibilities, and motivations with regard to ICT in society in general and in the face of an electronic teaching and learning.

The ICT are not only "media", in the sense of channels through which information is transmitted. An electronic space is an environment where things happen, individuals act, collaborate, and interact, and this is highly formative. The relationship between individuals is placed on center stage: technology is not instrumental and unilateral, but takes place within the framework of "an in between or relational framework", that includes culture and values. So, the ICT are not a set of tools, but a cyberspatial *public environment*, in which human interactions take place and social activities of communication, construction, and expression intertwine. They are also described as a cooperative environment where the users and citizens - and not only faculty and students, investigators and professionals -, share ideas, co-construct new concepts and interpretations and design new products within the "global" context, to promote greater humanization.

We must remember that the ICT, besides presenting the risk of proposing information - which could be partial, biased, or simply false (because it is always selected, filtered, interpreted, and extracted from a set of implicit assumptions from obvious and accepted experiences) -, are tools for communication.

The critical perspective - to which we adhere- understands that technology is derived from a particular cultural and historical formation of a relational approach, where the criteria of means and ends are interpenetrated and interreconfigured with and through ICT. It would mean surpassing the idea that they are simple means to continue doing - although sometimes better and faster- what we were already doing, or which are innovations that allow us to do things that were previously unimaginable, to conceive them as artifices that modify the perceptions that individuals have of themselves, of their mutual relationships, their interpretations of time and space, the concept of speed, their insertion in their lives, etc., with their potentialities and weaknesses.

It points to consider the inseparability that overflows any imagination and to think that we are (in fact, as always) facing the unknown, which inspires fears, unique thoughts, extreme positions (Kenway and Bullen, 2001), which describe "utopian" and "dystopian" social alternatives and that, thus, arrive to act in education. This is the reason for the incorporation of a critical and realistic perspective, not of rejection nor infatuation with regard to ICT, but analysis of their "risks" and "promises" or their dangers and possibilities (Burbules and Callister, 2001; Fainholc, 2004).

## Technology and ICT, the “Divas” of the Digital Culture

Concurrent to the information society, we see the appearance of cyberspace (or virtual reality) as a dematerialized digital environment (Maldonado, 1998) that produces a greater contraction of the universe of material objects. In fact, we can only see the tip of the "iceberg" in reference to these new realities: a great challenge for users as protagonists or producers beyond their role of readers, navigators, consumers, recipients and/or spectators.

The adoption of this protagonism lies in direct relation with the learning of competencies and the teaching of technological procedures that enable it, through the creation and practice of:

- a new hypertextual and nonsequential reading
- a new writing arising from the storage and the provision of programs supported in enormous and fast multiple and various data bases, instantly communicated and in aglobal way; and
- a transformation of human perception due to the appearance of new perceptual phenomena given among other elements by the possibility of erasing borders and/or fusing the human with the machine (Benjamin, 1968); in other words, the *hybrid-*

*robotic*, that redefines the new technoperceptions of image and sound when offering, among other new elements, new objects of art.

The digital culture (Montagu, Pimentel and others, 2004) is formed by the superconnected space (now without cables, or wireless society), where the vision of the classic theory of information (Shannon and Weaver) with the presence of a transmitter, a receiver and a channel is surpassed.

The new parameters for communication are given by interactivity that involves a perception and ways of appropriation of the new characteristics that the technological social systems establish and that the new subjects would have to execute: all of them re-creators of subjectivity. It basically means this: being located and available in a constant permeability, no matter where we are; in other words, that his/her presence, proactive predisposition, and actions are felt or perceived. In these social frameworks and electronic programs, the relevance is in being in simultaneous and permanent communication, invisible but available, of resources, "superconnected" individuals, groups and organizations, who format human relationships in very complex connections to form, finally, their very existence and subjectivity, since, otherwise, they would disappear.

This occurs because there is a direct relationship between the conception and the use that is made of technology and the beliefs, ideologies, and values of its users, their way of visualizing it and judging it as effective. Of course, it restructures in time the basic nuclei named, conducive to a slow but irreversible reorganization of social situations, where the pertinence is judged in addition to the effectiveness of such-and-such technology. It also means recognizing that technologies are not spread and distributed equally, nor at the same time, but that there are (more or less) various asynchronies in the changes seen in the cultural lags in the various social contexts in question. Which is why it will be necessary to respect not only cultural and subcultural pace, but also origins together with cognitive styles and multiple intelligences of the individuals or groups of various regions of the world, if we are dealing with distance education programs distributed online.

In order to deepen the explanation of what it means "to exist" in this virtual context (Queau, 1998), we should remember the existentialism of Heidegger, with his concept of "being there" or being in a place. Nevertheless, as well, "to exist" means *ex* (outside of) and *sistere* (place), in other words, it also means "to leave the place where one is". Thus, not only conceptual, but existential *nomadism*, is derived, accepted, and promoted, which occurs in these cultural times and contexts of the virtual, liquid society (Bauman, 2002) and of ICT, within the informational postmodernism.

Being nomadic is not something new in the history of humanity but that, according to the different historical periods, appears transferred by other profiles and characteristics. The passage to the digital social settings shows the mentioned sign of "lagging" of the social units, due to the lack of "adjustment" on the part of subjects and groups to the virtual culture. The process of reconsideration with disintegration of the social connections crumbles because many of the collective agencies disappear: everything becomes more unstable and lighter, because the structure of the sociopolitical, economic, and cultural power is increasingly fluid or slippery.

Sometimes we arrive at massive breakthrough points, with the dismissals of older workers or those who haven’t been "updated or recycled" and/or recruitment of new social levels; both include differentiated social groups: ethnic immigrants or groups, in the first case, and qualified women and youth, in the second.

The sociopolitical instruments pertinent to the liquid, light or portable regime (like practical telephones) that are described, point towards a lack of commitment and flight. On the one hand, they are professional nomads, civil employees of the network economies, and flexible teleworkers, free of ties and barriers, with insignificant social controls of their mobility, of virtual or cybercultural registry, that "fit" in a *light* way in any socio-organizational connection, beyond their territorial base. On the other hand, it implies for individuals and groups an irreversible loss of territorialism and, consequently, a sociocultural marginalization. This way, two opposite and fragmented realities appear: the powerful and famous people do not cling to their places of residence, the place where they belong, and their jobs because these change very fast and are ephemeral. Whereas those who occupy the lowest place in the social scale are most vulnerable, and struggle to make their fragile positions last.

If we considerthe information society and knowledge society as part of a cyberculture, with the consequences of nomadism, we refer, thus, to the transitoriness, precariousness, vulnerability of human and social bonds - now in networks -, perceiving that the only thing that would save this situation would be to have a plug (or wireless equipment) to be able to connect to a good network of virtual links with recognized traceable contacts.

From a systemic sociological position, we could say that this sociotelematic space is conceived as the possibility of survival without forgetting that within itorder and disorder, stability and unstability, vulnerability and invulnerability coexist, within an interconnected social conformation in an active and open, changing and uncertain system in constant transformation. This system, understood as a combinatorial association of different elements, has an ecological character based on the active participation of all of the social actors through networks of circulation/distribution of information through the multiple nodes of access and interactions between different communicative levels. It has contributed to new visions and points of view to act in the world of distance education with ICT, as an interrelated world in telematic networks that form virtual educational subspaces.

Cyberculture (Gros, 2001) would not exist without the phenomena of digitalization and virtuality made possible by the information and communication technologies, inscribed within the globalization of the multidirectional flows of information, which break through the geographic-cultural borders and delocalize processes and phenomena. Phenomena that surprise and provoke questions: it is possible to speak of new types of association? or which are the new ways of building perceptions and digital communicative relationships of interaction? or how is the symbolic capital constructed through a virtual space like Internet? When forming virtual communities, what new type of sociopolitical organization do they possess?

The social capital of the network is part of the cyberculture and the virtual electronic communities, which although they can potentially tend towards social integration, they do not always do; it is a source of disciplining power and control, which presents a great contradiction.

The ICT, with their supposedmotor of cultural inclusion for all of the citizens, mask effects of exclusion within a same human group. In other words, the digital culture with ICT, the axis of integration, hides mechanisms of social exclusion through its symbolic overlapping that includes legitimate and illegitimate uses of these technologies depending on various aims.

The contradiction is that, although there are sectors that can adopt, develop and execute the potentially egalitarian symbolic-technological competencies of ICT, at the same time, (unfortunately) a great exclusion and social discrimination are reproduced and increased. The rhetoric of democratic equality of ICT in the digital culture prevents us from disassembling this pseudo equitable logic. The ICT form proposals that establish a unifying or cohesive script or story of illumination and cultural exaltation within thegroups of this digital subculture, while other sectors are overshadowed, marginalized, and discarded from the social system, as "wasted lives" (Bauman, 2005).

If this is what occurs within networks, we should do the impossible to overcome exclusions with the stimulation of the citizen's formative action to create awareness towards the sociopolitical participation that reverts these perverse and sectarian mechanisms; an educational task of appropriation with an equitable and intelligent use of ICT for a communicative and re-creative interaction. Possessing and equipping with a prospective, constructive, and strategic vision in the long term with regard to this educational task and task of appropriation will contribute to an exact visualization and understanding of the potential, with its limitations, of various technologies, for education in general and distance education in particular, above all if we take into account the elimination of the differences between near and far, through the continuum between the conventional face-to-face education and distance education mediated with technology.

Encouraging virtual relationships that are activated in nodes of continuous cultural sociopolitical and formative participation would form in the long term genuine structures of equitable and representative bonds of power and participation with common goals and a sense of belonging to a group through a formative electronic organization. Stimulating the authentic participation promotes the development of the citizen's competencies to overcome the currently reduced inclusion possibilities, mainly in the south of the world.

We believe that the ICT inaugurate symbolic supports, contexts, registries, and attributes that are different with regard to the customary from the industrial and postindustrial society, whose characteristics of volatileness, deterritorialization, and lightness along with their invisibility, multiplicity, and enormous speed arrive at distance education, after "liquidizing" (Bauman, 2002) the society in question.

Questions: How do we keep these distinctive contextual characteristics of social entities, which are not solid, but fragile and fluctuating, from the risk of being transferred to the present electronic educational programs? Which tasks await the educational modality at a distance so that, in spite of operating with "robust" devices, it fortifies the concepts of quality and consistency, to overcome light and ephemeral social contexts, of diverse fragmentation and fragility, even more so if we are dealing with canned online programs of low cost? What critical registry is being made of this technocultural time from the existing educational/academic offer? Does it confirm the ideals of a more open and democratic society? Or does it only highlight the archaism of certain customs in the ephemeral and trendy social relationships?Will the electronic educational programs be agencies of authentic social change?

How does one face the multi and interculturality, a parameter that causes one of the greatest frictions and maladjustments in the present globalized virtual culture? How is most of the present virtual symbolic production, distribution, and consumption (general and online training) (Garcia Canclini, 2002) carried out in settings designed and controlled by the globalizing tendencies with social actors whom, although they can promote the openness of new interconnections between cultures and groups, they hide absences of necessary regulations of state policies?

## The Knowledge Economy. Distance Education and Lifelong Learning

In this new social model of information, as we have seen, the main source of productivity is in the training of the individuals who generate ideas and knowledge if they possess the means of production supported by this economic logic. The generation of knowledge, the resources for symbolic communication, and the mastery of technological equipment are what makes possible and forms the economy of information and knowledge.

It is an immaterial economy that is supported in the following four components, which are registering the greatest growth as much in terms of added value as of use. These are:

- information and communication technologies and Internet;
- intellectual property, which not only includes patents and copyrights, but also, in a broad sense, trademarks, advertising, financial services, health (or medical) knowledge, and education;
- libraries, media libraries, and the electronic data banks, as well as all of the audio-visual and telematic media, etc.;
- the biotechnology, traditional data banks, and the biochemical and pharmaceutical industry.

Education in all of its modalities and formats, face-to-face and virtual, is formed as an intensive brain activity supported in hard (or artifactual infrastructure), soft (or software), and invisible technologies (when involving different strategies of thought, feeling, and action). It reflects and is the reflection of material and symbolic resources situated in a culture that decides not only here and now, but also strategically for the future - even without meaning to do so -, and which for reasons of socioeconomic support it should be based on a triangle of balanced economic-social benefit of quality, cost, and coverage. This is why the nonconventional routes - electronic with ICT- should achieve, with virtual distance education, a greater social equity.

# THE KNOWLEDGE WORKERS, NEW ROLES AND NEW COMPETENCIES

In the context of the knowledge economy, the *knowledge workers* emerge, characterized as "human processors of information"; in other words, they use information as a *raw material for their everyday performance*, from which they extract, reinterpret, and produce the knowledge that needs to be transferred and applied to the respective organizational context. For this reason, they demand constant proposals of update-improvement-reformulation of what they know, through *just in time* training offers that today propose products and services in electronic education programs with ICT. Why? Because they hope to acquire what they need, in other words, valuable, precise, rigorous, clear information, adjusted to their expectations, without wasting time, to be directly applicable to the resolution of the problems that appear to them. They are demanding users, with a great development of specific competencies and with mastery of the field in which they are working. They are demanding and practice *self-directed lifelong learning*, which accompanies the passage to constant cultural and technological change, with its advantages and disadvantages, since panaceas do not exist.

Thus, the information and knowledge society moves due to the energy that represents this production of knowledge (or *knowledge-powered society*). Its energy is in the individuals, whose power lies in learning, productivity, and sociocultural integration. Thus, strengthening the abilities of anticipation or prediction of the future to oppose them to the linear conventional thought, within a reflective and ethical perspective to identify, share, contribute, distribute information jointly, leads us to think that if an organization of individuals is not moved by the power of knowledge, it is and will be obsolete.

For this reason, new occupational insertions must be recognized –in spite of the terrible contradictions and consequences that are cast and that were pointed out – in the information society and the knowledge society, which not only require education/training for the development of new competencies, but that form new social positions that generate a dynamic with its own expectations and values. They are occupations of " symbolic analysis, production, and interpretation" to be carried out on site/off site, with services offered by connected organizations and suppliers. Within the horizon of possible roles for knowledge workers, in which online distance education may have an increasing significance, there are:

- Talented and expert consultants and lecturers in various fields that present areas of knowledge, motivate, and inspire actions.
- Tutors, advisors, and coordinators with talent to work online with virtual presence for the personalized guidance of distance, individual, and group students and anyone who may be interested.
- Specialists in building the components of simulated cities, instruments, landscapes, biological systems, or physical phenomena.
- Experts in evaluation and certification of programs and projects that reassure that mediated knowledge and competencies agree with what is socially and occupationally demanded.
- Experts in disciplines, areas, or subjects who work in universities, research centers, professional societies, certified organizations, or companies and who define the requirements for an instruction or teaching necessary for innovating and strategic programs.
- Software engineers in teams who build, develop, and maintain systems and components of virtual simulations and environments as synthetic surroundings, for use in a great variety of situations of interrelation, communication, and learning.
- Developers of tools for continuous evaluation, "personalized models" for motivation, various diagnoses, decision making, etc.
- Administrative roles and of technical support with a variety of services of registry, administration of information and data, maintenance, repair, etc.

The new knowledge workers must be prepared to decide what is the most valid and valuable thing depending on the actors, settings, and their needs, in present and prospective terms. It involves, then, emphasizing ability (or the lack of) in societies which must channel and grant a meaning to technology and ICT, which are strategically decisive at this historical time, in which although the technology *per se* does not determine the evolution of social changes, it codetermines the capacity of the societies to transform (Castells, 1996).

Historically, we can observe the impact of the techniques in the social transformations; the railroad not only shortened distances, but also modified economic exchange, ways of production, communicational habits, etc. (Mumford, 1982). It is remarkable, therefore, how the constituted thing becomes constituent: it happened with aeronautics, and it is also already happening with ICT: the instrumental logic (or technical rationality), whether we like it or not, will dominate the will of individuals and groups, remaining under its responsible protagonism the possibilities for their appropriation, resignification, and adaptation to the local sociocultural needs. Since technological objects are creations of the mind that later are confused with the perception of reality, we have no choice but to know them, deconstruct them, demystify them, adapt them, and apply them in an intelligent and critical way.

Apparently, there is a need to train people in general and the new knowledge workers in new competencies, who as symbolic analysts, experimenters, solve problems, develop critical abilities of thought in general, and particularly, of analysis and synthesis. They cover the dominion of "informational" competencies (or what is known as information literacy or information fluency) articulated in a special way with the interpersonal abilities of empathy and emotional intelligence, with regard to diversity, solidarity, and collaboration, that strengthen, as well, the self-guidance and autonomy of the users, their capacity of negotiation and adaptation within a framework of social responsibility, and not only of increase of the quantitative productivity, which characterizes all organizations today.

Without the existence of these fundamental competencies, individuals and groups accept erroneous information, make the wrong interpretations, think that they already know enough and for always, get carried away by prejudices and, in sum, make partial, inadequate decisions.

In order to illustrate, for a sociological analysis of an electronic training of the required competencies, we may point out the following, without forgetting some risks or limitations that simultaneously and contradictorily may be shown.

Among these competencies there are:

a. *The stimulus for interpersonal communication*, one of the central pillars of the virtual learning environments, in order to increase discussion and b. *active and interactive participation*: derived from the previous, the users are called to look for, ask, develop, and engage in dialogues, discussions of controverted points of view, add, and receive new information from varied near and distant sources for intense telematic discourse (all of this applicable to connected, virtual synchronous and asynchronous distance education).

c. *The invention of flexible sociocognitive pathways and protagonisms* that the participants may establish and cover depending on their interest and need.

d. *The use, support, and follow-up of statistics and materials for consultation*, confirmation of what has been done, which is part of the process of management and administration of an organization or program.

e. *The monitoring of the self-control over skills*: when knowing and executing self-evaluations of processes and results of actions; individuals and/or groups can come together around a subject of mutual interest, need, evaluation, etc.

Among the risks or limitations to consider, there are:

a. *Possible low levels of social participation*, not only due to the personality and cognitive styles of the users, but to the profile of social interaction established in the design of actions.
b. *Low levels of abstract reasoning*: while the previous limitation reflects the amount of participation and interaction, here the *quality* of said participation is observed, which does not trigger higher thought strategies nor a leadership for the good putting in practice of interactive abilities through ICT and others that "scaffold" with detail what is required, presenting the criteria to evaluate the contributions of the participants.
c. *Various resistance* from administrators, managers, professionals, faculty, students with regard to the new electronic environments, so that step by step and by means of the removal of prejudices, the exploratory stage may begin towards the corresponding acceptance and dedication involved.
d. *The need for constant training, which is not made possible by all social contexts*: Although the ICT, with their possibilities of interactive communication, are increasingly ubiquitous and easier to use, users need to resolve and practice new technological skills and of cooperative communication-work for the effective use of these resources. The same occurs with regard to the technical support, whose cost is frequently not stipulated as an additional aid for online interaction, surfing, and using Internet or another network with the skills of technological interaction.

Although distance training with ICT today is recognized as proposals of "intelligent flexible learning", which surpass what is known as "educational communication through theInternet", it is possible to reflect on the possibility not only of standardization of the training given from the offer (in general in the hands of private sectors), but of the need to formalize academic regulations with a formulation of public policies referred to the specific subject, still little existing. It is possible to demystify the new tools of Internet (weblogs, wikis, Web 2,0, etc.): although they stimulate a greater socialization of the users-students, it is the network that approaches the user and not the other way around, in the best way of sales or marketing, of fast absorption in the global context: the market exists as long as it continues producing and distributing objects after advertisingthem; many of which point to "false needs".

## Lifelong Learning

Until recently, it was conceived as education for life, continuous education, recurrent education, non-formal and informal education, communitarian development, popular education, sociocultural animation, postscholastic education, education for leisure and free time, permanent learning, education throughout life, educating city... In some cases, these various names refer to different spheres of permanent education; in others, they are synonymous.

The same idea of lifelong learning, as the idea of permanent education, constitutes a kaleidoscope of different possibilities where education is no longer circumscribed to a phase or a space of life; rather a universe in expansion is considered, which contributes to the development of the person throughout his/her existence. In recent years, it has acquired a special cross-sectional relevance as continuous education to train the emerging citizenry in the new conjunctures, contribute to the communitarian development, the defense of human rights, and the understanding of other societies, within a sustainable development of cultures.

Today the cultural development of the emerging citizenry requires other logics of production and diffusion not rooted beforehand in the sociocultural, educational and labor context. Training cultural and public citizens of and in ICT means placing lifelong learning as an inescapable *service* of and for the modern development of institutions, independently of directions of a state centralism like that of the business profit. It means placing the cultural development of the emerging citizenry, lifelong learning, in the center of the formative actions inscribed within interculturality, innovation, the reduction of the digital gap, and critical thinking.

Among some of the significant milestones of lifelong learning, we may recall, historically, the discussion organized by the Council of Europe (Paris, 1967) which declared that the minimum right to an education for each individual must be continuous. Another milestone is represented by the Green Paper on European Social Policy (1994) which stated that it is fundamental to dedicate special attention to medium and long term education to determine a system of continuous training with meaning, or the Report of the International Commission on Education for the Twenty-first Century, presided over by J. Delors (1996), *Learning: the Treasure Within*, that dedicates the fifth chapter to lifelong education. The concept of " lifelong education " is inscribed within the reality of the facts, represents the key to living in the twenty-first century and is the central requisite for a greater self-control, if we seek to guide people's own destiny and offer the means to reach a better balance between work, learning, and the exercise of a locally and globally committed citizenship.

The concept of lifelong education surpasses, in the twenty-first century, the distinction between academic formation, update and recycling, reconversion, and promotion of adults, because it points to equity as a condition for personal and social harmonic development.

If it were necessary to further highlight the above-mentioned concepts, we could say that the demands of the training of citizen awareness in the twenty-first century through lifelong learning with ICT are: recognizing others as equals and those we learn from; expanding the area of interests as a wide horizon; engaging in dialogue and investigating with others; participating and becoming involved in a solidary common cause, and learning to coexist with respect for diversity. Unfortunately, we are still far from it, not only from the fulfillment of the above-mentioned conditions, but also from their inclusion in public national, regional, and international policies.

Lifelong learning is a consequence of the deep transformations that are taking place within globalization. The planetary dimensions transform all of the orders of a society: the capital tends to integrate the national markets in a single global market; the world of work presents new demands; the effective performance of a profession demands the resolution of complex tasks, etc., and ICT must be appropriated to satisfy this need and increasingly as a democratizing means of collective promotion to counterbalance the new forms of exclusion and violence in the social weave. Societies are increasingly multicultural, multiethnic, and multireligious, and these social, political, economic, and cultural changes affect the field of education and training, specially with new attitudes and qualified knowledge as a necessary response to diversity.

## THE ICT AND THE CITIZENRY

The ICT and their articulation into the continuous training of the knowledge workers are new phenomena in the recent cultural or cybercultural evolution of great impact in social dynamics and now in a global citizenry, not exempt from conflicts in reference to the great sociological issues of all time: stability or permanence, and social innovation and changes.

Sociologically, the technologies that are used for interaction in the virtual world have a dialectic relationship with culture. The virtual cultures are mediations between society and technology, and form systems of symbolic exchange in virtual networks by means of which reality is formed.

The citizenry today has an epistemologically and politically strategic role within tension of the everyday sociohistorical mediations, since we would have to give it another meaning and the possibility of actions and critical thinking. The technological media inserted in technological-formative mediations are not only material artifacts that communicate and transmit contents in the form of concepts, ideas, etc., but they also trim, distribute, communicate, and indicate what is fundamental with regard to what is accessory in a culture at a specific moment. They are physical and symbolic elements previously selected and hierarchized – in terms of their validity, opportunity, and effectiveness- for ideological reasons, dressed up as current, scientific, and technological which hide biased and hegemonic interests.

For these reasons and others, the citizenry must learn to analyze with reflectivity (Giddens, 1998) media, mediators, and mediations - in form and content -, because it constitutes an essential chapter of the sociological criticism of ICT in education that seeks to rescue the specific weight they carry as part of a "hidden curriculum".

The information society means the control society as it generates information tools useful for hegemonic interests. Nevertheless, sectors coexist which alternately resignify this information to turn it into more pertinent tools, which must be extended to all of the citizenry.

With regard to this, we propose a communicative and relational (as opposed to isolated and instrumental) substantive conception (Feenberg, 1991) of science and technology (in other words, socioconstructive and interactive). From this sociocultural position, we should emphasize ICT as the technological mediations where they merely stop being instrumental to thicken, become denser, and become something substantive or structural (Barbero, 1987).

## Towards the Integration of a Critical and Reflective Sociology of Distance Education with ICT

With the aim of forming a practice of the critical and committed epistemological-socio-cognitive perspective from the above-mentioned, the search, reflection and investigation, the deconstruction and anticipation are valid input to think and anticipate alternative designs of human interactions and for proposals within distance education programs and materials. This is even more so if we seek to surpass the sociological problems named with the appreciation and limitations implied in the common sense of everyday life and the natural unfolding of common social situations, for our case, of technological-economicist implementation of distance educational programs with the use Internet or online programs. We will encourage readers and designers, users and managers, faculty and students, to deconstruct with reflectivity, explore and elaborate various possible interpretations by deepening sensitivity and critical-ethical rationality (communicative, according to Habermas) to overcome the inevitable, the natural, what is considered immutable in the interactions proposed by the programs, technologically created and mediated. It would be necessary to be aware that all of the distance education proposals in general and with the use of ICT in particular:

- are not impenetrable nor unmodifiable, but cognoscible and improvable, when they cannot be surpassed by other alternatives;
- are inscribed within elaborative frameworks or broader conceptual and methodological networks and of mutual multidisciplinary interdependence that grant them their significance with projections for the real and possible behavior of the users of such programs; and
- should encourage interaction in order to overcome mediated, mercantilized, and disciplinating socioeducational reductionisms that make the ethical character that provides moral meaning to the formative human relationships move backwards.

Some of these statements refer to what a distance education program must and can do, considering options from the sociocultural angles that soon affect the semiological, technological, didactic, and so on, aspects of the system or service in question. For example, questions like: in what sense and why is it important that in certain distance education programs at least 85% of the accomplishment of collaborative tasks with ICT in each module should be indicated, considering that they establish real communicative-productive exchange between users.

This way, the sociology of distance education points to a way ofthinking about the distance human interactive universe or mediated by technology and ICT, which in terms of a specific educational proposal involves a conception of the design, execution, evaluation, and impact, in our case, of distance education systems or programs from a substantive perspective of technology.

Therefore, the goal is to sociologically think what the modality incarnated in distance education programs involves today in the information society, which certainly is quite different from what it would have been like in the industrial society of the nineteenth and twentieth centuries, beyond what is held by common sense.

Sociologically thinking distance education refers to a "landed" educational practice depending on sociocultural settings and with various actors; daring to imagine and contrast, in and from practice, various ways to solve the innumerable and complex problems that this modality mediated by ICT in such heterogeneous contexts is facing now. This strengthens options of freedom, at the same time destabilizing rigidities that prevail in many of the distance education programs with ICT through the relationships of power of some protagonists over others, who try to demonstrate the eagerness to reach a technical rationality of cultural hegemony and unique thought, assigned to control or discipline the current social order.

Other contributions wish to establish relationships with other disciplines; for example, with political science, when an aspect of human interaction in asynchronous communication through a forum conceals an impact created in the name of asymmetric power in the interaction mediated by technology; with socioanthropology, which will wonder about the consequences in the cultural behavior of profit and student development as a result of attending a distance education program and another different one.

Additionally, among the central concerns of a sociology of distance education, we ask how the widest networks of mutual interdependence that contain and give meaning to the educational program under consideration, condition, reciprocally expand or limit all of the actions and the freedom of the individuals in charge of this project: starting with the one who makes the decisions, the online didactic text designer, the conception of the role of the tutor existing in the organization, the presence and degree of importance given to technology, to how they conceive the socialization that the distance student will have to accomplish to be integrated into the educational service and be susceptible to academic achievements, etc.

It is perceived that only with the above-mentioned it would be worthwhile for the programs and materials of this - modality to be reviewed from this perspective of reflectivity. This is important also so as to be more cautious about external and internal dynamics represented in negotiations, commitments, and obstacles that must be overcome within the programs and which lie in direct interdependence with the greater concrete sociohistorical context.

All of this leads us to review the meaning of education in the knowledge society so as not to confuse the methods with the principles, since the referred society is not the wired society of ICT or the one connected via satellite, but rather it represents a set of forces in struggle, conflict, and susceptible to election for disciplinating, demagogic, manipulative, or re-creative and intelligent use of mass media and ICT.

As we may see, nothing new is being said, because it is the same classic struggle to overcome unique thought, the superstitions and myths given throughout the history of humanity, culture, and education, in order to reach the greatest possible humanization, criticism and reflectivity, the collective values of the citizenry and civism, the respect for differences in coexistence, participation, local and universal solidarity, which aims to strengthen autonomy and freedom.

Today, all of this appears to us in more complex settings, and the challenges are more serious. We think that technology, among other forces, as a cultural sociohistorical process and product can help to maintain -at least, proposes the communicating vessels - a shared and distributed thought, if communities of learning are organized into networks to strengthen the mentioned values.

Being more understanding and solidary, supporting innovations and exercising the freedom to think alternative ways of designing and carrying out distance education programs mediated by technology in the face of routines (in general linked to lucrative economic projects, so popular in the global educational era with Internet), rises above and resists the coming improvisations, in general, of technological areas that are not concerned with biased stereotypes nor understanding the internal logic of the development of thought in its highest form, which is what any educational effort must maintain.

*Chapter 3*

# SOCIOCULTURAL ASPECTS OF DISTANCE EDUCATION AS AN ELECTRONICALLY MEDIATED FORMATIVE COMMUNICATION

## CONVENTIONAL AND TELEMATIC MEDIA, MEDIATIONS, AND MEDIATORS APPLIED TO TRAINING

The technological acceleration, that begins in the late twentieth century, is accentuated in the early twenty-first, and will continue at a feverish pace, not only introduces into societies an unusual amount of new tiny or nanotechnological equipment that penetrate everyday life in acute technological convergence, but also establishes a new kind of relationship between individuals and groups, the symbolic-cultural processes, and the ways of production, distribution, and consumption of goods and services. Individuals and groups relate through communication in general and through more or less formalized specific distance education proposals until they reach the present online proposals. This has turned knowledge into a direct productive force within the information society and the knowledge economy.

In this society, the social space of culture is crossed by the infinite technological mediation now turned *structural* context, because its processes have been symbolically densified. Therefore, when referring to "mediations", it is perceived that they are not only "artifactual" - which would be the approach with a lesser explanatory scope -, but sociotechnological, in other words, they have historical roots, and hence politicaland ethical contextualized/localized roots, in relation to complex concepts and the appropriations that each group and organization have been able to perform.

Anchoring in the social meaning that is established by these processes of sociocultural, semiological, anthropological, and pedagogical mediations (Fainholc, 2003) as praxis, forces us to recognize the endless contradictions and existing paradoxes within them, fruit of a negotiating interpretation of meaning, that technology and ICT in particular face as process and result of a global world in local articulation.

The mediations are constituted as new ways of perception and language, cause the emergence of new sensitivities, narratives, and writings (Barbero, 2003), generating new discursive practices, product of the dialogic exchange by"unofficial" protagonists (youth, ethnic groups, women, etc.) with the use of more horizontal resources (weblogs, I-pods, etc.)

– which are also displayed by cyberculture -, resistant to hegemonic stories via reappropriation not only of the technical devices, but of the affectivity and sociabilization of individuals and different groups given by these mediations.

We should point out some clarifications in the conceptual distinctions that are present in the construction, distribution, and consumption of the new discursive practices of the technological-educational mediations, representing the continent of electronic distance education programs in particular.

When referring to media, mediators, and mediations, the analysis comes from withina critical sociology of educational technology that contains distance education, which deepens the possibility of scientific work as it interrelates culture, history, and society, with concepts like *sociological imagination* (Mills, 1983) and others, to help anchor, give meaning, apply information, develop reason, and obtain clear summaries on what is happening in the world and what is perhaps happening to individuals, groups, educational programs, etc. In this way:

1. *Media*: The goal is to reach the generic form of communication associated to a particular way of representing and organizing knowledge through various symbolic codes, formats, or styles of representation. Thus, any content can be transported by various technological supports, more sophisticated in terms of their *mass mediation* or mediatization through social mass media and telematics. We are dealing with devices, equipment, or artifacts used to transmit information among individuals, groups, and organizations.
2. *Mediators*: They deal with human and nonhuman proposals of communication that allow a person, group, or organization to carry out, totally or partially, the functions of scaffolding, assistance, and negotiation of meanings in various supports and so that distance communication is materialized as a cultural practice.

   To paraphrase Chartier (2001), it can be argued that the mediator is the space of reunion between the world of text in various forms and supports, personal styles, nonverbal language, etc. and the reader/enabler (or not) - by means of competencies- of the practice of comprehensive and critical reading of any message, today increasingly in support of ICT, which is given back to the context in productions re-signified by individuals.
3. *Mediations*: In the sociology of social communications and semiology (Barbero, 1987), we point to a *cultural critical reflection on the multiple heterogeneity and temporariness* of mediations as the space that triggers, or link that re-creates personal and group meaning within an interconnected global world. The mediations start off from and return to a precarious local "here", socioculturallyand cognitivellyre-signifiable towards a globality that takes more into account the production, distribution, and consumption of material and symbolic goods and services organized from a strategy of global market – in other words, aimed at a techno-economic, financial, and administrative business -, more than the search for a philosophy that strengthens the sociocultural inclusion and difference, despite more participative telematic proposals like Web 2.0.

   Media, mediators, and mediations are inscribed within the phenomenon of globalization, with multiple processes and related to the ongoing dynamics of the global society. Among them, and to name one of most outstanding, we may highlight migrations and their "established" and "foreign" subjects (Bauman, 1999), involved in intense conflicts and prejudice disseminated in their mediated interrelationships. Communication not only takes place there in verbal, written, or gesticular form (through videoconferences), but rather there are multiple symbolic forms of communication processed and represented by the convergence of the technological codes of ICT and Internet, as was previously mentioned.

We re-signify here the concept of *nomadism* which, beyond pointing to repeated hostile ruptures of communicational links, and far from relying on postmodernist relativism, is inscribed within a complex framework of formative communication mediated by technologies at a distance where endless elements participate, which act as multiple and biunivocal emitters and receivers. In other words, it will be understood as an opening to dialogue crossed with other discourses by individuals and groups, and as a hope for the future of other protagonisms in constant transformation, to result in new perceptual and representative products that impact on social imagination, and which would also penetrate training efforts at a distance.

## Revisiting the Communication Process

In the postmodern, liquid society or of late Capitalism in which we live, there is a paradox where the most perfect instrumental (or technological) rationality corresponds to total irrationality, through the promoted fetishization of what is technological and through the sense of high pragmatic contraction that is contemporarily granted to almost all of human accomplishments, in particular within the social sciences.

Consequently, there are tendencies that study the relativization, if not cancellation, of the historical validity of everything that is not characterized mainly by the production of concrete, tangible, or measurable goods. A projection of this would be reducing the communication science to "media science" (or science of devices), without considering the phenomenon and the implicit process in human communication, on which individuals and cultures have been historically and socioculturally built.

Other aspects that help these interpretations have been those that, starting fromthe physical route or electronic engineering, end up at the (schematic) linear model of communication (Shanon, Laswell and followers), inclined towards the control of human behavior.

The scientific study of the phenomena and processes of communication, of its signs, languages, and formats, in various times and contexts, with multiple actors and intentions, would tend to overcome these limitations, given by:

- the negation of the communicative phenomenon and its exclusive consideration in terms of the artifactual aspects of what is mediatic (today increasingly sophisticated); and
- the false conception where devices codify realities, with produced or manipulated effects, extensive to other elements of history in general.

This way, it is essential to revalue the complex and specific character of the communication processes, with their incidence in educational arguments, and distance education in particular, where they play a central role.

In practical terms and in relation to our teleeducational task, it means considering the communication process as:

- a dialogue that defines the mediated relationship and therefore of distance existence;
- a relationship of proximity and/or re-signified dialogue to be established not only in physical terms; and
- the development of people´s discursive capacity through innumerable dimensions when appealing to various codes (words, images, signs, icons, etc.), in order to communicate at the heart of factual and virtual social relationships.

This communicational approach is understood as a concrete and specific part of the relational practice of the human being, and not as a foreign entity which can be accessed by artificial mediation or technological distribution. For this reason communication is *communicative action* (Habermas, 1986). The development of this communicative action must be deepened in the processes of interaction and interactivity in general as a permanent practice of elaboration and re-elaboration of symbols and meanings in the new spaces of the electronic culture. Consequently, it is easy to understand the need to invest in the development of the communicative competencies of the person who interacts and studies/learns through distance education programs. Otherwise - and here lie the risks -, the discourses, their programs, and materials will be the support for controlling, mechanical, and "reproductivist" societies, in whose uncertain and complex framework - individuals and groups reassemble their lives. The postmodern and liquid derivations that as a consequence may appear - and in fact appear- could be:

- uniformity: the sciences and education are placed at the service of an hegemonic global production embodied in a logic of control and generalized subtle domination;
- the negation of the person and the collective projects that revalue the precarious present, neutralizing the past and the future;
- the accomplishment of actions referred to tangible objectives and not to superior values that transcend what is pragmatic to tend towards what is paradigmatic.

This way, the issue of values and ethics cannot be circumscribed only to the selection and combination of communicative media or supports of any type, without aconsideration of the pillars on which they support themselves.

The criticism of the highly technologized postindustrial society based on its alienating character, aims through these warnings to transcend its risks or limitations from a surpassing and humanizing sociopolitical formative project. Could it be possible? Here, the concept of person and human groups is paramount to the extent that it becomes a point of departure and arrival of all the communicational processes and educational designs, if it is to promote and improve the development of all of the human potentialities in every social organization.

It is imperative, then, to review the mediated process of communication because in the digital stage it involves recognizing and integrating different protagonisms and their interrelationships with the devices that come together in different communication contexts. In this process, the technology will have to be articulated according to the dimensions of the communication, from the *intrapersonal*, or self-communication; in order to pass through the *interpersonal* kind, or between two individuals; to the kind that takes place in *groups* or within a relatively small collectivity; and *collective* or of bigger groups, where the receiver is anonymous and dispersed, does not directly receive messages but rather through social mass media (like the radio, television, press, or posters); in order to reach the present *digital* stage of telematic networks that subsume the above-mentioned modalities through technological convergence, in ICT and Internet.

Although Mc Luhan´s historic phrase which stated that "the medium is the message" has been relativized, we mustremember that it means that, independently of the content which is communicated, it is also the profile of the design of a combination of media, mediations, and mediators, which gives shape to and controls human interaction.

We should point out that in the evolution of social mass media, starting from the existence of an *oral culture*, where creating and telling stories from generation to generation was the key, to a *culture of writing and the printing press* (with Gutemberg, in 1456), with linear thought and the universalization of reading as mass media, there were restrictions suffered by the manipulations of the ruling power and, with them, only grudgingly offering the possibility of including or excluding individuals with regard to information and knowledge. Today we have reached ICT by re-editing similar excluding problematics from various fronts.

The emergence of the digital culture reinforces the interactive and ludic aspects, and images; it develops new mentalities and communicational habits that require more sophisticated ways of thinking, organizing information, and transmitting what is elaborated to apply it to concrete actions of greater reflectivity. The electronic culture - of social mass media, mainly of digital television and ICT articulated in telematic networks - invades vital spaces and modifies experiences of the world, interaction with the universe of hypermedia in the network of networks of Internet, and weakens fixed traditions, in exchange for the "nonplaces" of virtual social situations.

The communication sciences in general are inscribed today within the context of "technological rationalism", that entails a new way ofseeing or understanding the world, life, and individuals (or world view): the dominant hegemonic rationality, understood as a scientific-technical *instrumental reason* that considers and privileges the *media*, not always the most suitable and transparent. Founded historically and culturally, it forms a part of the representation system that legitimizes or justifies an hegemonic socio-political-economic structure, and even colonial (in certain social contexts), through sociopolitical power structures and struggles that still fight to remain and to not be democratically surpassed.

## Deepening the Theoretical-practical Understanding of the Communication Process

When deepening the understanding of the process of communication to support the set up and development of communicative competencies in nonconventional educational frameworks, it is convenient to relate the contributions of the "critical theory", successor to the School of Frankfurt (Bunge, 1995) and hermeneutics. The "critical theory", within a "humanistic-philosophical" sociology, criticizes capitalism and its derivations of varying order, in that they inhibit an individual´s expression, while denying the distinction between science and technique, and between these and ideology. It also denounces science as lackey of the ruling political power and rejects positivism and rationalism as proposals of the social sciences of scientific appproach, the goal of social reality towards an interpretive-qualitative immersion. The contributions of some structuralists and poststructuralists like Althusser and Foucault are also included.

Among some of its philosophical elements, the "critical theory" proposes the analytical practice of a sociology of distance education, where it would be possible to anticipate and list, among others, some contributions:

*Neomarxism*, by adopting Hegel´s dialectic and conceiving that the whole is a unit of opposites in conflict, and believing that the sharp contradictions that today tear the world apart by the opposition between small globalized offshore elites and the impoverished peripheries of "wasted lives", migrantes, etc., branch off and polarize human experiences. Here is a valid interpretation of cultural consequences, of the category of analysis of "nomadism" as an example of the rupture of wandering lives. To this we must add today other "colder and more rational components", like the ones associated to global exchange, scientific cooperation, technological innovation, etc., where the generation of new interconnections (and the need for new competencies to be able to understand them and to operate) has real relevance and impact on social life, and therefore, on distance education proposals, as we shall see later.

*Phenomenology*, *existentialism*, and *hermeneutics*, mainly the last one, through the contribution of Gadamer, who picks up where Dilthey and Heidegger left off. The hermeneutical thesis maintains that everything that is social is as much symbolic as intentional, and that social facts are discourses "to be interpreted" in terms of intentions, instead of being explained in terms of causes and accidents, because the human being is a biological, social, emotional, and intellectual being, as well as artificial and symbolic. The hybrid perception of two worlds: globalized and localized is in keeping with the postmodern communicational narrative that is produced, distributed, and consumed in the ludic settings of cybercafés and social networks with Internet. The phenomenic reality appears to us through an oversized transfer of information and enormous possibilities of instant communication, which paradoxically coincides with an infointoxication/overinformation pointing to a breakdown in communication in general viewed between the producing global elite and the local marginal consumer (human) waste.

The interpretations of the *simulations*and the *liquidity* of the phenomena and bonds of postmodern society. Baudrillard (1993) refers to the worlds of signs and images created by media. He reflects on postmodern societies, describes how individuals live on *hyperreality* from the media messages sent. In other words, the realities mediated by technological media through signs, and for the alienating consumption of individuals and groups, pulverize or move away what really happens in real life. Bauman, refering to the "liquid society", writes ofhow this characteristic permeates all of postmodern social life.

Among the *core competencies* - originated from the perspective of the information and knowledge society to increase strength (solidity) not only for survival in general but towards a personal and social self-realization, to achieve sociocultural integration by overcoming inequities, successful achievements in social, personal equality, and solidary with the group, at the place of residence or work or in deterritorialized distance situations, within the immediate community and the global community, in harmony with nature and the environment-, the following may be listed:

a) competency of self-management of an ethical life project;
b) communicative competency as expressive possibility;
c) audio-visual competency for decoding images;
d) mathematical competency for the rational handling of symbols and abstractions;
e) mediatic competency (incorporating b and c) for the comprehensive and critical decoding within the interaction with the new information and communication technologies (ICT), which involves the handling and the processing of the information for an intelligent use of telematic resources in an autonomous management of knowledge;
f) critical-reflective competency in order to confront, with discernment, quick changes to self-regulate human behavior, in a metacognitive way;
g) competency of democratic leadership and respect for intercultural diversity within an effective communicational process of negotiation given by the emergence of new citizenships, according to the demands of social and cultural, organizational and communitarian environments, with a sense of solidarity.

While differentiating the various contributions from mediations, media, and mediators within the communication processes may remind us of the functionalist theories of mass media, of great influence in the fifties, reexamining them in light of the revisionisms that are imposed by the new contexts from the theoretical-conceptual and methodological points of view may be useful to extract some suggestions of sociological analysis of formative interest.

Today it could be noted that mediations, media, and mediators act as a kind of *surveillance*provided by the enormous, fast, penetrating, and continuous flow of global information that is consumed all over the world. This, on the one hand, contributes to *cultural* socialization, although of class differentiation, of great power due to its incorporation of input in the construction of knowledge, and on the other hand, with this control the individual and group privacy is invaded as it is penetrated with liquid values.

It is interesting to consider the sociological context of distance education communication with the mentioned phenomena and processes of mediations and mediators, even more so, when inscribing it in relation to the studies of communication from the situated perspective of the periphery of the world.

In this framework, we propose a "new sociology of education", frequently identified with the "sociology of knowledge", which deals with how knowledge is socially managed and transmitted. The inherent negotiation within situations of conflict and power in every social situation is postulated and recognized: from the family, school, company, social organizations, etc. It contextually surpasses, questions, and amplifies the understanding of every social phenomenon and, therefore, of the same educational process and the behaviors that are confined to it, when recognizing that every "cultural experience" is political. This way, from the actors or agents interacting in everyday activities, a "microsociological analysis"is proposed, which demonstrates the creative, unpredictable, and relevant ways by means of which individuals and groups construct their subjectivity, amass knowledge and/or solve their problems, from *other parameters of coherence*, beyond local identity and global hegemony.

## The Mediations

The mediations - term coined by J. Barbero in 1980- constitutes in the sociology of social communications, in semiology, as well as in this proposal of a sociology of distance education, a contribution that allows us to surpass the reductionism centered in the "artifactual" media considered a mere transport of information.

The goal is to replace the monopoly and anarchizing processes of equipment or devices through the consideration of communication processes, within a new interdisciplinarity of the strategic spaces given by the sociology of culture, the cultural studies of communication, the new anthropology, etc.

This way, the media are a part of the *social mediations* that include the processes of interaction and cultural reconstruction, which depart from communication and everyday experiences, characterized by individuals and groups, and which form the socioculture. Social mediations as the distance study or work in various spheres of society (in NGO, ethnic movements, popular urban manifestations, etc.) show various sociological manifestations supported by communicational mediations which often do not use or do not have access to technological media for everyday communication.

This allows us surpass the artifactual and consider the *sociocultural aspects* and their impacts originating from organized activities where individuals assume roles as decision makers, administrators, designers, among others, and establish interactions and tasks to be executed on the part of tutors and students, for example.

If seen through the prism of the sociology of distance education, it is perceived that the authority is behind the norm - vague and anonymous- and that we areobliged to observe, for instance, the telestudents, that act in favor of a modeling, which is not the same as a *modulation which favors their idiosyncratic development.*

The same may happen with regard to the alleged current and specialized "vision held by experts ", which prints the profile for a distance project. Although we are dealing with elements of an intangible and abstract, heavy and influential culture, they are not so invisible because they allow, to give only one paradigmatic sample, tutors to demand, for example, "at least one field work for each point to be studied in the program, which can be sent by e-mail, although it must be handed in beforehand on paper and disk to be presented in the mandatory face-to-face oral examination, if you desire to keep the status of regularly enrolled student in this program".

Thus, the sociocultural communicational aspects of the distance education systems mediated by technology are processes that model purpose and reasons for interaction between individuals and artificial objects, with a specialized established know-how and a tacit knowledge, a product of hidden conventions and agreements, existing in the minds and wills of the users who in the practice carry out a distance education program. Consequently, within these distance education courses, we should consider:

- *computer and regulatory* aspects of the context from which sociocognitive and educational-communicative processes of the designed social interactions and pedagogical interactivities (Fainholc, 2003) are produced;
- and *modeling aspects of purpose and motives* with regard to the course which, in the practice, is carried out with a distance education program.

The first or communicational aspects make it so that the *organizational and communicative*, tutorial and student life, of the educational program in question - as we shall see in the respective chapters- is less eventful, as it foresees and even controls all of the administrative, pedagogical, communicational, management, execution/monitoring aspects of the project and others (even more so if the distance education proposal with ICT is articulated with Learning Management Systems (LMS) and Content Management Systems (CMS); the second or modeling aspects point to the constituent *morale of the team* of the online pedagogical proposal. This means that managers and designers, producers and evaluators, tutors and students, etc., feel inclined to select and discriminate motives and targets for action in these proposals, which would have to be registered in the programs as data pertaining to the users within the portfolio of the organization.

These are aspects that are not independent nor mutually excluding, but complementary of the *management* of a distance education program and which the critical or analytical sociology that we present should not overlook.

## Electronic Educational Communication as a Mediated Construction

Understood as "new forms of everyday life" (Diaz, 1999) represented by ICT as well as devices and languages through which the previously mentioned educational-technological mediations are formed, they appear throughout all of the transactions of the social world, and, particularly, within an online electronic educational program.

Electronic educational communication as mediated construction is formed by cultural tools of varying degree of materiality, historically and culturally situated, and leads, through interaction, to various domains in the cognitive structuring and in the development of higher sociopsychological functions of the person who communicates, interacts, learns, changes, etc.It is a polymorphic, interdisciplinary concept, mutirepresented in various realities, which enables the exchange of infinite symbolic flows between the sociocultural agents and the technological devices, codetermining the conditions and forces of mediated production of meaning.

We choose the sociocultural approach in general, and cultural studies in particular, to approach these mediations for two reasons: on the one hand, to conduct a general sociohistorical analysis of the specific and changing relationships of human activities mediated by technological processes and devices; and, on the other hand, to explore the dynamic and specific relationships of these planned and modifiable practices - in content and intention- of online educational programs.

In all mediations, conflicts coexist, since the goal is to reach some hegemony (Bourdieu, 1989). In structured spaces, positions and individuals in struggle appear or who constantly vary in their relationships of *power*. In this context, also the concept of *articulation* (Jameson,

1994) helps to understand the way through which mediations are combined and dispute a space of practical and explanatory power.

The technological-educational mediations which specially take place within distance educational programs in general and with ICT stop being instrumental to become part of the structure of the new social relationships in this civilization called information society and society of knowledge and digital culture. They form networks of meaning, not only contextual but intertextual, due to the enormous convergence of languages in which they appear. Due to this magnitude, it is impossible "to map all the mediations of a general, mediated, and specific communicative action" (Araujo, 2002) such as the one this contribution is analyzing.

The *network of discursive practices* considers the locations of the mediated actions or mediations, where the social and communicative interaction process is installed, a multiple, complex process, too vast, where contradictory reactions take place in various directions and various connections coexist (Orozco, 1994).

Analyzing, deconstructing, and identifying the factors within mediations allow us to recognize the strategies of production, circulation, and consumption of technological products and accounts or discourse, from different social, cultural, semiological places; some agreed on as legitimate and others - among which those of greater social propagandistic penetration stand out -, which are in dispute over some *hegemony of symbolic power*. Consider, if not, the enormous proliferation of electronic distance education programs by Internet that incessantly compete today world-wide.

Thinking this way points to perceiving, analyzing, and disassembling the political-social and technological conditions of production, distribution, and reception/use of the discursive practices proposed for distance education. The socio-political-cultural macro and micromechanisms of power are revealed so that in a given situation, those who make the decisions and the users (or readers or navigators or students) may recognize their participation as authorized and/or allowed, stimulated, inhibited, subjugated, etc., in other words, recognizing which voices compose the positions held or from where the discourses take place, as a possibility of presence of local, general, or specific knowledge, within a strategic mediated educational relationship, which bonds and moves (because it is never fixed) the various roles and functions that compose an educational program.

Today mediations need a critical cultural reflection on the *heterogeneity* presented on the basis of a globally interconnected world, of violent penetration and hegemonic relationship, from a peripheral "here", as is the case of Latin America or the South of the world.

## Socioeducational Mediations

These mediations are represented by the action or activity, intervention, resource or didactic material existing within an educational situation to facilitate the process of education and face-to-face or distance learning, which is why it has, by definition, relational character. Its central goal is to facilitate intercommunication between the student and the advisors - in this case, online at a distance- to encourage through intuition and reasoning a comprehensive approach of the ideas through the senses (Eisner, 1994) within the horizon of an education conceived as participation, creativity, expressiveness, and rationality.

The didactic processing of the information within educational programs is also included, to make various contents apprehensible, to allow the visualization of treatments and forms of expression within communicative relationships, which at the same time, select and combine media and formats to scaffold (ZONE OF PROXIMAL DEVELOPMENT, according to Vigotsky, 1988) face-to-face and distance learning, and thereby strengthen the potentialities of dialogue of the proposed interaction and interactivity.

It is interesting to recall the contribution of Gadamer (1973) - within the hermeneutic philosophical school of thought already mentioned -, who proposes the development of interpretive work to clarify the *dialogue* within said relationship. Interpreter and text are two interlocutors through whom the dialectic articulation of mutually related questions and answers try to reach an understanding to communicate something. Sociologically understanding the hermeneutic dialogue helps to understand the formative work of the pedagogical mediations where face-to-face or mediatizedinterrogation leads to the deepening of the relationship from the answer given to a queryand to modify the horizon of the interpreter´s own understanding, highlighting his/her limits and asking for new openings.

In this context, one privileges both the dimension of the sociocultural, organizational, and historical setting of the actor, protagonist subject within a dialectic relationship, and the "agent and agencies", acting with "cultural tools", in a "located" and "distributed" way.

There are different *levels of analysis* of mediations, which relate to the cultural, semiological, communicational, and technological aspects in order to shape the educational technological mediations.

Itis also interesting to link that which is stated about education in general (Eisner, 1994) and which by extension could be applied to all of the modalities in which it appears, among them online distance education. We mean this task is linked to the intentions and chosen actions, that is to say, directly linked to the users, which is why the presence of democratic and representative leaders becomes essential to enhance the capacity to understand the world in a broad and represented way, to face problems with equity and effectiveness and to acquire ample varieties of transferable meaning.

The development ofsocial, situated, and shared cognition in an ethical-solidary way is central to these ends.

## The Phenomenon of Social Interaction and Educational-technological and Pedagogical Interactivity for Electronically Mediated Distance Education Communication

For the sociological analysis of the phenomenon of social interaction and educational-technological interactivity of electronically mediated distance education communication, it is necessary to refer to the investigations on virtual interaction focused on four areas: the study of interaction, the intervention of the tutor/professor in the collaborative space, the collaborative construction of knowledge and the mediating tools.

The interaction that takes place in virtual collaborative environments is different from that produced face-to-face. Obviously, a common space is shared, there is an encounter with others, but the specific characteristics of this space are conditional on the pre-established forms of interrelationship, the technological procedural mastery that possessed by the users, as well as their level of representational abstraction and the level of commitment to undertake electronic communication with the tools available for this purpose. In addition, for learning to take place, it is not enough to exchange messages and chat. It is necessary to achieve a designed dialogue that promotes the development of knowledge.

However, what is the role of dialogue in the mediated interactive process? How do we learn from dialogue? Should we also learn to engage in dialogue? Is the type of argumentation that takes place within dialogue relevant as apossibility for construction of knowledge? In other words, the issue of how virtual learning is promoted through dialogue mediated by ICT – which depend on the decisions of design and implementation of each educational program and organization-is central.

These are some of the most important issues that appear in research on virtual interactive process, in general in collaboration, and which each situation will have to take into account and consideration.

Crook (1993) believes that the study of the role of dialogue in learning and the observation of dialogues is fundamental to enable us to design learning environments which are conducive. To accomplish this, he proposes the creation of experimental environments that allow us to connect the learning theories with the analysis of interactions.

Baker et al (2003) believe that the important thing is to analyze argumentative interaction - a type of dialogue- along with the negotiation of meaning. It is a dialogue in which the pros and cons of the contributions are combined; during this process of discussion an important level of substantiation is required. The negotiation of meaning takes place during the problem-solving process in a manner that creates a space between the problem and its solution.

Ultimately, so that there really is argumentation – generally favored by cooperation- in the construction of knowledge, a negotiation of knowledge, and a learning by means of collaboration, it is required that the subjects acquire a common frame of reference that allows them to negotiate and communicate sources, meanings, and points of view with respect, sincerity, and peace of mind, to reach at a common base of inferences within a program.

Thus, a complex aspect of the analysis of the interactive process and a group collaboration through ICT, comes from establishing categories for the analysis of the respective exchanges and messages. The challenge of the present sociological study lies indeed in the study of the content and format, quantity and quality of transactions within the process of interaction in online electronic educational programs, within the present framework of the communities of network learning.

## THE INTERACTIVITY OF THE INFORMATION AND COMMUNICATION TECHNOLOGIES AND ITS CONCEPTUAL DIFFERENCE WITH SOCIAL INTERACTION

The analysis of the interactivity that characterizes the ICT, in addition to being a topic of complex discussion, is at the beginning of its investigation. It is a theoretical-practical gamble to study, from different disciplines and looks, the mechanisms through which pedagogical relationships act for the development of the higher thought processes of the face-to-face or distance learner. This calls for a more detailed explanation of the mediations that occur within the phenomenon of interactivity, in light of pluridiscipline.

Both the interaction and the interactivity mediated by ICT occurs in "learning environments", that constitute the "physical and psycho-social" space of a virtual class. It includes individuals who relate and communicate; technological resources enable this relationship and the process of cultural and pedagogical mediations to be conducted,processes that do not set aside the resistance of the mental representations, erroneous conceptions, fears, and the appearance of various imaginary mental representations.

We must understand the conceptual difference between "interaction" and "interactivity", if we wish to design various proposals for genuine participation of a user (student, participant of a program, etc.) in an educational context.

Whereas for the study of interaction it is necessary to articulate concepts originating from psychosociology and cultural anthropology towards respecting *diversity* in the assembly of the subjectivity (and identity) of the learner, for the study of interactivity attention will be given to the combination of technological advances of *hardware* and *software* with the didactic designs and the symbolic languages of ICT selected and combined in order to facilitate a user-friendly navigation and a reading that enables understanding and transfer of learning to specific situations.

Within social interaction, cultural (and subcultural) matrices of communication are recognized which are possessed by individuals (or groups) and which take part in the interaction processes, with their communicative sequences and guidelines. The same include values, social beliefs, stereotypes, etc. of varying type, and their involvement with local or regional communities, different labor groups or organizations, will grant said social interaction its own cultural profile.

Within interactivity we may not only observe the power and the technological-telematic support of reciprocal communication, but also the structuring and the presentation of the content for teaching with didactic activities of application, transfer, and evaluation, which will strengthen (hopefully) the development of autonomous and intelligent individuals, through technological mediations.

In all of the cases, the possibility of combining and promoting the world of computers, telecommunications, distant images, etc. as particular attributes of ICT offers a not at all insignificant interaction and interactivity for an expressive and communicative education. We may add to this the removal of the physical coordinates of time and space which expands the possibilities of distant sociocultural access, the possibility of flexibility in the design of didactic programmings in order to understand the professional formative relationship of facilitation and inescapable aid (Zone of Proximal Development, according to Vigotsky).

Thus, it is indicated the type of educationaldirection that will characterize social interaction and pedagogical interactivity in general, and mediated by educational materials especially, if we wish to foster an "education centered on the development of the student".

These are innovative features, where the *processes* that are generated have more meaning than the products, intimately related to the characteristic of interactivity that distinguishes the ICT and which we shall see in this chapter.

## Communication Mediated by ICT

Both interaction and interactivity can occur through various types of communication: in real time (or synchronous, such as chat, videoconference, etc.) or virtual mediatized (or asynchronous, such as e-mail, forums, etc.). Many electronic learning environments have both options, and they offer them by means of different types of software specially designed to enable this situated and distributed communication.

We shall also consider the various situations linked to interaction and interactivity that are encouraged by ICT, from the different dimensions of analysis, like the pedagogical dimension, that promotes the referred interactivity through the design of didactic activities for the understanding and the application of contents in individualized and collaborative virtual learning situations, in order to strengthen the participation and autonomous work on the part of the student. We should add to this today the platforms of *Learning Management System* (LMS) and *Learning Content Management System* (LCMS) that co-configure structured learning and teaching environments. This occurs with greater emphasis in the second mentioned environment, with the pre-established treatment of the contents, where the student is bundled up with instructions on practically everything he/she must do to learn, including the dimension of administrative management, that considers the interactive interrelationship relative to the planning and evaluation of the course, admissions, registry, follow-up, and student support, etc.; the dimension of the synchronous and asynchronous tutorial communication between faculty and students, and of follow-up of the collaborative work; the dimension of the design, production, evaluation, and interactive distribution of educational materials in the network; the social dimension in encounters in various virtual locations, from the virtual library to the informal cybercafé etc.

The introduction of ICT as the hallmark not only of the "information society and the knowledge society ", but also of the distance programs that promote life-long learning, points to the continuous process of construction of meaning through the design of virtual teaching environments and has many benefits but also limitations that must be pointed out. Among the former are reducing the time and cost of the arrival of information, and stimulating constant interpersonal communication, active participation, cognitive flexibility in the thinking that should promote self-control in students with regard to progress or the possible difficulties encountered in study, evaluations, etc. Among the latter are recognizing multiple resistance to new electronic learning environments – because they are innovations of unfair reach- that may lead to low levels of participation, weak arguments, impoverishment of vocabulary and thus higher thought functions, and so on.

For this reason, it may be noted that the quality of the interaction and interactivity needed for new teaching environments points to breaking the unidirectionality and the "repository position" of education to opt for constructive and self-learning proposals, cooperative and solidary, which give the control over communication to the network user and who, with ICT, becomes a real protagonist.

It is necessary to insist on the critical technological training of professionals in the field of education in general and especially those in electronic distance education, to strengthen the mechanisms of social interaction - that involve social interrelationships with and between individuals from near and far made possible by these technologies in an unprecedented way in the history of electronic supports -, and of pedagogical interactivity which, through the didactic design of powerful learning activities, increase the possibility of self-examination and practice in these electronic, synchronous or asynchronous (off/online) teaching environments.

When integrating the critical approaches of the new communicative paradigms that capitalize on information technologies (ICT) - with the above-mentioned risks- for training and teaching, we emphasize its possibility of technologically relating to other educational projects, students, faculty, and experiences in general in a fast and versatile way and, above all, through the design of intelligent learning environments, which should help build interesting and useful knowledge in dialogued, discussed, and shared ways. That is, with ICT there is the possibility of promoting not only the access to the information - which still has its limitations with regard to a much-needed equity in the socioeconomic order and infrastructure in contexts and users -, but also of helping to build knowledge in a situated and shared way.

Nevertheless, the ICT do not determine the interactivity nor the interaction, but are intervening factors that shape them, since they depend on the social and cultural meaning that has been given to the technology within a specific educational situation. The ICT have the technological characteristic of establishing the opportunity for interaction, unlike the previous (more conventional) technologies applied in teaching, such as radio and television. But they will not create by themselves environments of pedagogical interactivity, but rather must be inspired by a reformulation of the meaning and quality of social relationships for reciprocal pedagogical exchanges which educational programs should pursue in order to overcome the traditional, unidirectional, and repository conception of information.

The pedagogical interactivity conceived in this way enhances the ability to discover and seize training opportunities, because it will emerge from technological-socio-cognitive designs pertinent to specific social situations and actors as well as to didactic objectives and disciplinary content. Thus also the flexibility of the ICT will be capitalized to promote the control of communication on the part of the learner and allow his/her protagonism as builder of messages within cooperative and solidary proposals of self-study.

It would seem that it is necessary not only to train in technological-educational skills, but also to remove mentalities and reach new attitudinal domains which allow respectful horizontal communication and a sense of solidarity, if the goal is to propose alternatives and solve problems in a joint or collaborative way.

However, we must recognize that there is still a lack of unamimity, awareness, and social consensus in the face of the above-mentioned and the appropriate and reflective use of ICT in teaching in general and at a distance, due to the existence of resistance, fear, ambivalence, lack of qualifications and practice, etc., which is why the training for interaction and interactivity is still a challenge.

## Electronic Networks In distance Education. Their Genesis and Sociocultural Impact

From a sociological educational point of view, social networks are comprised of the group of people, communities, institutions, or organizations that produce and receive, distribute and exchange goods and formative social services, today mediatized by the advances of technology, within a squeme of expected development and well being. Such exchanges can occur at a local, regional, national, and international level.

Social networks are inserted in the conception of the theory of collective action that argues that "the social capital formed by such networks is of reciprocity, voluntary corporation, and commitment" as part of the very dynamics of the social system (Vargas, 2003).

They also share today different types of information and involve mutual benefit, trust and coordinated work with the globalized world ( neoliberal of information) in general through social political control (Aranda, 2002), operating in various forms of domination which influence the new social movements that emerge, are organized, and developed with more or less capacity to facilitate the collective action of technological articulation of the local in the global.

Therefore, the exchange of ideas and thoughts and the dynamics ofactions of varying scope have been caused and transformed by the practice of the networks within the globalization that governs the current destinies ofindividuals and social groups (Flores, 2001), even unintentionally.

Such networks require a human organization (*or basic primary networks*), defined as those institutions and organizations –public as well as private –which produce input, output, or basic services for their sustenance and the community's, at the local, regional, and national levels, through ICT, depending on how different areas are socioculturally prioritized. Their main features are their horizontality, voluntarism, interdisciplinarity, coorperation, flexibility, solidarity, common goals and objectives.

Social networks may also be defined as "the set ofmanagement or administration, participation or association relationships, which encompasses a wide group of individuals or microorganizations"; they bring together families, companies, ministery offices, political parties, churches (PAHO/WHO, 1999), etc.

Because of the above-mentioned,social networks are not distant relativesof the concept of community as social organization of the relationship among individuals and groups where close human ties, shared values (many of them emotional) and solidary actions take precedence.

While this is what counts for the quality of human cohabitation in networks, due totheir sociopolitical implications and of action, it is necessary to acknowledge that they can be a source of differentiation with the risk of segregation. The "we" of a network can mean people *like us*, and the others or "they" mean people *different from us*. It is not that "we are identical" in all respects: but while there are differences between "us", despite common features, the similarities could become small, dissolve, and neutralize the possible impact in the face of differences (Bauman, 2006).

## Virtual Communities

The virtual community, as well as being defined from the point of view of a telematic network that connectivelly and communicativelly shares several elements to build knowledge, should be regarded as archipelagos of islands situated along lines of communication in a rapidly globalized world. Those heavily guarded enclaves of society resemble the marginal enclaves of poor groups (Bauman, 2006).[1]

The virtual community is also defined as "the social aggregate that arises from the network when a sufficient number of people carry on public discussions with conversations, exchanging ideas, words, feelings, concepts, and so on, over a sufficient period of time, to express human feelings in personal relationships of the cybernetic space" (Rheingold, 1994), in the same way as it is done in real life, but leaving bodies behind or in an invisible way.

This lack of corporality is one of the first elements that should be re-signified within virtuality, bearing in mind that in face-to-face communities the body is one of the most important factors that define identity and factual communication among people. Since the physical channels of meaning are absent, it is necessary to create alternative channels, with which users develop new systems of meanings, mainly based on what is textual, verbal, on images, and on narration.

The virtual cultures of these communities are constituted in mediations between culture and technology, and are systems of symbolic exchange in networks through which collective meaning, ways of representing what is real, and new sensibilities are configured.

In virtual communities, the hierarchies are present, on the one hand, through those who hold technical knowledge and make them "work", and, on the other hand, by printing some form of interaction, for those roles of greater passivity. To participate in this form of communication, you need a certain speed of thought that allows you to keep pace with the the current that flows and a high speed typing. Emotion, as said, is also present. It is noteworthy that feelings of responsibility, looking after others, reciprocity, recognition, fraternity, friendship, love, and also hostility and hate are created. The fisical environment is virtual, but the emotional is real, both in the virtual as in the "factual".

While these virtual communities are heterogeneous, since participants come from different parts of the world and use different languages, from the cultures where they belong, this common environment is constructed –in its own symbology and meaning - in a more or less creative way, as a "copy" of external reality, to boldly form an alternative reality.

It may be the only feature that characterizes networks as a compatible, conceivable, and realistic unit within the conditions established by the "liquid modernity", where with high interaction with ICT, beliefs, values, and styles have been decontextualized or "uprooted", and the sites offered for a "re-rooting" appear as something temporary, of stable pretentions, but does not become permanent. Therefore, everything contributes to fragile identities and "with expiration date", stripped of any determination of its agents to keep them integrated. The vision of community is like "an island of warm and domestic tranquility in the midst of an inhospitable sea and turbulent transitoriness" (Giddens, 1972). The "we", as Richard Sennett (2000) repeatedly claims, is today an "act of self-protection".

Moreover, many etymologically argue that the word "virtual" is non-existent, supposed or implicit, and for these reasons would be inapplicable to virtual education. However, it is impossible to conceive it in a virtual way because all of the new media and existing technologies aid in a real way, and not in a supposed way, the training of individuals. Virtual reality is real and education has never been as benefited as now with the use of ICTand in particular, the network of networks, Internet.

The online or virtual electronic educational modality that is being analized, is only implemented thanks to the processing of data and sending/reception of distance information, with a telematic orientation of tutorial messages, which is why we cannot do without technology and ICT.

Virtual communities –inserted in the society of liquid precariousness, are presented as proposals for collaborative systems, increasingly common in the production and distribution of information and knowledge. Three esencial conditions for their existence help to solidify the social system:

- They make synchronous distant encounters as realistic as if they were carried out face-to- face or in the same place;
- They transport essential "meanings" for the continuity of synchronous encounters; and
- Coordinate these interpersonal encounters with other technologies at the service of communication to interact and take advantage of the necessary information through machines and automated telematic procedures.

These new technologies for collaboration central to the production of knowledge can also reproduce not only the oral word, but use and transmit drawings, graphics, still images (photographs) and moving images (videos) to give the participants a sense of fluidity in the communication and to increase the naturalness and the solidity of the experience with immediate *feedback.*

It is to be expected that this type of collaboration, in telematic convergence with the telephone, cable television, wireless equipment, the new generation of synthetic cameras, and satellite companies, provide communication service, not only technologically effective with high speed and fidelity, but at lower prices to increasingly more people, in order to achieve equitable services that help overcome social inequality.

The challenge of collaboration through the use of information technologies is to convert the incredible mediated human proximity into valuable relevant collaboration, useful to individuals and organizations (Dertouzos, 2002), through communications by means of all the possible combinations (from person to person, person to machines, and machines to machines). Individuals and groups should be able to work together in synchronous and asynchronous ways covering different areas, no matter where they are, appealing to ICT, highlighting that communicational coordination is centered and conceived from and for the people.

If virtual education or electronic distance education with ICT is the issue, we may observe that the process of teaching and learning is mediated by computers and telecommunications: it is desirable for this process to be inscribed in an approach of interdiciplinary educational technology with critical revision.

Since it is virtual,is a concrete, "factual", and potential reality. It is linked to the concept of origin in the lens as discipline that differentiates between a concrete image, and a virtual, present, and active one, and by the benefits and real functionalities that it provides through technology and ICT. In other words, the issues of formation and interaction for the configuration of subjectivity and personal and group identity have the same effect in this mode (Diaz, 1999) regarding face-to-face relationship, although withdiverse profile.

The virtual educational environments, like the "factual" ones, are of wide interactive power (some of them real and others made possible by devices), both centered in the user, and should promote the active and collaborative learning of the group in different types ofcommunities, namely: learning, search, production of knowledge, investigation, etc. In other words, these virtual learning environments would enable learning-without having to place people in the same space or at the same time- assuming the functions designed for the learning systems that are developed face- to- face (Duart y Sangra, 1999).

Interactive technology offers an enormous source of stimulation for learning, since the user possesses a greater self-control over the regulation of his/her learning process and can make decisions about its meaning and direction, as well as, how, when, and what to learn. The use of connected multimedia and digital materials is central to developing these possibilities of mediated learning and teaching.

Virtual education articulated with ICT produces transformations through the converging languages of mental categories, namely, in the way human beings think about themselves, others, and the world (Echeverria, 1991). In these network contexts, users, as members, build their community space from the interaction with others. They must access and appropriate a symbolic system and multiple textual meanings that will ensure the exchange, self-regulation, and understanding as they reach agreements of survival and a sense of belonging, from which they give meaning to their practice and the practice of others from the narrative, in spite of a lack of conventional physical channels of communication.

## KINDS OF TELEMATIC NETWORKS FOR ELECTRONIC DISTANCE EDUCATION

Among the kinds of telematic networks applicable to increase interaction and interactivity, productivity and sense of belonging in electronic distance education programs, we may name the following:

### 1. Learning Communities

There are no recipes for their construction, but rather some principles with theoretical foundation and pedagogic methodologies that give them their raison d'etre and can be consulted in any manual of educational design for networks. Seen from the social point of view, the priority of this study, these ways of associating in communities and networks to learn together appear as support groups, providers of security and identity; due to the coincidence of learnings, it leads to the construction of a formative proposal generated in a shared way. The meaning of learning springs from or is shaped through a process: each user becomes a full member building and sharing sociocultural practices related to a goal and topic which brings them together.

In general, these communities emerge and developed from the individuals or students who wish to learn and be together; also, due to the appearance of opportunities and agreements to cary out educational tasks together. Virtual interaction is accomplished in different environments: the classroom, workshop, self-learning centers, online courses, places of work, libraries, etc. In general they are characteristically free, solidary, productive, self-regulated and creative, democratic, and recognize diversity.

Learning is a process and product of a communication situated within a particular context in relation to a broader situation and of combined interrelation. The administrators of virtual educational programs (as well as tutors, coordinators, etc.) are the protagonists and participants that possess the duty to explore and deepen the diverse mechanisms of the networks through which people participate in communities. Rogoff (1994) emphasizes the importance of prioritizing instruction –electronic online in our case- which builds interest from collaborative proposals. It is also important to acknowledge that relating various programs enablesproactivity and mutual participation within a specific virtual group.

However, in order to relativize the potentialities of groups in networks, it is necessary to remember and be clear on the following:

1. Collaborative groups, of either investigation and/or learning, take up again the definition given by the *conditions in which the collaboration appears:* madepossible by communication and interaction mediated by advanced networks of ICT. Such collaborative groups of investigation and/or learning can only be defined as temporary or permanent modes of interaction among faculty, investigators, students, participants, etc, and as proposals of organization for the exchange of teams, schedules, and products.
2. Collaborative groups of investigation and/or learning are not new. Historically, Plato with the Academy, the first University of Paris, the Bauhaus School, the Viena Circle, the colloquium of the greatest physicists at the beginning of the century, and others interlaced their search and confronted their teachings. Today this exchange continues; they are more than necessary, easier, and quicker, due to virtual communication with ICT (Crook, 1993), in the hope that the greatest number of people involved could equally benefit, apurpose that has not materialized yet, beyondtechnological reasons.
3. It is not always necessary to form collaborative groups of investigation and/or learning: it will depend on the epistemological framework, disciplinary content, selected methodology, the meaning and pursuable goals, etc., in each particular project. Many faculty members think that knowledge is constructed through individual effort. Moreover, the different levels of training and specialization of the participants –whether they are teachers, investigators, students, etc.- make us think that the learning of complex concepts and theories needs solitude and the hard work of each student. In consequence, there cannot be many fluid discussions among participants,if someone doesn't know or is only taking his/her first steps in a discipline; it's impossible to organize deep debates and contrast diverse opinions in virtual groups, as it would be in concrete social environments.
4. It is not always easy to structure collaborative groups of investigation, knowledge management, and learning: it will depend on the mentalities and the underlying ideologies, beliefs, prejudgements, fears of losing control of the situation, ignorance of the methodologies, the emergence of socioemotional and cognitive conflicts due to competivity and rivalry, the lack of acceptance of shared evaluation, etc., which scientists, investigators, faculty, students, and so on, may be subject to. It is necessaryto revise and adapt solutions (not mechanically and linearly adopt) in this case ofcollaborative proposals, from contrast and invention; trying and learning new techniques to develop competencies, organize the work and communicate various

points of view, among differentgroups of remote colleages. The goal is to overcome resistanceand personal misgivings, " open minds ", respect diversity, share feelings of solidarity and coorperation.

## 2. Communities of Practice

We are dealing here with groups of people who decide to learn in an environment of collaboration and solidarity, taking responsibility for their training processes through self-management and collaborative proposals. They could be more or less formal or fluid, are joined by common activities that have been learnt through mutual commitment and interrelation (Wenger, 1998).

Various dimensions define the communities of practice as:

- *what they are about*: the objectives and the content approached in order to be together; it refers to professional practice;
- *how they work*: by way of mutual commitment, inscribed in a social entity; and
- *how they are capable of producing knowledge*: from the shared repertoire of common resources (routines, sensitivities, artifacts, vocabulary, styles, etc.) over time.

The communities of practice cover a lot more than the technical knowledge or special skills associated with a task: they are wrapped in a fabric of relationships given and sustained over time. From the sociological point of view, a community of practice –like the above-mentioned - needs to generate an apropiate shared repertoire ofideas and develop various resources (tools, documents, routines, symbols, etc.) which in a sense will characterize it as a "community". In other words, it involves its practices as action proposals shared by its members, which is linked to informal mechanisms of communication.

They can also be viewed as organizations with characteristics and benefits provided by this associative life for the generation of social capital (Putnam, 1993). The interesting thing about these communities is to highlight how they differentially generated these groups, associations, networks, etc. to which they are committed.

Therefore, more than observing what kind of sociocognitive process and conceptual structure is involved, it is necessary to ask what kind ofsocial and cultural committment is managed in these contexts for the contrasting with practice to take place and for these communities to materialize. It is not enough for the participants to acquire shared mental structures or models of understanding the world, but to be inserted and participate in frameworks of pre-existing structures, in new processes of committment and accompaniment, so they may become active participants of practices in these social communities. In this way, they build their identity in relation to these communities and view learning not as an individual acquisition of knowledge, but as a product of a process of social participation.

The concept of community could also be the means of rescue, development, and long term maintenance of the memory of an organization, a important element which is not always acknowledged as valuable and enriching of motivation and commitment to learn. Without contact points and relevance systems there is no learning or memory. Learning does not belong to each individual, but to conversations as exchange processes where people take part and develop various products.

Centered on the focus of interrelationship, this proposal is both a challenge and a deep dilemma. Learning to solve problems from experience in a contrasting way is the same as learning by doing. Education should involvepractices of informed and commited actions in this sense.

Accordingly, the issue of how information and knowledge are managed within the communities, groups and organizations is of great relevance. Which are the mechanisms of communication and coordination of teams to organize and sequence tasks, which sources should be consulted, how autonomous the parts are, and how work in networks is done, are, among others, questions to be faced in each situation of group contrasting. The same with regard to how to increase motivation and give meaning to information for the community to be sustainable and use it later.

"Knowledge management" is the process of capture and transformation, not directly observable and accessible, to appropriate information depending on the needs of the actors and situations for present and past uses. By *management* we understand the process which, in general, includes four functions: planning, organization, leadership, and evaluation of information. It is a process: creating, planning, storing, managing, evaluating information, in order to share and inscribe it in contrasted experience with insight and clarity in each community´s context for the communication of individuals, groups, and organizations with similar interests and needs.

ICT are today foundational for this process characterized by the continuous transformation of information, in specific contexts, from the appropriation of past and present information, processed according to an organizational prospective.

However, beyond the ICT, there is the process of "knowledge management" (Brooking, 1997) in the above-mentioned phases of planning, organization, shared leadership, and evaluation. This management forms a collaborative science, referred in our case to research and teaching in networks (of intra and Internet); the central focus is found in the values that the agents or "symbolic analysts" must possess in diverse settings as managers of knowledge.

On the other hand and in the same way, networks of intensive knowledge also are formed, which gather a high level of development of endogenous competencies associated to good channels of production/creation, circulation, and distribution oftechnological-scientific knowledge, as we shall see as follows.

## 3. Knowledge Communities

These networks represent the highest expressions of individuals and groups as producers of knowledge. Their features of creation, exchange, and transfer of information and knowledge arise from a social interaction today mediated in general by advanced technological systems. A knowledge network could be defined as a community of individuals who in a formal or informal way, part-time or full time, work with a common interest basing their actions on building, developing, and sharing mutual achievements of systematic conformation of knowledge.

The production of scientific and technological knowledge from formal organizations and research processes is the result of an integration of both sociopolitical and technological organizational decisions as intellectual and financial resources guided towards producing knowledge to meet and anticipate general and specific social needs.

It is a complex issue, associated to the sociological conceptions in force in the historical past as well as in the present, that include the agreed perspective for a technological development and sociocultural innovation, the desired country project within the scope of selected values with regard to what is understood as science and technology, inscribed in today´s technological culture, where the agents in mediated interaction transform the raw material or energy (Quintanilla, 2000) which is information.

According to Casas (2001), these networks of knowledge production "involve the formation of professional and training networks,as well as networks of diffusion and transmission of knowledge or innovation, which would be leading to the formation of regional spaces of knowledge".

The social knowledge networks are constituted in human interactions for the production, storage, distribution, transfer, access, use, and analysis of knowledge produced in a systematic way by investigation. The personal or group interest in sharing information of any kind through, generally, electronic means, in order to develop the capability of creation, understanding, power, study, and transformation of the historical territorial and economic-social, real or virtual reality, is one of its main characteristics.

Such networks have been developed since the twentieth century from the dynamics of the industrial society, the information and knowledge society, articulated with the characteristics of the scientific technological systems that constantly generate and exchange information; and also, by the dizzying expansion of investment in certain key areas and systems of communication and transfer of digital data and images in real time, of easy, quick, and economical registration and access, at a world wide level, though not always for social aims but mainly for economic, financial, and military goals.

Some basic characteristics of the knowledge networks are expressions of human interaction in a larger social context, linked to the development of civilizations, such asproducing, storing, and distributing scientific knowledge by technological transmission. Their goal is to transform the social environment in the constant search for enrichment/improving the quality of life and deepening the innovative, creative, and pluridisciplinary work, inscribed in an socio-historical field and of specific local, regional, national, and international impact.

Among the different models of social knowledge networks, there are virtual networks directed towards knowledge management, structured into three basic elements: the members of the network, the tools of the network consisting of a telematic platform, and discussion topics defined by its own members, other persons, or organizations (Rodriguez, Araujo, and Yulianov, 2003). In general, what is important here is the social, public, and organizational character of production and transfer of technological scientific knowledge. This is why it is a chain of networks, from the primary social networks, the institutional networks, cooperation networks, and transfer networks. In all of these, the generation of knowledge of fundamentally two types is relevant: 1) *local generation of knowledge* through activities of investigation and exploitation of native knowledge; and 2) *adaptation of knowledge available in other parts of the world*, through appropriation, assimilation, integration, or incorporation of the knowledge to the productive process, encouraging respect for the sociocultural profile of the social unit that receives it through institutional networks of local agencies.

The process of generating knowledge and transfering technology in these networks is a complex process that takes place in basic environments: scientific, market, legal, and financial; it involves various actors and depends on a number of critical factors: registration of intellectual property, the technology brokers that gather members and organize them in an effective way to facilitate agreements, the creation of new businesses, venture capital, and the development of technological capabilities of the companies, where the small and medium play a leading role (Garrigós and Hidalgo, 2003).

## 4. Cooperation Communities or Networks

They are public or private organizations at a local, regional, national, and international level, which are able to cooperate technically and financially with knowledge and institution networks in order to manage joint projects with pertinence, effectiveness,efficacy, efficiency, and relevance for self-sustaining development.They may include researchers, research centers or national research systems, communication and information networks, academic networks, telematic networks, reseach networks, innovation networks, technological service networks (Sebastian, 2002), and transfer networks – closely linked to processes of technological innovation and scientific development-, that group individuals, entities, or organizations to intermediate and transfer the knowledge produced.

In this framework, today it is interesting to establish alliances, which are central to an intelligent international cooperation. An alliance points to the group of associated entities, formed by social organizations, communities of collaborative learning, practice, investigation, etc., based on certain self-regulated and agreed relationships, within a socio-scientific-technological coallition, which in general is supported in virtual higher education programs. They are based on collective values, norms, and principles of collaborative work. They have clear objectives to achieve common and representative goals of each one of the institutional members of the associated group to ensure benefits for all.

Nevertheless, communication, agreements, and representativeness within the alliances is not always easy; there are sometimes imposed hierarchies and diverse discrimination from the decision-making levels with regard to its institutional members; tasks to be addressed and overcome in the action with the help of ICT.

### *Research Communities or Search (or Inquiry) Networks*

They are communities in which their members learn together from the experience of others (Wertch, 1995). They are not learning or academic communities but rather of individuals who in the face of a doubt or difficulty, propose a self-corrective search or investigation in order to build hypothesis to solve this problem. The epistemological contribution to re-creation and "participative appropriation" as a central process in these communities is acknowledged, where participants transform their understanding and responsibility through various activities carried out jointly.

Among some of their features, valid for proposals of electronic online distance education,we find that they encourage the inclusion (or inclusiveness)of all of the participants within a squeme that takes shape as a *gestalt,* with multiple interconnections to penetrate and analyze an issue. Thus, they infer, define, assume, suppose, imagine, distinguish, anticipate elements by appealing to the mental acts of the members who are mediated or in communication. The relationship among them, though not essential (as in communities of practice, as described), is advantageous because they establish complex meanings which are constantly reinterpreted. Moreover, the existence of the feeling of social solidarity within these networks is fertile when deliberating and proposing alternatives according to the reasons given by each participant, forming an opinion,making decisions, and facilitating contrasted debates, in an open, self-corrective, defiant, reflexive, and contextualized way, considering all existing points of view and interests.

***New Settings of Cooperative Networks of Online Distance Higher Education Programs***

The new settings we have been describing, analyzing, and criticizing show, within theprocess of socio-economic, cultural, and technological worldwide change, the adjudication of roles central to higher education institutions, universities, and research centers, to meet in a critical way the new training needs, inscribed in the framework of globalization; many of them should be consideredurgent demands in the mentioned networks.

In the emerging setting thus characterized, there is in progress a thorough revision of the premises and traditional ways of conceiving organizations, their functions, and management to achieve specific objectives, which today tend towards the improvement of the quality of higher education managed by the development and implementation of new strategies (virtual among others), expanding and rethinking the spectrum and educational-cultural contexts where they take place.

Education presents two core values: one, "intrinsic", which refers to itself in direct relation with the historical dimension of a specific time; and the other "extrinsic", in interdependence with other individuals and groups, in relation with the sociocultural and natural environment and its institutions, to enable a global understanding of the culture and help the development of creative and imaginative potentialities.

If the construction of a knowledge society requires understanding that the raw material is information and its energy is knowledge, competencies that promote this production are required.

Thus, the pillars of this society are the power or force of self-determination thatindividuals and groups possess in terms of their knowledge to carry out actions with adjustment and revision of the values and attitudes which sustain them. The construction of a knowledge society should consider “alternative” ways to configure encounters between cultures and knowledge.

Proposals for higher education, in line with the above, should be systemic-holistic, flexible and dynamic, variable and diverse, formative and valorizing, transcendent and pluralist, interactive and respectful of diversity. This involves a challenge to the power of learning, productivity, and sociocultural integration, with sustainable gains, in other words, sustained over time, today, in global networks.

Internationalization is part of the phenomenon of mundialization of communication and information due to the great technological advances of ICT, which allows us to consult and operate with databases and navigate in telecommunication networks with interactive multimedia services for the development of professional, economic-financial, education and entertainment, public and private activities. The phenomenon of internationalization is understood as the incremented relationship among nations through the action of telecommunications, which increases the geographical extent of the above-mentioned activities beyond national borders; in other words, they are deterritorialized.

All societies inserted in a global social space (Bourdieu, 1991) are found in a force field that is imposed through agencies and agents. They are presented in turn as social subspaces in differentiated structures established in the distribution of the forms of sociopolitical power and economic-financial capital, efficient within a considered social framework.

The telematic educational proposals today shape national and regional identities and cultures saturated with references to deterritorialized global social subspaces. Garcia Canclini (1995) argues that the current culture is a hybrid because of the impact of the accelerated interaction of fast ICT within a multi-ethnic and intercultural interdependence.

Globalization is a more advanced and complex form than internationalization, as it involves a certain degree of functional integration among disparate activities. This has also reached online distance education because its programs, telematically crossed, surpass all boundaries, belong to a world strategy, and are directed at a global market.Distance education has thus every chance of transnationalizing with its programs of “local” version, which does not necessarily mean, with this local commercialpenetration, that it possesses or maintains a high level of excellence.

ICT foster such development in the internationalized space known as *cyberspace* (Gibson, 1995) or *globalvillage* (Mc Luhan, 1981), an extension of the sociocognitive and cultural reality made by our mind, which offers unprecedented experiential dimensions provided -not in a egalitarian way- by transnational connectivity.

Online education and the growing use of technologies of information have become indispensable for the development of programs offered by higher education institutions, to the point of forming hyperuniversities with the not simple modification, of their organizational structure. The possibility of sharing resources and equivalent formative processes should be accompanied with serious studies to face the risk of such processes being uniform and not respecting different cultural manifestations within the interinstitutional training alliances.

The new formative settings for the construction of knowledge in a collaborative way, inscribed within a new educational paradigm, introduce new methodological formulas. These frameworks, where individuals and groups create knowledge, impact on the activities of those who design, produce, and distribute symbolic goods, as well as the users´ activities within educational processes, which is why, among other things, faculty and students should instal themselves in a process of critical self-evaluation and reformulation of their roles in this new paradigm, of course, not without varied conflicts (central power *versus* local power, percentage of local contents *versus* international canned goods, etc.)

### *The Contribution of ICT to Collaborative Research Networks within the Mundialization of Distance Education*

Although ICT prove to be a good support for online distance education programs, the virtual collaborative work for research and teaching, as an inevitable contribution for the co-construction of knowledge, is in fact in an initial stage. They present various difficulties in their acceptance and concretion in universities and organizations in general (and specially in Latin America), not only for economic reasons.

From the standpoint of sociological analysis, there are two dimensions of work relating to research, teaching, and learning in the concerning programs that incorporate ICT and Internet, which must be considered.

- Ensuring a *conscious professional development of the specific competencies* necessary for a virtual collective creative process in environments mediated by ICT: the main goal and concern for the optimization of technological equipment and sophisticated investments that are increasingly made in universities and higher education institutions; and
- *Ensuring the proposal and development of research*, which to be such, must not only rely on the distribution of information through ICT, but must also be sustained and evaluated within an articulated framework of substantive and powerful theories; receiving an enormous quantity of information (statistics, cases studies, or other) through networks without theoretical support is not scientific, nor is it of serious academic interest. Any research and teaching practice must be permeated by theories that should be known, proven, verified, and/or refuted, if it is a genuine scientific work and not "illustrated essays" with numerous quotations and bibliographical references, but superficial and arbitrary in substance.

So, the two dimensions of work for the reflective analysis of ICT in higher education with collaborative networks are of interest in order to:

- Investigate whether ICT have reached all users and have really helped to change the way in which knowledge is built through teaching, to know if the way in which people learn and apply knowledge in their reality has improved. To do so, we will consider if there is local appropriation of the fast connective arrival of data with high definition, if the invisible sociocognitive strategies have been strengthened, represented as technologies of *mindware* – and not just solid *hardware* and *software*-, if virtual dialogue, discussion, and cooperative construction of knowledge, etc. are deepened.
- Recognize and teach, in this direction, what is and what is not a collaborative scientific research in the social sciences, where the subdiscipline of distance education in networks is inscribed (unavoidable chapter of a critical current educational technology), with the goal of studying what kind of scientific research may be carried out in virtual collaborative contexts and groups with the use of ICT. So for this, we should be talking about theoretical conceptualizations and not only advanced networks of connectivity.

Therefore, the analysis concerning *interactive work* and *research* is of interest.

- *Interactive work of collaborative groups through ICT:*it is perceived that this interaction will be sustainable in the long term if the organizations, groups, programs, and individuals possess the skills and attitudes consistent with the cybercultural times, with powerful strategies of thought, intellectual work, and socioemotional maturity, to risk and anticipate elements towards the resolution of problems, with balance and solidarity. In spite ofthe complex issue that is being addressed, there is some consolidation of a sociocultural framework that supports collaborative work for teaching, learning, research, etc, when recognizing and articulating valuable scientific input given by theories and practices of situated, constructive, perspectivist, confrontational, tacit, distributed, connected, etc. knowledge; these contributions, in turn, seek to dismantle beliefs and prejudices sustained in the interactive and shared spaces of high technology for a "socio-construction" (Edwards and Mercer, 1988) of a demystified knowledge.

- *Research:*in a time of great change and reconsideration of the conceptions and operations of all sciences, the research process is also reconsidered. It is understood as the reconstruction of empirical evidence, developed from theories where rigorous procedures and scientific-technological methodologies (Wainerman and Sautu, 2001) are applied with validated instruments. From the standpoint of content, all scientific-technological research is historical, limited, and cumulative, subject to innacuracies and therefore, biased and refutable. The scaffolding of any investigation responds to the theories, models, and the framework of concepts that structure the knowledge of any area in a given time, to which are added- in a spiral way- new ideas, doubts, issues, etc. This will build the general and specific objective of any investigation.

The reconstruction methods of the empirical evidence and the substantial contents will depend on the adopted or selected theoretical approach because, as everyone knows, there is no observation without an underlying theory to support it, which in turn is reinterpreted and reconstructed from the empirical evidence. The systematization and description of the processes, phenomena, etc, in their interdependences involves the observation, measurement, and registry of data, where ICT can be of use.

Beyond this work, the content of the investigation will be the reflection of the current historical cultural socio-economic tendencies and of international and local decisions to beadopted, as well as the support (or sponsorship ) from the various organizations that facilitate it (Bourdieu, Chamboredon, and Passeron, 1994), above all through long-term economic support.

It is also important to acknowledge that research topics are born, developed, become trendy, and decline. This occurs with our work, namely, the "social incorporation of ICT"; although it is central to the electronic educational programs within the knowledge society, it must be included in the agenda of the institutions so it does not become marginal with regard to the leadership of the dominant institutions.

So, the focus of the research does not depend on the ICT, unless it is a topic to be researched in itself. The objectives, methodologies, contrasts, generalizations, etc., lacking in rigor, without methodological control or epistemological monitoring, which are in the hands of untrained researchers, are not considered scientific. The same can be said ofteaching and learning processes with faculty members who haven´t been professionally trained.

In academic or general research networks and from collaborative and distributed actions in virtual environments, it is necessary:

a) To learn to explore, exploit,and evaluate the ICT to obtain strong collective processes as products of consciousness, feelings, commitments, cooperative accomplishments and attitudes, and not just the performance of technological skills for the use of ICT. When a person recognizes that knowledge is associated to his/her context of work or life needs, he/she will see it as even more valuable if it is shared and confronted with other knowledge and with other people. He/she will feel more motivated and committed,and will form networks of mutual collaboration, beneficial for each and everyone.

b) To keep in mind that identifyingthe benefits of appropriation of high-speed or advanced technical definition ICT, will only be relevant if it serves to deepen socioproductive interactivity and to make attitudes, mentalities, and procedures flexible towards the satisfaction of the collective work in various programs, organizations, cultural environments, etc.

The virtual cooperative academic groups for research or education do not emerge out of nowhere. Their members know perfectly that subjectivity, and its continuous reframing, arises from exchange as aresult of the cohesive and interdependent co-construction of individuals with common goals.

### *Some Tentative Sociological Conclusions and in Open Discussion*

Although in this context of work in networks and virtual communities it is important to teach respect and acceptance, negotiation skills and techniques for building consensus, all belonging to the category of "emotional intelligence" (Goleman, D. 1996), to strengthen coordination, self and co-evaluation, and increase the synergy of divergence in associated groups of individuals who hardly known each other, it is worth mentioning that it is not easy nor simple. Despite acknowledging its importance, it is still associatedto the mastery of technical devices or the possibility of receiving largenumbers of documents “at high speed”.

Although specialized literature highlights accurate results of the collaborative groups enriched by ICT regarding achievements of individual work, it can only be said that cooperative groups are useful. It will be more fruitful in academic terms if criticism and contrast of frameworks continues with different methodologies relating to the collaborativeproposals in the field, where it would be useful to associate and to correlate some variables, as well as to analyze the interdependence of a specific virtual mediation, with which actors, for which topics, with which activities, etc.

These are complex processes, which are not solved by just being connected to devices. Although equipment can help in the educative and investigative professional work,-since ICT are increasingly ubiquitous and feasible, of course depending on the regions and institutions -, this does not invalidate discussion on the reasons and conditions, objectives and disciplinary content, in implementing proposals of collaborative work mediated by ICT. Thus,it is argued that ICT, beyond their own intrinsic rationality - technical-instrumental, of social disciplining and cultural control- become a useful resource for receiving and communicating data, processed information, and others, to build shared forms of knowledge, to re-create general and specialized knowledge through global and local communication, to explore new directions and points of *serendipity* that arise during the work, to surpass conflicts through extensive debates, etc. Therefore, nobody will argue against their articulation in any kind of work, although efforts must beredoubled to deepen their analysis, study, and impacts.

The main drawback of these or other approaches, incorporating procedures and technologies, lies in personal sociomotivational problems, anachronistic beliefs and organizational structures, institutional rigidities and reluctance relative to sectarian political powers, in addition to economic hardship, not due to limited resources but to embezzlement of funds, null strategic planning, and unrealistic diagnoses. Although panaceas do not exist, and serious feasibility studies are required to analyze strengths, the evaluation of ICT in collaborative environments of virtual higher education and research, as well as the evaluative investigation in action, confronted in each context and discipline with specific users in the face of a technological combination, etc., are central and indispensable tasks.

### *The Context of Academic Capitalism, New Economic Markets, and Virtual higher Education*

In the new technological-virtual settings and acceleration of economic competition mentioned, a new axis of competitiveness appears, with the incorporation of technology and ICT into productive activity, which influences the transformation of higher education as part of the public policy and global geopolitics. The construction of the knowledge society is being processed and settled through a competition between the higher educational systems, which marks a new role for the State, who re-focuses its public policies and integrates them into the optics of internationalization of increasingly virtual education. The expansion of transnational education promotes today new geopolitics where education will trace the future borders between nations.

In these previously unheard of settings, there are new proactive and permanent instances that the State must assume to guarantee quality and the regulation of the internationalization of higher education. It is here where re-directing aspects of public investment, the formation of resources and decisions for applied research, which attracts students to a program or university, the export of certain educational services and not others, or the decision to cover with equity the access of more people to information are introduced.

ICT are present in all these issues, when formulating new technological-educational and sociopedagogical conceptions based on telematic communication models, of simulation, that assign new roles to faculty and students, among others; or when emphasizing or promoting an effective equity and incorporation of ICT in marginalized sectors (ethnic groups, indigenous people, women, the physically challenged) within a reform of university institutions. This is now necessary within the framework of life-long learning, with institutional flexibility and greater openness, the search for new sources of finance, high external competitiveness, etc.

The proposed work on academic capitalism in the information society and knowledge society, within the "new economy" (Slaughter and Rhoades, 2004), explains the process of integrating institutes, colleges, and universities when considering groups of actors in networks that cross borders (increasingly blurred), to interlink them with companies and business firms, nonprofit organizations, public or State agencies, and so on, through the participation of schools, students, university administrators, scholars, and professionals.

These players use a variety of state resources to create new circuits of knowledge that link higher education institutions with the new economy. They also use public resources to create interstitial organizations which complete a great variety of tasks, such as bringing the corporate sector within the university, developing new networks that intermediate between the private and public sectors, and expanding managerial capacity to supervise new flows of external resources. These resources go towards investment in research and infrastructure for institutions that are in the market and offer products and services to students (travel agencies, lodging networks, publishers, etc.) "under the umbrella of the new economy". The now expanded managerial capacity is directed towards the restructuring of the work within the schools to reduce instructional costs and bring them to the lowest possible levels. It is here where online electronic educational programs with an aggressive marketing of their teaching programs, *instructional* distance materials, etc.enter the stage.

In other words, academic capitalism is defined as being directed to the market and adjacent activities to generate external revenue. It is linked to the theory of dependence on resources, which takes into account new networks of actors as suppliers external to the university organization, forming the new universities which are integrated through knowledge.

Knowledge is the critical raw material recognized and extracted anywhere, sometimes unprotected, sometimes patented or copyrighted, marketed as a brand to be sold in the market for economic profit.

In this context, the students are considered to be flexible consumers of higher education programs, who after graduating become the products (or output) of such programs, contributing to the shaping of the new economy, through virtual educational institutions that act as traders of knowledge in a vigorous competition against other organizations in the market.

In the new economy, the market and its mercantile activities (with its new enterprising ideas) constitute the perspective (or foreground) to be achieved, whereas the State and its subsidiaries are suppliers of funds through the collection of taxes, charitable donations, etc., for background or support. With these activities, the public and nonprofit institutions create profit centers, which engage in aggressive marketing of instruction, educational materials, software, and distance education courses, among other goods.

Thus, there isa change in the supply of higher education seen in the passage or shift from the learning regime offered by the public sphere - which emphasizes the value of knowledge as something public for the benefit of the entire citizenry -, towards the regime of academic capitalism for learning and the pursuit of knowledge, within a competitive market, built as a private good, evaluated by flows of high technology. Both models coexist. This shift is also seen as a proposal of the networks of actors in universities, corporations, government agencies, etc., which cross transnational borders where electronic distance education plays a central role in teaching, research, and learning management.

This model or regime of the new academicism of capitalist knowledge, within the logic of the hyper and postliberal market, tends to lower the prices of products with regard to competitors and seek greater efficiency and quality of the services, which in our case are educational. For this reason, many believe that it appears as non-transparent; it flies over borders seeking grants for higher education, which redefines the public space of the academic and fosters a displacement of work fields and professionals.

The international academic community needs a serious debate on the issues to be outlined between the public, non-profit, and profit activities related to educational programs in general and online distance programs, in particular; what must be established, as well, is who will draw the line, with regard to knowledge and learning, since it points to a change of values in the world today. On more than one occasion it seems that the only concern is achieving greater economic progress, with monetary benefits, revenues, and financial goals instead of striving for academic excellence through the higher education programs and research needed in the twenty-first century.

It is possible that, from a critical framework, alternative designs for distance education should be proposed for the conjuncture, described above,of electronic higher education programs at the international level. These should be formed not only with and for the production of general knowledge, when capturing and studying the specific regularities of the social and educational action, but fundamentally, they would have to consider an equitable extension of their goods and services for all citizens and be enriched from the multiple cultural perspectives. The goal is to start from and reach a broad, synthesizing, critical framework to design and implement online educational projects and materials that point to a different international distance education; in other words, which make academic excellence and public and private resources more compatible with alternative, equitable, and innovative learning.

*Chapter 4*

# SOCIOCULTURAL CHANGE AND CONTROL THROUGH DISTANCE EDUCATION PROGRAMS AND PRACTICE IN THEIR VARIOUS ELECTRONIC MODALITIES

For us to be able to understand the process of technological change and its management as the related social control and cultural disciplining, it should be inscribed within the digital culture or *cyberculture* of virtual reality within the information society. Among its characteristics, there is the complexity of the weave of actions and reactions, of events and associations, that transform human perception with the possibility of erasing borders and merging people with machines, resulting in, for example, new objects of art, of high impact on the training of individuals and groups, as well as in the emerging citizenry.

In this sociotelematic space, where order and disorder, what is stable and unstable converge and coexist, in interconnected frames in an open and active system, which is changing and complex, distance education programs and organizations are found.

These systems - consisting of multiple access nodes and interactions mediated by technology among different communicative levels- are understood as a combined association of different elements of an ecological nature, based on the participation of all of their social actors through networks of information flow and production of communication.

Cyberculture (Gros, 2001), within globalization, is the new sociopolitical, economic, scientific-technological and formative setting that is enabled through networks, which with infinite, fast, and intricate flows of information crosses allcultural boundaries, and also fragments and delocalizes processes and phenomena.

How is the symbolic capital built in the virtual space of these instances favored by ICT, which enable communication, sociopolitical participation, and social change? What new characteristics do social and formative organizations possess in order to allow it or not?

# The Process of Innovation, the Management of Technological Change, and the Possibility of Social Change Mediated by Technology and ICT for Distance Education Programs. The Management of Technological Change. Conceptualization. Prerequisites, Characteristics, Problems

Social change includes aspects such as the success and/or failure of the various political systems and phenomena like globalization, economic development and growth, democratic expansion, etc. Social change involves the study of the evolution of societies, from the large-scale changes to the small adjustments with their consequent alterations. Social change is considered a core chapter of study and reflection within sociology, but it also applies to political and economic sciences, anthropology, other social sciences, and technology. In general terms, social change is the creation, the evolution, and the dissemination of the material culture (financial assets) and of the symbolic culture (social values within human relations) when introducing new features or when creating a new potential for wealth and knowledge.

The impact of new information technologies (ICT) has raised concerns on several issues related to social and technological change, including: 1) how to face this challenge in all its dimensions, as it is not only material, technological-"artefactual"; and 2) how to manage, in uncertain contexts, the analysis of various necessary personal and group skills for problem solving, if it is accepted that we are in a society and economy based on knowledge and which requires very flexible skills for extremely changing life and labor conditions.

Technological change, required to meet the demands of an information and knowledge society, is characterized by the series of interventions planned (Fainholc, 2003) and sustained by the mediated interaction of ICT, towards the achievement of technological knowledge corresponding to the domain of *hardware, software, and mindware;* in other words, sociocognitive strategies supported in higher thought functions and in interaction with others within a constructive and agreed exchange. The goal would be to dispose of anachronistic ways of thinking, feeling, and acting with standardized routines to solve problems when viewing the interdependence of organizational subprocesses, produced and required by an organization in a particular social-historical moment, because they are useful, valuable, ethical and profitable in a sociocultural and economic-financial sense.

Any technological change should seek to increase the quality of processes, products, and services through generation and management within a program or organization. This is linked to the integration of subprocesses that prove to be, in practice, timely and pertinent depending on the processes, products, and services that may be required.

Therefore, technological change should prompt an intelligent and sensible incorporation - coherent and non-consumerist- in general of technology and ICT, supported in the values of respect, equality, trust, authenticity, openness, and support, to sustain the personal and group efforts of a solid organizational development and work towards its gradual improvement. As technological change within social change is understood, it seeks to review, adjust, and change the organizational structures and mentalities – in other words, systemic, attitudinal and moral aspects -, more than the "artefactual", which is essential to eradicate stereotypes in social relationships and in the rigid perceptions that disturb fluid communication in the construction of joint knowledge in and towards a personal, organizational, and social development, if the goal is to increase committed participation, creative and self-sustained openness and productivity of the social units we are dealing with.

The organizational structures of education in general and in particular, higher learning, concerned about countering traditional rigid and bureaucratic structures, should remove rigid attitudes, in other words, personnel who are not qualified nor stimulated to produce and adopt sociotechnological, cross-sectional, and democratizing changes. These measures, which point to sociostructural change, would allow a transformation of the traditionally vertical structures towards a horizontality that supports a transparency of the processes sustained in the electronic educational services.

Since we are dealing with the incorporation of ICT in an educational organization and/or program, one would perceive this innovation as a planned proposal of introduction of change devised for improvement with a greater quality and equity of the educational processes, products, and services. Nevertheless, we must consider that changes, in addition to being costly and risky, do not necessarily cause all the actors to become involved in a reframing of the know-how and make them feel favored by significant technological improvements.

Therefore, caution is a great counselor in these cases, since the unpredictability of the consequences may be very high. When we address organizational innovations, we seek to perceive sociocultural processes with devices, but beyond these, to consider the individuals and the groups characterized by their ambivalence and contradictions.

The concept of technological change is also articulated with a new, conceptual, procedural, attitudinal, and moral *know-how*, in this case referred to ICT in processes of production, management, and evaluation of information to set up new administrative and pedagogical structures or systems for online training programs. ICT are central to all of the areas mentioned as a positive influence on innovation, the facilitation of flexibility, and adaptation, since they make the flow of information that is now shared more transparent. However, we must keep in mind that they are central but not the only ones, and even less so, a panacea.

Of course, it is necessary for all actors to be associated and committed to innovation, in particular, in relation to the decision-making level of the organization or program, which provides legitimacy as regards the what for and how the tasks must be carried out to obtain the desired outcome.Any innovation requires and is nurtured on resources which allow an organization to bear the cost (beyond the economic sphere) of implementing them as they absorb/readjust the weaknesses and failures and/or their inevitable mistakes.

## Technological Conflict and Change

The approaches to the study of social conflict make it advisable to include the concepts of *contradictions and paradoxes* within every social process and phenomenon. Social conflict is understood through the structural key of the power which is based on the unequal distribution of social wealth and prestige (Dahrendorf, 1973). It is a necessary universal social fact which is solved in the rethinking of the processes that lead to social change. In relation to this, we find the Marxist economic interpretation of superstructure as the dominant ideology, given by the possession of the means of economic production, in turn, based on the principle of contradiction to build a dialectic of transformation.

The goal is to start from a transforming utopia, with a criticism of the modern post-industrial society where social conflict, marked by historicity and crisis, is different from other theories, which do not emphasize the conflict between opposing material and symbolic interests within a particular contextual configuration. This is opposed to the positivist conception of society, which understands that social phenomena can be seen as understandable, expressible things or events in an objective way, and cannot be changed by the action of men, which proposes a neutral view of social phenomena.

The theories of social conflict are useful to explain how any social unit requires order and integration, which can be achieved by consensus and /or coercion. In any case, the conflict will be the factor of social change, through personal actions and those of social pressure or interest groups, in the search for integration, through the transformation of structures or through pacts with the rest of the social artifices of the change sought.

The *mediations, media, and mediators* existing in any society in general, and especially within an organization and educational electronic program, do not stray far from the previous explanations, since those instances are and will be instruments of power in the service of the dominant - local, national and international- pressure and interest groups, which design and use them in accordance with their preferences, not always representative or majoritarian in the social unit in question. In general, they are used for the vertical transmission and /or search for legitimized consensus of their objectives and ideologies, resulting in the materialization of social control and the configuration and consolidation of frameworks of thought and action in users, which must be acknowledged, and which resignify messages and meanings depending on various settings and needs.

Therefore, among the various inputs that form social communication models and policies, we must consider the political economy of media and mediations, referring to their propriety and economic interests-in general, private corporate interests that support them.

Adorno and Horkheimer, representatives of the Frankfurt School, mentioned the development of an industry of culture that conveys pure motives of economic benefit to the existing social ways, linking the concept of industry with cultural ideology.L. Althusser, also made reference to this with his conceptual contribution of "ideological state apparatuses"belonging to or independent from the former, which reproduce the dominant ideologies, within *mediations distributed by media and mediators*, existing in any social unit; this is something which is questionable today and/or overcome since there is no doubt that audiences are active entities and with independent resignifying decision-making ability.

There is no doubt that the changes that drive mediations and media have affected and still affect –within a set of variables- the way in which individuals and groups see things and behave. Similarly, the planning, management, and leadership of an electronic training program has multiple impacts, in accordance with new approaches, management, and evaluation of the contents of the programs -with decentralization and autonomy- made possible by ICT.

In addition to this, the value of knowledge and know-how -driven by the above mentioned mediations- is one of the most valued organizational assets for the creation of collective knowledge, which has a direct impact on all their measurable and intangible results.

At the heart of any organization, and even more so in the educational ones, the learning process in general and, now, the electronic one –with ICT-especially, should be recognized in forms of pure electronic or blended learning.

These educational modalities fuse into scientific and technological knowledge, although they have become strategic political and economic resources of the States and industry and exacerbate the sources of social conflict intrinsic to any social unit. To this we should add that citizens today are more aware of the benefits and negative impacts of the technoscientific development of electronic mediations, in relation to the quality of life. Much of the above is seenthrough the impact of technological change which lies at the base of infinite environmental, social, and cultural problems existing today.

While the "technocratic rhetoric" has been denouncedin the service of political and economic interests, its consequence was the legalization of the technologies introduced without the possibility of revising their configuration and implementation. This implies we should understand these phenomena as a manifestation of social control and cultural disciplining.

An understanding of technological change today should be inscribed within the context of philosophical and cultural criticism, to include proposals for constructive evaluation of technologies, with emphasis on the need to develop political strategies that allow democratic control of the innovation and social change, technologies that reflect conscious decision making in the service of shared sociocultural and environmental values, respectful of survival and diversity.

To overcome the negative sociocultural impact of technoscientific development, we should identify those responsible for the technical choice and intervention, that is, those who decide, and based on what interests. Identifying the "hidden agenda" present in every technoscientific project is more than relevant when facing the remodelling of the material and symbolic conditions of human life, as it produces unwanted effects or negative consequences for the majority of the population and the future of the planet.

These technologies include not only their material aspect (or artefactual), but include organizational aspects related to economic and industrial, professional, etc. activities, as cultural aspects seen in goals and values that are affected by them.

Anything that sounds remotely evaluative –of a moral or sociopolitical nature- is often criticized, if the goal is to judge the subtle and often unnoticed ways of social control of the technologies implemented from the proclaimed viewpoint -not always valid - for improving the quality of life. If technological logic predominates, without reconstructive sociopolitical, valuating, and reflective questions, choices and decisions to combine technologies in general, and in particular for electronic educational mediations are instrumental, in other words, they only refer to the media or technical side.We hide and devalue the fact that this technological selection and implementation, at the same time, are revealed as non-representative options for sociopolitical ways of life, which are established, and build the subjectivity of individuals and groups within a society.

The revisionist role of various pressure groups -environmentalists, consumer associations, advocacy groups for "alternative technologies" (including the educational, appropriate, and critical), among others- reflect a rational, reflective, and critical ideology when participating and influencing decision-making on specific interventions, which shows great commitment to the analysis of pertinence, rather than a simple flat-out rejection of the various "innovative" contributions of technology and science.

It should be noted that "public participation" and being in the service or under the public power at hand in the selection of technologies to be socially or organizationally incorporated, are not the same thing. "Democratic control" of science and technology involves not only strengthening representativeness and the participatory regulation of the social users in opposition to the political power when setting up and implementing technoscience, but also demystifying and withdrawing these decisions from the hands of the "experts". As science and technology become more complex, in addition to becoming increasingly politicized, it is perceived that their image and operations are not linearly progressive, but even less so: contradictions and irreversible negative impacts appear.

Changes are inherent to human condition. Learning in a realistic and fair way about the mechanisms that enable them, helps to make them available and, above all, to plan, guide, act, and evaluate them. There are countless changes that must be faced along a road taken, and there are others that must be introduced and also reviewed, from different perspectives, analyzing the basic problems that condition them in theirstructure and contextualization.

## Towards a Theory of Social Change

Each context, setting, and actor is inscribed within historical and cultural times with special characteristics. Every social situation has always possessed various technologies that were relevant to the satisfaction of individual needs according to the cultural frameworks, which is why they have proven to be dominant or hegemonic for the operation of the context in question. This is not to say only that technology/ies determine/s the model of society, but that the sociocultural and organizational development of a particular specific historical time designs and promotes the development of certain technologies over others. Therefore, there is a strong and reciprocal relationship between society and technology that, while not decisive, should be taken into account.

Change is sociocultural and implies innovation:it involves the organized and systematic search for renovation and the analysis of its opportunities; implementing a new idea to create or improve a product, process, or service (or all of these) and which, in general, is carried out by a person or organization. Accordingly, it involves the articulation of a variety of sources, including the unexpected, and is based on the appearance of what is incongruous (the discrepancy between what is and what should be). In other words, it is conceptual and perceptual. The need for a new process (in an industrial structure, in the market, or in services, among them, the educational) often appears favored by changes in the greater society (in its demography, the emergence of new knowledge, and so on. ) and not necessarily linked to material elements because it includes invisible or intangible content.

As understood, the processes of change are not necessarily tied to the introduction of material technology, since one of its central features is that they include and possess intangible, invisible, non- "artifactual" content, as those already mentioned.Among the factors that can lead to technological and cultural change there are:

Today we all recognize as a challenge the reconstruction of the sociotechnological and cultural variables to be taken into account in introducing innovations and flexibility through various learnings. The novelty of introducing such changes is not in the level of external control, but in the needs and intrinsic motivation and, increasingly, in the committed awareness of those who undertake the changes and learning.

**Factors of Technological Change**

| | Cultural factors | | | Social andinstitutional factors | Political-economic factors |
|---|---|---|---|---|---|
| | Cognitive | Practical | Values | | |
| Inventions | Scientific andtechnical training | *Know-how.*Efficient practices | Efficacy, efficiency, social pertinence and cultural relevance + innovation | Institutions andpolicies that promote R&D. Creation of patents | Political decisions. Financing of R&Dprojects |
| Dissemination ofinnovations | Level and ability to communicate and access information | Production andconsumpt ion habits | Evaluation of risks and environmental impact | Creation andmaintenance of technological centers | Support ofinnovation at public and private companies |
| Social changes | Representations of society.Technol ogical demystification | Revision of customs, ways of life | Evaluation of thesocial consequencesof technological development | Education and training policies in higher educationinstitutio ns.Evaluation oftechnologies | Industrial promotion, financial investment, etc. policies |

Source: based on J. López Cerezo, J. Luján, and E. García Palacios (1998), *Filosofía de la tecnología.* Madrid, OEI.

Any change proposes seeing concepts and carrying out processes and procedures differently. Often it is necessary, it is possible, and we must plan a change, which intentionally and in a guided way searches for other goals because the previous no longer meet the requirements. In the current times of shift to new paradigms, change is no longer regarded as linear and mechanical but multidimensional, discontinuous, or disruptive and recursive. It covers all of the dimensions in which a process or phenomenon manifests itself, even if this means we cannot predict when it will take place or to what degree and level it will affect the rest of its components. This degree of unpredictability is particularly relevant when it comes to educational efforts, even more so in educational programs in electronic form.

There are people regarded as "agents of change" who act as catalysts and assume -also lead- the liability and risk of introducing new concepts, planning and managing activities of change within an organization or program. However, change does not have a great reputation, because in general, individuals and organizations resist it. On many occasions it is felt as something that threatens security, including financial security. The fear of the unknown and ambiguity, in uncertain times such as these, also work against it. Organizational resistance points to various structural inertia given by existing mechanisms which in appearance produce stability and security. When you change (or move) something, all the pieces of a board are moved and this produces insecurities in certain sectors, which in turn tend to be overridden by the greater system. The inertia of the group with its predetermined rules, stereotypes, and misconceptions restricts change and favors the above-mentioned resistance.

**Restrictions on Innovation**

| Extrinsic origen | | | Intrinsic origen | |
|---|---|---|---|---|
| Institutional Socioenvironmental | | | | |
| Sociocultural | Environmental | Organizational | IndividualUsers | Nature of theInnovation |
| Cultural values<br>Social structure<br>Pressure groups<br>Political views<br>Scarce financial, cultural, and political investment<br>Scarce resources<br>Scarce innovative promotion<br>Legislative inflexibility | 1.Negative environment<br>2.Barely innovative environment<br>3.No "critical mass"<br>4.Unfavorable climate of immediate context<br>5.Minimum social, cultural, and educational communication and interaction<br>6.Lack of comprehension in communication<br>7.Unsatisfactory atmosphere<br>8.Problems with violence, lack of discipline | 1. SOCIAL SYSTEM<br>2. Closed.<br>- Centralized<br>- Uniform<br>- Authoritarian<br>- Huge institutions<br>3. Centralization<br>4. Hierarchical structure of communication<br>5. Minimum institutional incentive<br>6. Minimum technical support<br>7. Material and technological scarcity<br>8. Lack of motives. Insularity of the work or isolation<br>9. Limited autonomy in tasks | 1. Lack of operative control of innovation<br>2. Low level of profesionalization<br>3. Lack of study of cost-benefit relationship<br>4. Uncompensated effort<br>5. Uncertainty and risks in innovative process<br>6. Insecurity when dealing with new proposals<br>7. Ambivalent attitudes when dealing with change<br>8. Conflict of cultural values<br>9. Weight of former habits<br>10. Negative or slightly satisfactory experiences<br>11. Dependence on environment and low identification with the group<br>12. Minimum stimulus and incentives<br>13. Lack of time availability<br>14. Excessive work that demands giving up personal plans | 1. Confusion, ambivalence in goals<br>2. Non- visible improvement of the innovation<br>3. Difficulty and diagnostic errors<br>4. Difficulty in evaluation and measure<br>5. Unpredictable outcomes<br>6. Imposed demands on innovation<br>7. Precipitation in the establishment of time frames for actions<br>8. Fast move towards dissemination before completing evaluations |

Source: S. De la Torre (1999). *Innovación educativa*. Madrid, Dykinson.

Changes become threats due to several factors: firstly, consolidated experience (If we always did it like this with moderate success, why change now?); on the other hand, in terms of relationships with the entrenched power regime or due to a certain distribution of resources that may facilitate the completion of what needs to be done.

There are a number of factors to be taken into account because they drive us towards experiencing innovations related to ICT and their impact on the training of individuals and groups. Higher level education and the more progressive universities choose in this way -generally with varied conflicts within their units-to incorporate and use technology (Bates, 2001). This will be input to improve the access, distribution, and effectiveness of learning, at the same time reducing the cost of education and providing teaching that will generate job skills and everyday skills for citizens who will occupy new public spaces, confront ideas and questions, and present new demands.

## A Sociocultural Analysis of the Various Electronic Modalities of Distance Education: With ICT, Online, Virtual Education, E-learning, Blended Learning

There are various proposals for an intelligent application of ICT in higher education, and therefore promoters ofsociotechnological change, such as: a) the creation of virtual universities whose programs contribute to making educational processes of a non- face-to-face, combined, or hybrid modality, with a non-traditional design and management of education, b) the introduction within programs and curricula of the input and increasing added value of ICT with the redesign of the curriculum and the roles of the instructor and student, c) the change in the organization and structure to make all these programs entities with autonomy and the capacity for decentralized management for the development of non-conventional educational modalities (Ruiz Valdés, 2002) and others which will take place in the future…

Accordingly, a number of questions arise for reflection and decision-making in reference to the previous proposals: What is the current state of the art of the organizations of higher education and universities to face such decisions? How do we articulate the diffuse and off-center learning environments of an information society intermingled with multiple knowledge of a traditional still hegemonic education system represented by brick enclosures and books, compared with the versatile modalities of the electronic possibilities of ICT (Barbero, 2000 )? What substantive elements of reformulation -in a line of strategic planning- should be considered in the electronic educational projects with ICT, in a globalized, territorialized world of relocation, with hybrid logic and temporalities? How can we make distance education one of the main links in this chain of sociotechnological change by giving greater prominence to users within the hitherto unheard-of possibilities of configuring knowledge, emotion, and expression? What virtual campuses will be designed, what for, and with which partnerships between different institutions and universities, organizations and social services?

## Electronic Educational Modalities of Distance Education

Among the various electronic educational modalities that form distance education within the sociocultural analysis being carried out, now inscribed within the context of a sociotechnological change, we should consider those proposals of multidirectional communication for teaching and learning with various technological mediations.

The participants of varied ages, backgrounds, and residences study individually or in groups, close to their homes or workplaces, or remotelly, in other countries, with pre-produced and semi-structured self-instructional materials distributed by various means: from the most traditional to others with connectivity (or without it), to form pure electronic or mixed learning programs (e-learning or blended learning, respectively), monitored by the actions of individual and group face-to-face, conventional, or telematic tutorials.

This ensures that distance education can be offered (and in fact this is how it has been historically) through printed texts, now in electronic format, in convergence with unimaginable audio-visual and interactive telematic technologies, Internet networks, and so on.

Among the socioeducational foundations, which from a theoretical point of view have historically defined distance education, and which are now articulated and adapted to the electronic online modality, there are:

1. Theories of autonomy and independence: Charles A. Wedemeyer (USA) and Michael G. Moore (United Kingdom).
2. Theory of Industrial Distribution: Otto Peters (Germany).
3. Theories of interaction and communication: Börje Holmberg (Sweden / Germany), John A. Bääth (Sweden) and David Sewart (UK). Of interactivity: Michael G. Moore (USA.), T. Driscoll (USA), Beatriz Fainholc (Argentina).
4. Theory of communicative mediations: M. Barbero (Colombia); technological educational mediations: B. Fainholc (Argentina).
5. Theories of social connectivism: Siemens (USA).
6. Theories of deterritorialization, delocalization, hybridism and miscegenation, nomadism, interculturalism: Z. Bauman (Poland-England), N. Garcia Canclini (Mexico), M. Barbero (Colombia), and so on.

Electronic distance education with ICT absorbs the conceptual and methodological input mentioned which reconfigure social interactions and technological-educational interactivities within each program. This interactive dynamic occurs between proposed objectives and contents (as specific historical cultural pieces) and the decision of managers and designers in each program for a specific pedagogical semiological structure and organization.

The presence of tutors, instructors, and students of any age and origin, linked by remote synchronous and asynchronous communications within a cyberspace of infinite navigation requires the development of skills for the management of information, theintelligent use of technological resources, and the comprehensive and critical reading of texts generated in network spaces, among them the Internet.

Among the most outstanding socioeducational features of distance education, the one that carries great weight as a "must ", we find the necessary respect for the multi/ intercultural and multilingual diversity of the users, which includes both their previous experiences and knowledge, as well as their idiosyncratic cognitive styles, in order to promote their autonomy and self-control of: what to learn and what for, how to learn, where to learn, the pace in which to do it, who to ask for help, and so on.

The pedagogical mediations of this process establish the relational meaning of this modality which adds different connotations depending on the specific phenomenon of sociocultural and technological interaction given by the contemporary usage increasingly commonplace and multi-application of the technological resources of ICT. This modality should show proposals for educational designs, management of the instructional practices mediated by technologies and evaluation practices of the projects and learning materials, which reflect a connection with the demand, as well as a flexible teaching, depending on varied cultural aspects, languages, formats, and so on.

However, distance education does not mean open education, which refers to great openness not only in terms ofage and the space-time coordinates of the individuals and groups attending, but rather represents an open sociopolitical proposal as to the ideas and training methods that can be selected and combined to carry out the distance learning proposal.

Today distance education is considered a complementary means of conventional face-to-face education, with a strong connotation of educational innovation, within an educational continuum of teaching offered by an institution, region, or country. Among these, we may find the modalities identified as "connected education" (Gilbert, 1999).

Distance education does not necessarily mean or imply open education, since many distance education programs adopt the same stringent face-to face criteria of the mainstream institutions that house them and do not operate under the educational philosophy of openness and flexibility, especially for those over 25. The open teaching is primarily a sociological goal and a part of an education policy given by the possibility of flexible educational opportunities, built to overcome the geographical, social, cultural, and time limitations of each student. Distance education is a means to that end,as it is a way through which students may study in a flexible manner, distant (but not absent) from the author responsible for the teaching materials produced, the instructional designer who has processed these "to make them learnable" and a versatile administration of learning environments mediated by technology.

This proposal takes place at an available time, in a place of choice (home, work, or learning center), with or without physical contact, although direct and customized, today telematic, communications should always be included between the instructor/tutor and the students.

While open learning and distance education can mean different things, the only aspect they have in common is an attempt to provide social equity in the access, the pursuit of quality, and satisfaction of the various demands of those who were unable to attend conventional institutions. They also involve design proposals to continue learning throughout life, to update knowledge in the information society and knowledge economy; to provide in remote areas effective and low-cost opportunities for education and job training; to expand opportunities for participation in an emerging citizenry in the new public spaces for a competent and judicious use of networks and sociotechnological resources.

From a sociocultural and organizational analysis of the electronic online educational proposals mentioned for distance training and education, some central issues deserve to be considered:

1. *For the conception, design, and management of contextualized educational electronic projects, including e-learning, it is important to*:
   - conduct a sociopolitical and organizational feasibility analysis of the strengths, obstacles, weaknesses, and opportunities of the educational program in question;
   - contextualize the proposal by assessing, formulating, and prioritizing needs (such as discrepancies between where the organization is and where it should / needs / wants to go) to achieve which principles and objectives;
   - study in a strategic way the viability, feasibility, and cost / benefit of the project in its sociocultural integration to achieve quality with equity and relevance.
2. *For the phases of administrative, socioeducational, and communications management of the e-blended learning project, it is necessary to design, implement, and evaluate:*
   - present and future strategic contextual sociocultural, economic, and political decisions;

- didactic and technological decisions for a flexible and intelligent, collaborative design, of potential applications to the social, occupational, etc.reality;
- decisions about interaction and communication through the technological material and resources to provide educational guidance on the tutorial roles, student performance, and responsiveness of the program offered;
- • decisions about verification, adjustment, assessment in the short, medium and long terms of the processes and products of the program and the necessary economic and financial gain.

3. *To investigate in action and beyond it:*
    - contrasting assessments to make changes and decisions that will ovecome multiple barriers and obstacles in the design, management, and contextualized evaluation of educational projects with ICT;
    - anticipate contexts and formats for pure or blended electronic learning, from prospective studies with valid, feasible, and realistic assumptions.

The modalities of the electronic educational projects with ICT may be:

1. *Electronic learning* (or e-learning, according to Urdan and Weggen, 2000): aims at the learning process that relies on electronic means for its achievement, regardless of the distance or face-to-face modality in which it is contextualized. It is usually based/ supported on network technology as a complement to face-to-face learning or with various media in the formal classroom or non-formal learning groups where it is possible to include simulation exercises, participation in discussion groups, links to Internet sites, collaborative work, records of metacognitive action in portfolios, and so on.

    Among its central sociocultural characteristics within the information society, those that prevail are speed, the tendency towards low cost since it is linked to the electronic knowledge economy (e-business and e-economy), through a broad range of processes, telematic applications and technologies for digital collaboration for the construction and distribution of content through a variety of media: Internet, intranets, satellite, broadcasting, audio/videocassette sequences, interactive TV, CD-ROM, video conferencing, etc. (Urdan and Weggen, 2000).
2. *E-learning with ICT:* it is the learning acquired in the "artefactual" and informational interaction with the use of a network (Intranet or Extranet), interactive cable television and/or CD-ROM. It refers to learning environments for the use of such hardware and software with individuals who have technological skills, with prior training for their use. Such training has been designed, implemented, and managed using a variety of combined technologies developed locally or globally. Comparable and/or complementary to the previous one, the emphasis is on the connective possibility to surf/read/interact -we hope- in a comprehensive and critical way (Fainholc, 2004) on the Internet. In these contexts and supports, it is of utmost importance to make clear or plain the symbolic codes of the ICT involved and their combination of teaching, communications, semiological, and technological resources for an intelligent and demystifying use in terms ofwhat for and why, with whom, etc.. , the pedagogical work is carried out.

3. *Education through the use of Internet:* is the application of a set of instructional strategies socioculturally and cognitively geared for their pedagogical implementation in an environment of interactive, cognitive, constructivist, and collaborative learning, using Internet language and resources.

   Training through the Internet is also understood as an innovative approach to develop curricula based on hypermedia for remote audiences, using the attributes and resources of the networks and the ability to create learning environments designed and focused on the students in an interactive way (Khan, 2001).

   The teletraining through the Internet allows us to configure different training settings, which in the case of the mixed system (or blended learning), are combined and provide a more meaningful contextualized learning (Welsh, 1997).

   Intercultural communication will be the most outstanding feature to be highlighted in order to achieve these formative environments via the Internet, which allow students and tutors from different regions and cultures of the world to communicate so as to be able to share different points of view and build processes and results enabled by new human and technological mediators.

4. *Virtual. education:* virtual education based on computers, telecommunications, and educational technology embedded within the new digital culture of the twenty-first century is supported on and benefits from the use of the network of networks where interactive communication processes favor the constant tutorial pedagogical guidance among the protagonists of the system and the sending/receiving of learning materials.

   The virtual environments of extensive interaction promote and foster, in an active and constructive way, collaborative learning and teamwork to create learning, knowledge search, research, etc. communities. focused on the individual who studies and works in a remote way.

   Among the socioeconomic and cultural characteristics and considerations that should be acknowledged and taken into account from the sociological perspective of analysis, and which enable the access, assistance, and training in unconventional electronic educational programs, in times of international virtuality and learning throughout life (or lifelong learning), there is the fact that they (Bates, 1999):

   a) increase, in a democratic and equitable way, access for all users and students to technology in the context in which they live or work;
   b) reduce the costs of technology at reasonable levels per student, drawing on resources such as open source, creative commons, etc.;
   c) do not lose sight of the educational needs in different types of learning required from different cultural and pedagogical arguments in establishing various objectives, contents, and mediations with technologies which, in each case, should be improved;
   d) increase interaction and interactivity to exploit, with social and pedagogical activities full of significance, the advantages of technology, towards a creative adaptation of the digital culture alerting on the incalculable and negative consequences that may arise in social interaction caused by the selected and combined technologies;
   e) consider not only the sociocultural and pedagogical variables involved within online educational programs, but also place them in a restatement of the components of any social organization that is becoming "virtual" to analyse

sociocultural barriers that are presented and the stereotypes in the mediated communication that should be removed. This involves changes from the standpoint of values and beliefs, attitudes and mentalities to be adopted and technology to be appropriated according to settings and actors.

5. *Blended learning:* involves the combination of face-to-face or classroom-based training, used conventionally or in semi-face-to-face systems in traditional distance education, with the articulation of ICT. The proposals focus on or depart from a virtual electronic system, in other words supported by ICT, which operates with a management system of content and telematic communication (LSM) and forms a hybrid system with conventional face-to-face teaching; as we may see, we are dealing with complementary educational proposals.

In the blended modality, the effective combination and use of all technological media to be integrated in general depends more on sociopolitical decisions within the organization that offers the program, than on technological-scientific educational arguments or the strengths of the instructional design (Fainholc, 2004 -07). Unfortunately, we are still far from having reasons for action-research as the prevailing reasons for the improvement of the quality of education given in electronic formats. However, it may be argued that blended learning will try to overcome-especially at the university level-, the strong criticism received by pure e-learning in terms of its epistemological rigidity.

Blended learning is more ambitious and elaborate in terms of the combination of teaching strategies to be implemented and mediating technological resources, which will be articulated and evaluated by prepared professionals who lead and carefully monitor the proposal.

Among the socioeducational characteristics of blended learning, we may find -as already mentioned- : interactivity, the possibility of online and realtime communication, as well as on a global scale, quick access to information of all kinds, the requirement for a critical reading of the virtual sources, and so on. The concept of technological mix for the mediated socioeducational work seeks to mitigate weaknesses, since no medium is a panacea, and it is important to understand that technology is a great accelerator for verifiable conceptual and methodological proposals if they are suitable and work properly. In turn, it should be acknowledged that articulatingtechnologies in a risky way in poor socioeducational situations, or working with outdated models or traditional practices that haven´t been brought up to date or lack continuous assessment, not only does not improve the electronic educational proposals, but worsen them.

We, thus, appeal to and challenge the educational community to adopt an ambitious approach for the self-reliant creation of innovative teaching capacity and take advantage of the real opportunities offered by ICT as they help improve educational equity through broad coverage, relevance, and effectiveness of education services, according to actors and settings, in terms of a contextualized analysis for a sociology of distance education.

Yet, in general, the incorporation of ICT for online distance education is limited to virtualizing the existing face-to-face educational proposals; formats, objectives, and contents are repeated, perpetuating the same problems and defects. The student continues often in a state of mechanical passiveness, as the recipient of information mediated by the technological artifacts of ICT. In other words, the student does not face a rational, authentic, and relevant sociotechnological change as required by the participatory needs and cultural-historical times.

There are certain sociocommunicational frameworks that should be taken into account, since they promote, given their potential for connectivity, socioeducational situations and ways of working, which are not inconsiderable when strengthening pedagogical interaction and communication mediated by ICT. These include, among others, the following:

1. *Independent study:* Without schedules or fixed locations, students should access and interact with pre-produced materials. It is asynchronous or with/without direct communication between student/s and tutors. It demands autonomous behaviors in the organization of the study and pedagogical work carried out by the student, which do not always exist and should be mitigated by compensatory education in order to develop independent study habits.
2. *Strategies to increase interactivity* (Thornton, Jefferies, Jones, Alltree, and Leinonen, 2004) *and synchronous communication:* We are dealing with online meetings that allow the realization of collaborative group work with a great potential for socialization. However, these opportunities are often limited in practice due to various obstacles: lack of access to ICT, difficulty in scheduling between students from different time zones, absense of solidary socialization to strengthen socioemotional skills and respect for diversity, lack of deconstructions when dealing with attitudinal rigidities and others that prioritize the sociodidactic role of the tutors who must devise ad hoc situations impossible to carry out because they lack the necessary abilities.
3. *The broadcasting:* It is the broad access to information of different types, given by the technological convergence of the Internet, which is not always exploited due to a lack of knowledge of the symbolic codes of the various sources. It stimulates decentralized study from home or work, connected to the Internet.
4. Within the framework of *lifelong learning,* we have the versatile possibility to imagine and design interactive courses based on networks and the Internet for multiple learning activities and the development ofcitizen and community skills, in fieldwork, extension, or application work, and so on.

## Conflicts and Concerns of Online Electronic Education

As has been argued, while these electronic-educational modalities are in their early stages, and besides there are no panaceas for the same, there would be some warnings, possible criticism, or theoretical and methodological precautions to be taken into account. For example, there is indiscriminate transfer or copy of virtual training programs and/or education outside specific local or decontextualized situations. From absence or ignorance, without a relevant analysis of needs and feasibility, to conceptual and methodological flaws concerning interdisciplinarity which involve this modality, there are deficiencies in the design of materials, conception and performance of tutors, management of the organization in the interdependence of the various components, including the distribution of materials, asynchronous and synchronous communications, etc., to arrive at many other problems that reflect conflicts in the sociocultural non-correspondence of the formulation of the objectives of the program, the selection of content, the timely acquisition of technology, and so on.

It is believed that ICT should, through specific proposals, have a presence to allow greater access, coverage, and applicability of social interest, when provoking a credible and valuable educational projection depending on the training offered and not as a consumer good that will only mean symbolic social prestige.

If the goal is to prevent or manage conflicts, we will have to anticipate and develop serious studies of sociopolitical viability and commitment, as well as the economic-financial feasibility with regard to the real predisposition of the leaders of the educational organizations to incorporate sociotechnological changes, with serious initial analysis and constant comparisons. These analyses should not only relate to the sociocultural and economic needs and problems that exist or may arise, but reflect a proactive and flexible context in the incorporation of changes, degree of compatibility with previous experience, degree of technological literacy and the presence of skills in the users for a critical use of Internet resources, to name the most central.

Pursuing the idea of an organizational strengthening that is able to and knows how to face and manage conflicts in terms of the inevitable introduction of technological innovations, the goal would be to establish with realism the kind of education/training required and with a suitable combination of multimedia technologies. This includes a strategic and situated visualization, understanding, and appreciation of the objectives and goals, the actions to be deployed and how they will play out in the sociocultural environment in question.

Not having trained professionals in interdisciplinary areas related to the field of educational technology and distance education is also an issue that generates conflict, frustrating expectations, the wrong planning, and unsuitable performances with regard to the larger social context and the organization that contains the program and demands changes.

There are also conflicts relating to the lack of understanding of the macro-socialvariables, of the strengths and weaknesses of the organization that will receive the implementation, in a "timely" fashion, of the online program: in other words, factors that relate to the management of the proposal. From not discriminating options or alternatives (which involves a challenge to creativity) to not being able to face all kinds of adversity, negotiating with containment situations of friction, there are difficulties reconciling codes or languages, mental frameworks of the various segments of the program and the budgets allocated that disrupt the development of various "good practices". Understanding and recognizing what the goals of a sociotechnological innovation suitable to the context involve, requires working in depth and intensity and not just in length.

But, as dully noted, technology is not a panacea: not by having much and updated technology, are we able to understand the nature of the problems to be solved and the right decisions to be made. In addition, there are often misleading issues in the selection and implementation of technologies, so depositing too much confidence in them, univocally as something consistent and reliable for all cases, is not only an unrealistic approach, but also a succumbing to a typical reductionism of "unique thought" of a cultural hegemony. For contemporary authors who deal with the issues mentioned (Chomsky, Ramonet, Amin, among others), globalization expands techno-cultural hegemonic control through a privileged minority over a subordinate majority under the deregulated capitalist market thought that presently covers the entire planet.

It seems necessary to reformulate the meaning of this culture towards a critical project, which involves a great formative task. This requires the unification of criteria in collaborative work, devoting time and effort, appropriating ICT and deciding what for and why, when and how to use them effectively, starting from and towards which other sociocultural meanings that must permeate virtual learning environments to develop, distribute, and test contextualized and quality electronic proposals.

There are also other conflicts, no longer at the macro-social or organizational level, but which equally lead to misunderstandings, in this case about the role and performance of the tutor/s in their interactive communication, an issue that will be addressed later. And there are others, referring to the proposals of instructional design which since they are eminently didactic, will not be explored in this text.

From a sociocultural perspective, we invite a review of all the aspects of an online training proposal, leading to the deconstruction of preconceptions, unfounded or false ideas and simplifying generalizations. One of these states: "Telematic socialization leads to an updated learning by which modernization is achieved." Delimiting and rescuing realistic ideals and values to overcome the fragmentation that the very same ICT produce, would lead to learning about the contradictions that may be enclosed within these socioelectronic proposals, conceived in an unhistorical way and which often become apseudosolution.

Thus, the myths-views, many of which are listed below, are common ideas that, based on theories relevant to their development (and which have been taken up again to improve face-to-face education), have turned into false arguments or great promises beyond what can be achieved in contextualized socioeducational practice. Thus, ICT in distance education:

1. *Propose a great interactivity between the user/student and teacher/tutor.* Thus, the electronic connectivity and communication formats, such as chat, forum, or videoconferencing, with social interaction and pedagogical interactivity are identified, and "necessarily" so. Once their defining characteristics are known, although ICT, from the instrumental point of view, may operate to remove the feeling of isolation of the student, theyare still quite far from a genuine use to improve the quality of training by synchronous methods; these formats are not yet well integrated into the pedagogical design of the course and/or the sociocultural register of the user in question. At times, "the cure is worse than the disease".
2. *Strengthen the true protagonism of the online student in the learning management.* We should remember that if the student is not the one who takes responsibility for his/her formative process, with dedication and effort -as in traditional education-, thelearning does not take place. The role of the cooperative group is central, but the changes come from those who learn, according to their own idiosyncratic nature and culture.
3. *Encourage flexibility in the online proposals in terms of time, place, and schedule for asynchronous communication in virtual classes.* This is so, as long as the organization offering the program is decided, and there is commitment from those who learn. Being flexible does not depend on connectivity (although it helps), and even less so on the novelty of learning through these mediations. Motivational factors, empowerment issues, which enable an individual to move away from their usual framework and connect to their training program in an online framework, to name a few cases, influence the programs.
4. *They encourage interrelationshipsbetween all of those attending the virtual classroom, and hence boost the sense ofgroup belonging and participation.* It is not so simple: it all depends on the social and pedagogical conceptions that inspire the

program and didactic design, embedded in a social context and/or specific community context, which proposes meaningful collaborative activities, which promote the commitment of students to the group, the content, and so on. The degree of technological socialization can be a source of conflict in the communication dynamic mediated by ICT. Many times they are not used, since their benefits are not seen despite the recommendations for use. The training of the role of tutor as a virtual counselor and coordinator of a group or moderator for virtual discussions contributes to balancing conflicts and often monopolistic interventions. As can be seen, the technological platform is the support of connectivity, but it should be imbued with values of equitable representation and group solidarity, to be a genuine educational effort.

5. *Achieve greater equality in the training of students and among the staff of an organization.* Often this results in an increased social control with the risk of uniformity, but the problem is not so simple. An example: a document in electronic format or available on the Internet is protected and can only be modified by the system administrator, while a document or manual in print can be changed by anyone who transcribes, photocopies it, and so on. In both cases there are equal chances of re-signifying messages, thereby creating, or not, uniformity. Linked to this issue is the ease with which the Internet allows us to update the contents. In general, "updating topics" is identified with "distributing content", which relates to a greater reach of audience, and not with coverage, which depends on the access people have. Here, also, access is confused with "impact of the formative proposal": it is very different to acknowledge the number of users accessing the course, or refer to the impact of the course given by an evaluation where a change in behavior can be verified as a result of the new course.
6. *Possibility to access content on the Internet.* This is not just about being online. Ranking and analyzing information which will be used involves the prior development of skills, such as information management and critical reading of electronic sources (2004) in order to discriminate content and learn about the reliability of information, as is the case with conventional reading sources. Whether on paper or online, the task of perfecting the mechanisms of reading have a cost and require time and dedication.
7. *Improving the quality of education through the achievement of more effective learning with simple monitoring.* There is not at present a comprehensive study, but rather approaches in several investigations, which shows that electronic learning, in all its combined forms, is faster and better than conventional learning or that its follow-up is easier to carry out. On the contrary, the quality of an educational program -conventional or online- involves complex and dedicated tasks. Verifying that the students have changed concepts and attitudes, acquired procedures and methods throughout the training process in order to value their successes and supporting them in a personalized way when it comes to their weaknesses, are indicators of a quality face-to-face and virtual teaching. The technological mechanisms -some simple and others more difficult- should seek to strengthen the self-monitoring of the processes of individual, group, and organizational change, in which blind trust must not be given.

## Related Issues

The previous arguments highlight sources of change and potential conflicts in the central premises to be taken into account in the design and implementation of quality electronic distance education programs with equity and relevance.

ICT should help meet needs and solve problems with content which will bring meaning to the demands of the various actors and settings. These formative proposals amplify/semantify/ground their meanings through networks, in mediation, mediators and media, within sociocultural frameworks. It also means that they are not fixed, but are constantly developing/re-developing in practical contrast. They need added value, freedom and creativity to adapt; they also require ideas and expectations to grow and develop, and thus become truly formative: they are not final or perfect in general and even less so from the sociotechnological point of view.

The recovery of principles to prepare powerful and well organized individual minds and group mentality (to paraphrase Morin), will allows us to overcome encyclopedism and ephemeral procedural pragmatism, which appear in the online proposals, instead of creative proposals that renew attitudes relevant to the twenty-first century and which enhance creativity and anticipation that these uncertain times require to face life with ideas and responsibility, not only the consumption of devices.

# The Subtle Forms of Social Control and Cultural Disciplining in Electronic Distance Education

Social control, as well as social change, conflict, power structures and so on, are characteristic and constant social processes of the social actions carried out by individuals, groups, and organizations within a societal unit. The social processes can be cooperation or solidarity, in dealing with processes of association or social integration, as well as opposition or antagonism, leading to a social struggle, dissociation, or fragmentation. They may even become more or less customized, thus becoming a "rivalry" and/or "competition" among individuals, both very common but inevitable, in human environments in general, aggravated by the sociopolitical structures of the prevailing late capitalism and/or liquid modernity, as we have already mentioned.

Continuing with the sociological analysis, we may perceive how social processes (Weber, 1977) comprise various sub-processes detectable and mutually interdependent, within a historical sociocultural structure. Social processes present in education -in all its manifestations- typical behaviors generated from an elder society, currently liquid and fractured by late capitalism. Depending on the special place held by the individuals in this social framework (for example, socioeconomic place of the youth, who embody a particular problem in the contemporary social life), different possibilities and aspirations will be presented, as an expressive channelling of specific needs and sociocultural, labor, professional expectations is (or not) present in the search for identity.

We mustn´t believe that because we are living times of globalization, we are moving backwards in our central search for identity. The search for social identity, as aspace for identification and belonging, is the horizon and the key to overcoming the "precariousness of institutions and the self".It would help us understand the changes that take place within a particular historical and social structure, and in our case, referring more specifically to what happens and/or should take place, especially, within the electronic programs with the use of ICT.

These structural processes are complex and are seen in the emergence of socioorganizational and formative sub-processes which establish strategies for the inclusion and survival of the users in the programs. As they introduce clear goals and relatively safe options for the future, they try to alleviate the existing macro-social inequalities, and they turn out to be seductive and desirable proposals, especially for young people, but not always related to educational efforts…

It is not uncommon that when faced with crises in the public sphere, in the dynamic and chaotic postmodern social context, for institutional gaps to appear without the presence of speeches, as well as the legitimate practice of organizational forms with meaning, which support and build for a different future. It is believed that, among these, -mostly online-distance educationprograms carry real weight, which generally show high structure and regulation, particularly with acute social control over its values and rules. They would be proposals that would help ensure the integration and the incorporation of new members into the social dynamics-particularly young not excluded professionals that enroll in graduate and masters distance courses. However, there are many questions about whether they "solve", and to what extent, the tensions present in the paradoxical transformations that surround them, or are distraction mechanisms that postpone a "genuine" job placement.

Once again, we witness how social and technological mechanisms of exclusion and marginalization qualify/disqualify, reject/incorporate, fracture groups into those who are disconnected and those who are connected, in the search for certainties that the globalized world is willing to contribute through the "benefits of connectivity" and with the use of ICT.

Within this profound social unrest and deep crises, where we must remember that education –as well as other social institutions- teeters, in the socialization, shaping, and reshaping of the necessary social identities, the electronic distance education programs appear on the rise.

## Social Change and Control

The goal is to clarify both processes, which are central to the understanding of the various mechanisms that drive the information society and knowledge-based society, defined as innovation societies, or of constant social change. However, this involves analyzing what kind of knowledge society we are dealing with or what knowledge society we should shift towards. In other words, it is necessary to identify the processes of integration and reformulation of thestructural components that over time conform and change –although in a contradictory way-, within specific sociocultural (real or virtual) spheres.

It is also interesting to reposition in the twenty-first century, these questions or issues to be clarified, since they may offer some suggestions or answers open to discussion, when generally the work of sociological analysis has been formed in the nineteenth century starting from the industrial society in progress then: neither Comte, nor Weber, or Marx asked themselves "which industrial society the world was marching towards" at that time. It would seem that today sociology should be interested in the analysis and foresight of societies that are qualitatively different and require greater investment in knowledge.

*Social change* involves the introduction of elements previously unheard of, today in general of sociocultural implication and technological reformulation, leading to a restructuring of the interdependence between the parties which constitute said sociocultural field. We must remember, also, that not all social change necessarily means progress, development, and improvement of human welfare.

*Social control* is defined as the intentional social influence exercised in general on a set of individuals, groups, and organizations within a social unit, especially as a means of continuity, consolidation, and permanence of the current state of existing social norms and values. The goal is consistent with sociocultural integration and stability of a particular social organization, which in our case studies educational systems in online distance education programs while promoting the integration of students through their telematic socialization in the administrative, regulatory framework of didactic interaction for a consolidation and survival of the program in question. It should be noted how, from the perspective of social control, it can lead to the standardization of norms and values, as opposed to new reformist trends - some more non-conformist than others.

## OTHER RISKS OF ELECTRONIC DISTANCE EDUCATION

The *instrumental theory of technology*regards technology as dependent on the values of other spheres, such as the political, social, and cultural; while the substantive theory of technology ascribes to technology the role of autonomous cultural force capable of razing all the traditional values it competes with. The *substantive theory of technology* (Feenberg, 1991)- which goes beyond the instrumental theory, acknowledged in the contributions of J. Ellul and M. Heidegger- argues that technology becomes a new type of cultural system which restructures the social world entirely as an object of control.

Many theorists (Heidegger, 1977) agree that technology coolly "coopts" individuals and groups; it involves and sustains the transformation of nearly every social process -including people- to transform them into "reserves" (many of raw materials, others of human skills, to be mobilized or incorporated in the technological processes). Therefore, it is stated that the technical restructuring of modern societies is rooted in a desire for nihilistic power and degradation of the individual to the point that he/she becomes mere object.

The substantive theory of technology attempts, in this way, to raise awareness of the arbitrariness of this construction, or its cultural character: technology is not just embodied in supports or media "artifacts", but in a dominant and hegemonic way of life that is the controller.

A consequence of this reasoning is that the sociological analysis concerning the current electronically mediated education reveal and warn about social fragmentation: many social sectors do not have access to information, while others are under the influence of infointoxication and/or overinformation brought closer by the infostructures of the telematic highways of the information society at unpredictable speeds and quantities.

Because of this deployment of continuous flows of data, the "informational economy and culture" need to generate –so as to counter the influence of the consumistic and narcotic standardization of the new telematic environments- new "informational skills" (or literacy skills) to overcome the stage of technological and informational telematic "functional illiteracy".

These settings require a new intentionality, a communicative rationality, and a reappropriation of the formative architecture that strengthens from early on in people´s lives their "sociocognitive tools". The goal is to achieve a thorough understanding of the psycho-sociocultural phenomena of the information and knowledge society; in these coordinates, the skills to master information management, critical reading and surfing with the use of ICT in electronic environments are central in a lifelong learning.

This involves tending towards a new socioeducational hypothesis: teach everyone to learn and monitor (with metacognition) the learning generating by themselves and with others, by using the technological supports in a suitable and intelligent way, from which everyday and specialized information flows.

There is thus a new approach to understanding the formative tasks that many call "informational sociopedagogy" in assuming a rethinking of the "mediations" existing between human experience and the information of today's society, and especially realize that the information must be of equal access, which is regarded as a point of departure and arrival for its transformation into knowledge. In fact this can not be regarded otherwise, in this new paradigm, where the generation, processing, and transmission/ distribution of information flowing in networks become major sources of productivity and power (Cornella,1999) , which must reach all people with equity in all areas: domestic, industrial, and community.

## OTHER CONTRADICTIONS

Continuing the analysis from the sociocultural perspective of technology, and as a result of distance education, with the use of ICT today, it is necessary to point out some contradictions found within globalization as a general context, where telematic educational programs in particular are inscribed.

*Delocalization and the logic of the space of informational flows* (Castells, 1996) already mentioned, may cause, among other features, through ICT and online programs, the uprooting of people, which greatly impacts in the shaping of *volatile identities, a possible moral emptiness, and indifference in values,* a reflection of the frameworks of a liquid techno-cultural world of international presence.

Globalization exacerbates ethnic and cultural differences, not only from the north to the southern countries of the world, but also among the various regions within the core countries. This lack of respect in coexistence, almost always altered for political-economic reasons, is seen in the relationship between neighbouring countries. It is evident both in the developed world and in Latin America, or among the various countries of the former Eastern Europe, just to name a few of the excluded regions that stand out.

The hegemonic world transports and exports images and goods –released from their original realities- from one side to another: not only from the centre towards the periphery and from the north to the south of the world, but rather it is accompanied by large groups of migrants, who are attracted by the homogenizing "center" and thus, seek to, contradictorily, belong to areas that produce uniforming and dominant lifestyles through material goods or merchandise and symbolic objects that act as a social disciplining lifestyle.

The techno-economic logic and migratory pressure reveal the contradictions of the universal discourse of modernity and which characterized the West (Barbero, 2002). The risks with violence and threats regarding coexistence and the proximity of another who is different, who is not accepted because of the difference, in practice leads to violence and obtrusion, exclusion and stigmatization, which opened other social and cultural distances, sociological challenges for coexistence and respect for difference in the quest for equality with equity, problems which conventional and distance education can not always solve ...

Why? Because we are not dealing with online educational programs that collect or absorb students, but rather culturally denied or unrecognized identities, possibly the result of a dominant system. In other words, many times we are dealing with users (students) characterized by older prior social, cultural, political, linguistic, etc.. exclusions, the result of accumulated social injustices to which nationalism, xenophobia, and various fundamentalisms are added, which , as is well know, education or technology alone can not solve.

Education is an intervening variable in any macro-social analysis carried out like this one, now refering to the modality of distance education. It can help, cooperate, and even sustain the creation, configuration, and consolidation of the sociocultural, productive, and formative changes in general, required today, but can hardly inaugurate them independently because these inequalities do not emerge or are exhausted in the realm of the symbolic and educational-cultural

These are times of crisis, ambiguities, and contradictions regarding the hegemony of the instrumental reason, which affects identities. Identity (Barbero, 2000), is not what is given to someone just because they are agglutinated in a group, but rather the expression of what gives meaning and value to the life of this individual in a group. The identity that is expressed depends on, and therefore lives from, recognition from others: identity and citizenry are built on dialogue and exchange within an atmosphere of respect and peace, since that is where individuals and groups feel recognized or accepted (or not) by others.

Multiculturalism makes it increasingly apparent that the multiple figures of the cultural diversity supported by a society can only be overcome only by a policy of inclusion and practice of universal values that equally represent all sectors of a social unit and its segments (women, migrants, ethnic minorities, religious minorities, etc.). Online distance education program should not ignore these realities when supporting sociotechnological changes to demystify existing controls and disciplining.

The network society, where online distance education programs are inscribed, is not a pure phenomenon of technological connections, but the systemic disjunction (or contradiction) between the global and the local, which also covers the opposition between public and private when the time frames of personal experience are fractured, as they are run though situations of power. This is evident (Barbero, 2002) in the confrontation between an elite that inhabits the timeless space of networks and global flows, and the majority of the populations of dependent or emerging countries who inhabit the local dislocated space/time of their cultures. In other words, in facing the logic of global power, now telematic, local people take refuge in the logic of power that produces a local hybrid identity.

Many theorists (including Habermas, 1987) noted that decentralization today characterizes complex societies, with the absence of a central office. Power is dispersed, actors coexist with a myriad of new micropowers struggling to impose and express their views. One example might be that the excessive concentration of power, through the Encyclopedia Britannica, established around 1700, has been displaced by *Wikipedia*, a participative and free, voluntary digital encyclopedia on the Internet, twelve times larger (and steadily growing ), started five years ago.

Classic sociological theorists had already explained the fragility of what was supposed to be stable in a social unit and how it changes and is reformulated from the interplay of personal and group identities (Stuart Hall, 1999). We witness, therefore, the present need to produce *glocal synthesis* with the use of digital media to represent what it means to "think globally, act, and respect the local"... That is, in the same way that new technologies are reformulating the concept of what is global, new ways of thinking what is local are induced.

The evolution of the information society is marked, not without tensions, due to this dual communicative meaning. This is also reflected in the online educational programs, because technology modifies identity, interaction, and educational practice, in the same way that it impacts in a socioeducational reframing with regard to mediations, media, and technological environments; now with ICT the characteristics of the twenty-first century are emphasised, due to interactivity and facilities for participation.

However, it should be noted that the study of the interplay between society, culture, politics, and technology is not new. It is worth considering the references to the events of thought which stress that the technical objects of everyday life -constant or repetitive throughout history, such as the water mill, the wheel, the steam engine, the hydraulics plant, and above all, the printing press in its time, as now ICT and the Internet - has been involved in the matrix of other future inventions (Deleuze and Guattari, 1991). In other words, the exercise of power involved in the decision to produce the various technical revolutions that led to progress and disasters, or marked innovation in the different historical stages: pre-industrial, industrial, post-industrial, and digital.

The appearance –by no means final- of the Internet in the history of technology shows the opposition between written and oral, which is a sociopolitical strategy that distinguishes a time: while printing is the mother of capitalism, of transoceanic travel, of modern subjectivity, accounting, industry, experimental science, among others, the Internet, returns to the most primitive and intuitive transmission of experience, knowledge, and customs, even in an oral way, but written and socialized, because there no longer is privacy… Internet enables the creation of a large database where individuals, groups, and organizations are registered and classified in their key features, as never before. The universal tracing allowed by a "omnimemorizing gives credit to Deleuze´s idea (…) of the man of control". On the Internet, opposites as dichotomies appear together, are synthesized and converge: oral practice together with the written, private practice combined with the public, the factual articulated with the virtual, and so on. As perceived, much sociological research is needed to face such contradictory and unheard ofphenomena.

Only a deep democratizing transformation of the post-industrial civilization can solve the paradoxes and dilemmas posed by the technological changes that have pervaded the reality mired in a "consensus" leaving plenty few opposition elements in practice (Feenberg, 1991).

The contradictions appear and compete in a way disguised by the reality shows on television and the Internet weblogs, emotionally charged, which hide in a vacuum of public debate the lack of historical perspectives, the absence of alternatives seems to have left this place available to be occupied by small and trivial problems, characteristics that were anticipated over two generations ago by other theoreticians (Mannheim, 1936).

Raising perception and awareness for a critical analysis referred to the state of emptiness, dissatisfaction, lack of will power, and frustration over the unfulfilled promises of technology as a panacea -although highly-publicized- towards self-sustainable and equitable development in improving the quality of life and education is an inalienable duty. It will be necessary to reopen, deepen, and broaden the debate, based on a full democratic participation, truly representative, and challenged in various theoretical and practical objections, which should not confuse individual freedom with more market freedom. Inventing, anticipating, suggesting, and awarding coherent alternatives to preserve and deepen the threatened democratic heritage given by a technologized social control and cultural disciplining should be a stimulus to provoke the maturation of younger generations.

## A Possible Way to Overcome the Contradiction Control vs. Social Change: The Critical Theory of Technology within a Civilizing Change

Critical theory argues and proposes different avenues for a possible alternative technological development. The starting points for this should be rescued recovering elements in the existing technical social system, articulated with the constructive (agonistic) idea of a different sociopolitical cultural future.

Thus, this proposal is similar to the substantive theory of technology mentioned earlier, when it is argued that the technical order is more than a sum of tools, because it "frames" a more or less "autonomous" world, as it -consciously or not- configures by choice those technologies that are making us who we are.

In other words, because they are inscribed within the post-industrial and post-modern society, future choices and the act of choosing itself, are already technologically permeated and can not be understood as entirely free. It would be a "fatal freedom" because "it deprives us of what eludes us and rob us of what cannot be seized" (Finkielkrant and Soriano, 2006).

However, "modernity" does not define once and for all, through the choice given by a fragmented, controlling culture, guided by the consumption that characterizes the "enjoyment" of Western society, found anywhere around the globe today. The choice of a civilization of social control or change is not decided by some determinism or by the inherent flow of technology, but should be affected by sovereign, participatory, mature, conscious, rational and republican action of individuals and groups.

The autonomous social and political, constructive commitment, detached from economic and partisan commitment was, is, and will be what allows us to found free societies. It is central to review the implicit controls and decide by democratic resistance to the various forms of domination and introduce innovation in general, and technical -cultural innovation in particular, to renew all sectors in an ongoing and representative way.

Critical theory is against the neutrality of technology, and instead argues that the "technological rationality has become a political rationality", as an ambivalent process of development according to different possibilities for its conception, design, and use, which we believe must be reviewed and deconstructed. Technology and ICT, in general and for distance education, are not a destination, but are configured on a stage of representative decision-making and hence socioeducational formative decision and debate, which appraises civilizing alternatives to be confronted in the field, beyond all the contradictions.

A superior technological civilization should arise from the adoption of ethics, or a system of ideas and values, so that the technological variable is based on such a distinction and choice. Today, any major gestalt change in structures and sensitivities should happen from within the sociotechnological cultures (Ihde, 1990). The most significant consideration is a discussion of the category of power, organized from a variety of institutions which in general decide and lead -to be obeyed- with regard to technical systems and thus, install new forms of control. An example of this is seen in the economic interest that determines major investments in technological design formats for various objects such as technological platforms for electronic learning.

However, the social *contingency* of current technology seems to possess an unexplored democratizing potential, which should be considered in any educational proposal, as it would help to review and critique various situations of social control and standardization in order to bring about a transition to situations of change and reformulation.

The emergence of a *culture of responsibility* would alter, thus, not just the social, political, and economic institutions, but also but all of their sociocultural and traininggiven in gender relations, the role of youth culture, the synergy of cultural diversity, in shaping a more participatory spaces at work, networks, among others.

## A Form of Social Control through Quality Standards in Online Distance Education Systems

We could argue that the quest for quality education - mobile and the goal of contemporary socioeducational systems in general- is the raison d'être of any educational proposal. The search for quality assurance in mediated technological- educational systems today is the greatest concern.

*Quality* is understood as the integration into the product or service, in general, especially in education, and particularly in online programs, of those subprocesses that proved to be successful because they are useful, valuable, viable, accurate, realistic, insightful, wise, and ethical, and which, for this reason, have been incorporated into the *hardware, software*and *mindware* (invisible intelligent technologies) of this distance education practice with ICT. Seeking quality is continuing in the line of training the ability to continue learning, solving problems, produce critical thinking, building social solidarity, and strengthening the genuinely human aspects required by any society.

The quest for quality in electronic educational programs has been the subject of great theoretical and practical-organizational discussion: today it arises in terms of a confrontation with standards. A standard (www.wikipedia.org) is a norm or a technical paper that has the following characteristics: it contains technical specifications for application sometimes voluntarily, other compulsory; it can be the result of productions by consensus of the parties concerned, which in our case would be the designers and managers of technological platforms for online education, the teaching designers, the tutors, student users, those responsible for research centers and computer labs, participating and professional associations, and so on.

Some studies have made comparisons on satisfaction and academic performance of students in learning conditions with and without the support of sophisticated electronic distance learning environments. The observations made from these studies -that prove a strong social alliance between society and the conceptions that support social change through education- have shown that electronic distance learning is more satisfactory when it is a complement to more traditional teaching methods and not when it is used as a pure and even forced element in the curriculum.

Many voices argue that to assess the quality of technological processes in general it is necessary to apply the contrast of rules approved by a national, regional, or international organization with recognized standards, as may be the general norms called ISO, or for Argentina, IRAM, etc.and which are available to the public. In other words, without stable standards it will be very difficult for the technological processes and products, including programs that offer both pure electronic learning (e-learning) as well as blended learning, to evolve and be perfected. But it is also necessary to include in this analysis that, within such educational proposals, there are strong implicit levels of social control, which often do not have much connection with the educational context, and even less so the sociocultural context, and respond to economic and commercial interests, which contribute little to improving quality, as argued earlier. Other lines are expressed to incorporate open standards for education in general and thus for virtual educational programs: they opt for the non-inclusion of standards controlled by centralizing companies, often of a commercial nature, which would put down any improvement or innovation given more through a scrutiny of the quality of the concrete reality than the qualifications mentioned.

Among the central factors to improve and not to prevent reflection on and in socioeducational innovation mediated by technology, is the need to take into account several components, which are mentioned below.

We are dealing with the *infrastructure*that enables these systems where many are still in an embryonic stage and require a great deal of follow-up and monitoring, especially as they mean much more than the networks and their devices to access information; the *communication*devices, central to deepen the friendliness of the equipment for access and interaction with suitable content and the role of users in the construction of their participation, interaction, and knowledge; the *content* to be processed and distributed by various and combined media in technological convergence, which involves transforming them from traditional digital formats so they can be adopted in designs that will make various contents "learnable" in an electronic way, as well as recognizing the great historical challenges, their positioning, distribution with global deployment; the selection and training of *tutors* who contribute in a guidedway, with a personalized and interactive follow-up; theintelligent *training* of the users in a technological literacy, especially for those who can not yet interact with a computer, ICT, and the Internet, because they are not connected or culturally ready for it.

While the debate continues and there is no temporary closure, it is necessary to recognize some minimum quality standards for online educational programs, if it is a requirement for accreditation and continuous improvement of flexible training in the current historical and cultural times.

It is indisputable that if the greater quantity and quality of educational communication is mediated by technology in these socioeducational proposals, namely appearing in and through networks, there is a need to achieve telematic educational processes and products that are worthy and suitable from the sociocultural point of view: this should be sought in confrontation with standards for quality assurance.

In other words, within a framework of particular sociocultural and technological - educational relevance, it will be necessary to prepare and test monitoring mechanisms and perform "state of the art" actions, so that at any given time during the online program (or course) implementation, we may find out what levels are being achieved, how, what are the causes of difficulties and prospects, within a recursive process of knowledge construction, in this case the quality of education.

The quality of education is designed according to cultural patterns and is built over time. It is not possible to achieve it "magically", but as a result of a process that seeks quality through thoughtful and conscious actions carried out by individuals and groups.

Quality controls are carried out according to various methodologies in compliance with pre-defined standards; however, contrasted continuous monitoring of specific actions within projects is valued. The standards for e-learning were not accepted without difficulties, but rather, at first, were quite resisted and sometimes fought, as they were understood as tools to be transferred and be used from the measurement of the quality of industrial processes. Nevertheless, it has been shown that in combination with qualitative evaluation components, they may be effective for several educational processes. Proof of this is that Great Britain, France, Germany, and the United States (where 49 of the 50 states have adopted them) have been pioneers in their articulation and use. They can be used for purposes of self-assessment and group evaluation, audit, continuing professional development, personnel recruitment, and so on. although they are mostly used in the management of the programs, in the design, production, distribution, and support of the now virtual learning.

We may identify, in these coordinates of programs seeking a constrast of standards, four key areas with specific dynamic roles that intersect each other. These are:

- Providing strategies and leadership for individual and organizational learning;
- The management of organizational learning and knowledge;
- The provision of services, infrastructure, support, and learning resources; and
- The Encouragement of e-learning distributed in specific environments.

In other words, the goal is for quality standards in online distance education systems, to adapt and develop values, knowledge, and skills associated with one of the following areas: 1) identification and anticipation of emerging technologies for their influence in the development of organizational and training policies; 2) creation of an innovation culture with processes of management of digital symbolic physical resources for the overall management and management of the knowledge within a program; 3) continuous professional development, as well as development of learning and practice communities; 4) provision of technological support for communication and guidance for learning with tutorials (or coaching), diagnostic guides, and consulting depending on the particular needs of students with diverse cognitive styles and multiple intelligences; and 5) continuous development of ethics within situated and distributed electronic educational environments.

If the focus is on the relationship between education and society, in general, and in particular, concerning online educational programs with specific sociocultural demands, it is society who must reformulate purposes and trends, change, improve, and demand innovation, so that, education may, thus, improve, change, and resignify its purpose in all its manifestations.

*Chapter 5*

# A Sociological View of the Organizations Driving Distance Education Programs with ICT

A sociological view of the organizations driving distance education programs with ICT involves disassembling (deconstructing) their structures in order to understand the result of the extensive process of building consensus and establishing negotiations with the goal of arriving at such proposals, as well as conducting futures studies and investing in technological infrastructure for the knowledge society. It is also important to visualize the disputes that break the consensus achieved through the appearance of conflicts within the network of multiple players that make up these organizations.

The hermeneutic contribution, as it asks about the conditions of possibility and survival of these organizations, helps to discover their underlying structure at the local, national, and transnational levels. Deconstructing organizational structures and their processes involves confronting the order established with the contingency of its foundation, not only to find its meaning (or understand the not always conscious system of rules that underlie it), but to go beyond it and see that everything is intertwined with a meaninglessness if we adhere to a critical analytical method, which also emphasizes in a complementary way, the metaphorical and rhetorical dimension of the organizational texts.

The goal is not to deny the need for determining the significance (Derrida in Peñalver, 1990) -in our case, of a transnational online educational program-, but to consider what are the conditions for its possibility. In this regard, it is pertinent to relate the concept of hegemony, as a synonym for supremacy, whose origin is applicable to the military-political field and now is transferred to the social, moral, and cultural plane a tool for analysis (Gramsci, 1967) with dominant behaviors both in organizations and modern states today. The supremacy of one group is expressed, thus, as intellectual and moral domain and direction that intervenes in the socialization of the user/receiver/student group of an online educational program, for example, through its predominant standards and values.

However, conflicts between various real and/or virtual hegemonies or counterhegemonies in construction, are opposed to and face the spread of the culture of symbolic domination of transnational distance education programs -to continue with our example-, in their respective balance of power. They point to intellectuals -individuals or groups equipped with a specialized and critical rationality- which, as producers of consensus (recognized or alternative), are organizing leaders of other proposals called "legitimate violence" (Gramsci, 1967), which carry out innovative, adapting. and restructuring functions of the interests that characterize a social unit, program, or organization.

The hegemony of a transnational educational program is not understood linearly: each program is shaped through recursive and spiraled experience, relationships, and values, namely non-linear or not passive, but in permanent forward and reverse movement, also being challenged and/or resisted by the myriad pressures from the so-called alternative groups, among these an "emerging citizenry".

The transnational hegemonies –based on consensus, as well as the alternative- are not comprehensive or exclusive, so that sociocultural processes, and hence, education, should be understood as complex and living; in their course, domination and resistance are articulated and faced.

In light of these statements, a sociological view is given of organizations or electronic educational programs with the transnational/international use of ICT, as promoters (or not) of sociotechnological change.

## THE INTELLIGENT ORGANIZATIONS WHO ADOPT TECHNOLOGICAL CHANGE

Understanding an organization as a living organism, where every component is necessary for the suitable operation of the whole, leads to the consideration and understanding of the same in systemic holistic terms, keeping in mind the interrelationship and interdependence of its components, the technology to be combined and adapted in the electronic educational programs with ICT.

There are different organizational theories (Hodge, Anthony, and Wales, 1998) with regard to the inclusion of technology, especially in the service sector of the information society, characterized by processes and products of intangible value, provided to different social users (or customers). Within the various existing services (medical, legal, gourmet, tourism, and recreation, etc..), we find distance learning, which is an important area of analysis.

The inclusion of technology can be extended in the above mentioned educational sector from a reduced production adjusted to specific needs, according to individual demands, which makes it essential to have intensive labor-, for example in the creation of tailor-made software (such is the case of a manufacturer of airplane engines that produces small quantities of various kinds of engines, modified according to specific applications) to the mass production of thousands of units of the same product or similar products, such as the manufacture of software and/or tutorial courses, through a massive industrialization (with the intensity of capital and labor) and storage for future use, to arrive at the continuous flow processes where production is constant and requires little labor directly (for example, the petrochemical refineries and hydraulic businesses).

The concepts of organizational technology are useful in the development of these complex frameworks that should characterize the various organizational tasks. Among them, those that are central are those electronic educational services or programs with some of the following characteristics: 1) *intangibility,* referring to the realization or the abstraction of the outcome or transformed output; 2) *standardization,* considering the directions or specifications of the processes involved, human resources employed, their final products, and so on, for a suitable certification; 3) *synchronization or simultaneous production and consumption,* because the production of services (in online distance education organizations, in our case) requires users to use and/or consume the outcome produced; 4) *formalization,* as a method of ensuring that the different sectors, with highly differentiated tasks, coordinate their activities in a proper manner, which is achieved through formal regulations, policies, and procedures established with instructions, job descriptions and/or other documents seeking to provide a rational and contextual guide to behaviors within an organization or program.

It should be noted, moreover, that organizational theory is based on sociohistorical and psychocultural approaches to give a new role to the administration and its references, known as manager, leader, coach, or administrator. Their roles are evident in the design of situations of change, learning and/or improvement, as symbolic analysts who introduce, accompany, and investigate these practices from their confrontation in the field.

Today, however, an organization should be and should learn to be flexible. Thus, it would be the one that re-creates its reality and constantly expands its future capacity (Senge, 2000). Or, to put it another way, its future effectiveness is directly and proportionally related to its ability to learn new products and processes, make existing frameworks of thought and action more flexible, and promote collective learning practices. The trends show that those organizations that behave thus prove to be successful and become *intelligent* because they readjust/change/re-create approaches, in other words, expand the ability to create and perceive the world.

Accordingly, an intelligent educational organization - national and/or transnational-is the one that relies on an understanding of complexity, in a reflective conversation of research, and hence drives generative -and not just adaptive learning - through a leadership that proves to havepersonal mastery, handling of new mental patterns, a vocation to share a systemic vision of reality and make necessary changes to work, produce, and learn as a team.

In times of the information society, knowledge management, and technological change with innovation, the challenge is to build intelligent organizations able to constantly reinvent themselves. This should occur in higher education institutions offering distance education programs, as well as within the same electronic systems that provide online educational products and services. In other words, they would be the two sides of a coin, input and outcome of the organizational options outlined, where *generative* learning is seen - as the ability to constantly expand the creative tension or amplify the aptitude to produce the necessary or desired processes and outcomes. Therefore, the notion of *metanoia* -or change of approach or view- describes what happens in an intelligent organization of any kind as the mentioned shift or transcendent mental change (from the Greek word *meta*, which means beyond) involved in a situation of learning or improvement occurs.

As previously mentioned,the organizational and communicative life –of design, management, and evaluation, of tutorial support-, among other factors, of a distance education program with ICT, will be less random and more fertile, if we can anticipate and modulate the aspects that compose it, such as the: administrative, communicational, management, implementation, monitoring of the project and all other aspects involved, even more so if the education proposal is mediated by technology.

The goal is to recognize, and if possible anticipate, the interplay of various social expectations distributed and situated in relation to different happenings, events, and the critical paths to follow/adopt, which are embodied in the various roles of specialists and technicians within a national or international online distance education program. It is also essential to identify the profile of the students who would take the course, to systematize flexible rules or standards, as well as the more or less likely, more or less necessary events.

Choosing, designing, implementing, and evaluating/investigating a distance education program with ICT means, from the sociological point of view, shaping and criticizing a culture. These activities seek to investigate the probability of occurrence of certain events during the interaction within this program, since some events –supported on values and patterns of interaction- are expected for a necessary social cohesion, and others will become obstacles that break the group apart, reminding us that conflicts are to be expected. It also involves thinking about the possible particular structure of the sociocultural and technological areas that make up this distance education system, selecting preferences and priorities that make up its regular or characteristic aspects, through which its particularity will be recognized, for example, in terms of departments or areas of planning, design, production materials (print or non-print teaching texts, audiovisuals, computer software or hypermedia, online or telematic in connectivity, etc.); selecting and combining technologies to beused to mediate the content and didactic activities of the program; training, updating, and evaluating the performance of the tutors; the sector of monitoring and evaluation/research of theprogram, to know more about and make decisions about its functioning and achievement of quality, and increasingly considering the impact of graduates in the social life in question.

We recommend going beyond the quantitative way of conducting an observable and isomorphic assessment between the objectives set forth and the products and processes of the implemented electronic educational program; doing better than just considering the number of graduates in a determined amount of time that the program has taken place, to also consider the various cohorts and/or percentage of students who are behind the normal pace and those that drop out. It is necessary, in terms of processes, to phenomenologically describe the process of social interaction and educational-technological interactivity of the proposal, as well as, in terms of products, to consider the graduates and their provable skills, as well as their real or potential placement in key and dynamic sectors of the economy, graduates in non-conventional fields seeking to promote areas of innovation, research, and development, who drive local community development in the citizenry from virtual collaborative projects, among others. As the structure of the program is perceived from its sociological aspects, its functional co-ordination within the organization should also be visualized, as well as its inscription and articulation with the context.

In general, whenever there is an opposition or a juxtaposition in the ways of conduct or behavior in any area with social actors within an educational program, it is a reflection of a similar opposition in the broader social context. This surprising "overlapping" and correspondence between social reality and socially manifested behavior is explained, from the sociological educational perspective, by the notion of "culture code", which allows both to bearticulated and interdependent. This code has a record and a particular significance, built on relationships, differentiation, complements, and oppositions between signs, signifiers and signifieds, as its central components. Knowing and understanding this culture code allows us to adequately recognize, anticipate, and regulate a situation. But remember that the opposition (or contradiction) between the signs is what builds a new social significance; cultural signs, signifiers and signifieds do not necessarily correspond in linear causal connections between the phenomena, but are unpredictable. As in all social processes, the same appear as promising paths, but which are not easy to take; the current historical times do not tolerate mechanical transfers.

Thus, the frameworks that shape the projects of a social organization are shaped in the interaction between experience and woven in the light of the images of a society which is not more durable or solid (Bauman, 2004). In other words, they have become fragile and brittle because their "solutions", which were valid and useful at any given time for specific problems for which they were designed, are no longer applicable. For example, a professional with specialized knowledge may become incompetent or dispensable due to his lack of adaptation or training with regard to the emergence of a new technology, with a new vocabulary, conceptual frameworks and procedures related to the global and offshore, and so on.

In the digital culture and the culture of networks, of collaborative virtual teams, and of intercultural hybridizations of online educational programs, the use of certain metaphors, such as "surfing" or "navigating" illustrates the phenomena experienced "liquid" environments, rather than referring to "engineering" or "designing" situations, in somehow more stable ways. The same could be said of the preference to use the term "influences" rather than refer to manifestations of social control (which exist, with a strong presence).

Then, if the social units and organizations exist and are structured in fluid, unstable, and flexible ways so they may be assembled, dismantled, and reassembled quickly depending on twists and turns, even including changes without halting the march of processes, educational proposals should be increasingly flexible, changeable, and of rapid response to ambiguous, confusing and plastic, uncertain, paradoxical and even chaotic situations presented by reality. In this sense, face-to-face and distance educational programs articulated with ICT appear as modalities that should be adjustable within a multiple, complex, and fast worldview with regard to the requirements of today's, and thus local, world.

In this context, any kind of knowledge, skill, or know-how, isworn out and ages rapidly; which is why there is a tendency to reject established knowledge or accumulated experience. Instead of valuing the acquired capacity to do certain things, knowing (and learning) how to move in the world, involves being well connected, communicating easily and possessing/ belonging to a wide circle of also well connected people–in a real and virtual way- and in contact across multiple networks and in expansion.

The new sociology, which processes this new image of social reality and shapes new sociological strategies of study and reflection restricts or abandons the use of the term and concept "society", which is replaced by "network", which in turn presents overlapping institutions and interdependent existence. This model of social experience does not include prolonged or defined, but brief and fleeting life expectancy. On the contrary, its intrinsic relationship is to the experience of "consumer" as a life experience, understood as a series of consumer options without lasting value, responses to the attractions displayed by various alternatives to traditional proposals. In an extreme competition, advertising in shopping malls, television stations, and websites (Bauman, 2004) -which can also be educational and cultural- offer valid proposals while possessing the capacity to satisfy even without a permanent link between the objects offered and their potential users.

As a result, it is believed that the information and knowledge society requires individuals, groups, and organizations who, through the appropriation of ICT in general and applied to education in particular, will form symbolic analysts as critical users, train clear-headed citizens for the emerging digital citizenries, as well as train human resources in order to optimize the huge and fast production and flow of information for it to be valid and valuable to makedecisions when facing problems arising from an unpredictable reality. It is expected for this to take place in organizations that will become intelligent through innovative local, national, inter/ transnational projects. In other words, organizations that incorporate technology in general and ICT in particular with criteria, through e-learning and/or blended learning designs.

The introduction of ICT can not be carried out in an improvised or random way but requires a serious and careful *strategic planning*, if the goal is to obtain quality results, taking into consideration varied aspects and inescapable components. This relates to the need for:

- appropriation of ICT in local contexts where individuals and organizations carry out their work, which should reformulate their operational teaching and learning proposals through an intelligent management and application of technology; and at the same time,
- understanding that technology and ICT involves renewing and adapting communication, planning, management, organization, and evaluation strategies for an organizational restructuring of academic and educational situations where the organization -national and international- learns with others and from others in the network and as a whole.

It also means understanding that sociocultural and technological change in the network society of information and knowledge involves, for it to be managed and monitored, applying communication, cognitive and metacognitive, socioemotional, media, ethical, etc. skills, when incorporating these technologies within international projects. In addition to leading missions strategically managing and planning processes and products, social interactions should promote virtual collaborative contexts as a team. The technological infrastructure and technical support to those involved in the project are also central in any organization, which includes evaluation and research of management and the impact of technologies within realistic parameters of social relevance, cost, technological innovation and self-sustained financing. Lastly, and perhaps most importantly, it is important to not lose sight of the fact that we're dealing with *educational projects* so as no to succumb to the technological paraphernalia that characterizes contemporary life in the twenty-first century.

## THE INTERNATIONALIZATION OF A QUALITY DISTANCE EDUCATION WITH ICT

A good framework for interpretation of the above-mentioned could be worded as: "The internationalization of virtual universities and their paradoxes within the globalization/ contextualization of the cultural industries" or "Globalization, education, resistance, and technologies" or "How ICT affect the construction of social and cultural identity of peoples in the digital age", all of these interrelated issues.

We are living times of economic, sociopolitical, and cultural globalization, favored by the flow of information made possible by ICT, which are found in every society; a new kind of human relationship begins to grow, and we still do not know how they will be shaped and what their destiny will be. Among its most immediate impact -though not the only one-, we may findthe interconnection and convergence leading, through ICT, to the formation of networks without borders, generating hegemonic flows of information -often of argumentative discontinuity-, taken advantage of by the central economy as it exploits contacts and new business opportunities, but that simultaneously becomes an intruder and disrupts (Diaz, 1999) personal and social identity.

The current global technological-hegemonic practices (Gramsci, 1967) of ICT, although manifested by their claim of interactive satellization and a certain social standardization, shape a cultural hybridization as a set of social structures, processes, and practices which are combined in turn to generate new structures, processes, and practices. The components mentioned go beyond real social interaction and collide or are in sociocognitive dissonance with traditional or customary practices and mediations. We are witnessing the emergence of another *habitus* (Bourdieu, 1991), where the categories of perception, thought, and action point to another recognition of the legitimacy in the apprehension of the social world, now through virtual paths.

## Personal and Social Identities in Uncertain International Times

Achieving a reconstruction and/or cultural reinvention within the social relationships mediated by these technologies would allow us to recognize the domain that has originated them to promote reflective awareness of complex technological proposals given by the huge informational flows. This is not easy nor simple because ICT, as technology in general, develop faster than language and thought, which through intersubjective communication, help to build the identity of the individual during social, real, and virtual interaction. Technology appears today and establishes a complexity of technological, semiological, cultural, communications, etc.mediations, which is not necessarily negative, but demands to be acknowledged and demystified. Walter Benjamin (1892-1940), a critic of the Frankfurt School, stands out among the first to reflect on technological mediation, together with T. Adorno (1903-1969), M. Horkheimer (1895-1940) –authors who arerepresentative of the "critical theory" - or Erich Fromm (1900-1980), etc.., who also makes a critical-dialectic denunciation.

What is required is the development of critical sense and various resignifications in order to rebuild the discourses of the mediations as potential sources or parameters of identification/ reconstruction, even more so since we're dealing with proposals regarding media and telematic resources such as the online international distance education proposals, which tread across and arrive at various social units mediated by electronic technology.

ICT have much to contribute; they promote collaborative learning situations by providing strong technological frameworks for interaction, production, and social uses of contextualized and renewed digital meanings, and they can also maintain differentiating cultural territories as identifying parameters of generation and maintenance of social representations of undemocratic impact.

The centrality of education in these contexts, which are not always flexible, demands a revision, reinvention, and reformulation of the personal and social identities, while recognizing and promoting integration and social cohesion, diversity of actors, collective values and meanings, with guidance and practices that redefine the uncertainty and generate multiple strategic projects highlighting other possibilities for knowledge.

## THE PHENOMENON OF INTERNATIONALIZATION

The phenomenon of internationalization appears as the expanded and reformulated possibility of relationship between the organizations and groups of different national social units, today increased by telecommunications, which expand the geographical extent of cultural and socioeconomic activities beyond their physical boundaries. This deterritorialization associated with globalization -the phenomenon of modernity and late hypercapitalism-, aimed at the highly competitive international market- has subsumed distance education with ICT, now in e-learning format for real-time interaction and on a global scale. Internationalization is part of the phenomenon of mundialization of communication and information, where queries to databases are multiplied, and we navigate in telecommunications networks in a world of multimedia and interactive services that drive public and private professional, economic-financial, social, education, and entertainment activities.

All societies embedded in a global social space are being inscribed within a force *field* (Bourdieu, 1991) with actors and agencies. They are presented in turn as social sub-spaces or difference structures which are understood from the generating principle they are based on. These are differences settled in the contradictory distribution of forms of power and/or capital, both functional to the social framework under consideration.

The previously mentioned notion of *hybridization*- useful for the social and educational studies carried out- is not always well received because, with its contribution, there may appear situations of uprooting or loss with regard to the society and culture of origen, which should not be disregarded in the analysis pursued by distance education. The increase in intercultural mixtures also produces discomfort, due to the unequal exchange and inequitable access to global goods and services in general.

This expansion of global electronic training proposals –which will be seen later on- is not negative but rather makes options even more complex, generating new contradictions within a society as it broadens the educational and cultural offers such as the telematic communication systems which intermingle and grow -not without conflict- in the realities being studied.

## THE INTERNATIONALIZATION OF HIGHER EDUCATION

In the context of globalization, internationalization, virtualization, and delocalization established by general digital life, the new sociocultural processes mentioned appear, with unprecedented forms of social relationships, based on other parameters and approaches which, in turn, are manifested in various practical procedures for social action in general and education in particular. Accordingly, the new perspectives in higher education are heavily influenced by two parallel and converging processes of transformation: the impact of ICT and the mundialization of the planet, which for education, especially higher education, is linked to, today electronic distance proposals.

The Paris Conference in October 1998 stated in its World Declaration on Higher Education for the Twenty-First Century the challenges and goals of equity, quality, and relevance that should characterize it, along with sustaining that no country in the world could ensure by itself a real sustainable endogenous development, if new training environments were not created, which should include distance and/or virtual education programs to promote democratic socioeconomic and cultural development of the people.

In general, universities and higher scientific-technological research and experimental centers have been and are spaces for generation and transmission of knowledge. Accordingly, they should shoulder the historic challenge posed by the phenomenon previously mentioned. Among the many issues raised are the socio-political and cultural issues with relevant questions such as: What for and why educate in the globalized society? How or with which strategies? What values should prevail in a training inscribed within cultural mundialization? What does quality education mean to this international issue? What does it mean to prepare the future professional in global parameters of excellence and competitiveness? There are issues that exceed what globalization has traditionally focused on as concerns: foreign trade, monetary processes, and market economy.

The internationalization of higher education in general, although not a new phenomenon in the social history of education and intercultural contacts between peoples, is deepened after the emergence of ICT, basically with the possibility of remote interaction that favors the configuration of exchange, cultural, and educational programs in e-learning mode and the hybrid modality combined with face-to-face learning (or blended learning). Thus, the social dimension and international and intercultural technological ones are integrated with the functions of university teaching (Knight, 1997), learning, research, and extension offered by the institutions and programs in question.

Within this paradigm shift, higher education institutions, historically focused on classroom-based activities, require substantial changes in their organization, which may occur in three plausible strategic alternatives:

a) the creation of virtual universities whose programs contribute to non-face-to-face educational processes with a non-traditional organization; b) introducing in the educational units programs and curricula with an increasing added value given by information and communication technologies, with a conversion in faculty and students, in terms of roles; and c) changing its organization and structure to create an entity with autonomy -departments of virtual education-with management capability for the development of programs in unconventional online electronic modalities.
b) The internationalization of education, in turn, can be presented in a package of cultural industry, which constitutes an important topic for discussion, since it is one of the most important trends in the last decades of the late twentieth century, due to the impact of ICT in communication, interaction, and distance training.

Concurrently to the scope of internationalization, we see a shift in paradigms of co-operation towards the unspoken supremacy of the paradigms of competition. There is no doubt that the economic reasons are the factors leading to strengthen these arguments within the internationalization of socioeconomic relationships and trade of competitive markets, which then impact on education. In this context, generally the nomenclature "international studies" appears as a synonym for global studies, which also include multicultural education, intercultural education, international education, education for peace, and so on. The new nomenclature of *transnational education*, equivalent to "education without borders" or that crosses borders or education abroad and others, generally relates to distance education.

## TRANSNATIONAL EDUCATION

*Transnational education*is defined as the process of incorporating an international, intercultural, or global dimension in educational proposals within their sociocultural and legal inscription, curriculum, functions, administration, organization, and educational assessment.

The same assumptions made for higher education in general should prevail in virtual inter / transnational higher education, which is shifting towards the information society and knowledge economy with the incorporation of ICT.

Thus, higher education is distinguished by its production, research, and valorization of new knowledge in cultural, social, and economic areas.Therefore, if deprived of the possibility of performing the functions of research, discovery, and innovation, the functions that characterize it as an institution of higher learning will be undermined (Unesco, 2005).

As universities are somehow "mirrors" of their respective societies, any social unit should benefit not only from the practice of teaching, but also from the fruits of research, regardless of their cultural framework and level of economic development. In this context, it is also imperative to distinguish between descriptive knowledge (facts and information), knowledge of procedure (referred to the "how"), explanatory knowledge (which answers the question "why?") , implementation and evaluation knowledge related to the transfer in behaviour and above all the knowledge in terms of anticipation and research and development in its multiple relationships university- society-enterprise and culture, nationally and internationally.

The relevance of higher education -as emphasized at the World Conference on Higher Education held in 1998 - would involve taking into account:

- Public policies: higher education does not play its role when it neglects its duties of alert, research and anticipation, when not analyzing society's important problems;
- It is imperative that higher education is adapted to the changes in the world of work, without losing its production identity and dissemination of knowledge, without abandoning the priorities related to meeting society's long-term needs;
- The provision of professionals in general, of social workers, and the training of teachers for all levels of education lies, with rare exceptions, with higher education; among these priorities, university research should address the analysis and evaluation of education, in close relationship with the world of work within a genuine social project;
- Cultural development is built in space and time: higher education contributes to building it in its universal dimension and to that end should take into account the local and regional diversity of cultures;
- Social and community development extends to all groups without exception with the implementation of appropriate strategies to increase their participation and expression in general (especially of women, ethnic groups, etc.).

- The promotion of education throughout life is also seen through greater flexibility and diversification of possible proposals for education and university extension and/or higher studies.

National, international, and transnational higher education could really contribute to a socially useful production and distributed dissemination of knowledge, in advanced societies as well as those of so-called developing countries, contributing to the formation of the emerging global citizenry. In this context, it is necessary to reduce the digital gap and inequality of access. It is necessary to foster disciplinary, geographical, and sociocultural synergies, as well as creating appropriate activities for cooperation in a regional and international university level for further freedom of thought, dialogue, confrontation of views and expression as prerequisites for the generation and development of a truly global knowledge society.

In this transition to the information society and knowledge economy, and in relation to virtual inter/transnational higher education, a greater sense of localism and regionalism (commercial, economic, sociocultural, and educational) will be emphasized within a reformulated framework of the market economy, with fair bilateral and multilateral trade agreements, which will lead to greater demand for education and international mobility of programs, individuals, capital, ideas, knowledge, and technologies. This affects the international dimension of higher education, in developing and offering diversification and articulated scientific-technological innovations, with strategic alliances with other socioeconomic and cultural providers (commercial enterprises, community institutions, and other private non-profit organizations dedicated to education) which use telematic channels or online distance training, to adapt new types of training and qualifications.

Among the foundations of a transnational virtual higher education incorporating the intercultural dimension in educational programs, there are the:

- *Sociocultural:*that deepen an identity and intercultural knowledge, an alternative social development, of the world community and the emerging digital citizenry towards a mutual understanding.
- *Economic:* that promote economic growth and competitiveness in the commercial and labor market, exploiting the existence of financial incentives and new sources of income and international capital movements for the formation and development of new professions and research with strategic alliances.
- *Political:* because they strengthen the local and national identity, within regional and global levels, through the consolidation of foreign policy, security through blocks of countries, sustaining peace, and so on.
- *Educational:* because a positioning of quality towards an expansion of the academic horizon would be reached from the institutional power, with educational programs within the international context, as the development of ideas in general (according to international quality standards) and the production of knowledge through teaching and research are intensified.

International/transnational education is not new. It was globally and historically linked to the phenomenon of colonialism and post-war reconstruction in 1945. Then, in the middle of the twentieth century, it prevailed as technical assistance and cooperation for the development of exchange systems for education, training, and research. Today, driven by ICT, it continues as a proactive strategy towards internationalization of virtual education proposals.

From a prospective, it is believed that the process will continue growing, with variations in implementation depending on each organization, country, and blocks of countries, where each will define its role in accordance with their needs and possibilities in order to compete in the global education market from the regional, national, and institutional dimension.

Among the various models of electronic transnational higher education, the teaching models based on ICT and the Internet stand out, such as those:

- *Centered on the medium*: as a teaching proposal supported on a conventional educational technology of an instrumental type, where the electronic medium selected by the instructor becomes the leading provider of information;
- *Centered on the instructor*: generally in higher education, with the use of videoconferencing, which actually re-creates the traditional relationship, but now remote, with the distribution of communications resources, as well as with conventional or traditional face-to-face classes;
- *Centered on a mix of traditional technologies and other Internet-based* (blended learning), which, despite the absence of consensus as a teaching model, offers good proposals for the organization of the mediated learning and teaching, for the development of sociocognitive and technological skills required by the information and knowledge society.

## Paradoxes of International Distance Education

However, there are serious paradoxes within international higher/university distance education of a general nature, evident between the "internationalization" of the virtual educational discourse and the "pro-contextualized" pedagogical discourse, which is seen partly in:

- Access to online educational programs in a free market without borders opposed to reduced or no guarantees of equal access to ICT with quality and suitability of the proposals;
- Knowledge and experience of cultural diversity versus cultural conflicts of values, language, rules, etc.;
- Overvaluation of international aspects versus exacerbation (often violent) of regional/local identity values of various groups;
- Linguistic diversity versus social linguistic and cultural local/regional cohesion;
- National evaluation and accreditation regulation of courses versus creation of international systems for evaluating quality with convergent standards or parameters according to international criteria.

And there are also paradoxes of a special nature related to virtual educational programs, presented in the following variables:

- The *design* of international electronic programs of distance education adheres, through its dynamic, to general behavioral and attitudinal traits, in other words, beyond the sociocultural foundations of students, instructors/tutors and local support teams.
- In the *social interaction* of the programs, it is necessary to have a symbolic consensus to consolidate communication within the educational process, the informal language is neutralized in the virtual and telematic territories of a distant internationalization.
- The *sociocultural impacts* of ICT-mediated communication in connection with the identities of local communities in a program in question, which may benefit (or not) from an internationally situated learning. Although they may strengthen inclusion, cohesion, and theintegration of the program as they combat isolation and exclusion, they may result in regulatory and axiological frameworks which enhance biased judgments and prejudices.
- With regard to the *content* and *significance* of the local/regional accounts, stories, folklore, ethnicity, migration, etc.., which enter a global context, there is a mutual co-assimilation of knowledge resulting in a hybrid.
- *The articulation of the exogenous with the endogenous* with the appreciation of difference, neutralization of the routines and inertia that legitimately resist change, preservation of the identity of those involved, generation of creative challenges and opportunities.

There are no panaceas: the new structures of higher education with electronic distance education programs and new technological devices of the network society and digital culture generate positive and negative actions and reactions from the social and cultural structures, which must be taken into account for their study, evaluation, and research. The empirical certainty and existential uncertainty point out a cognitive, social, and cultural evolution of a still unknown impact.

There are trends that identify the items set forth with an analysis of controversies and risks, opportunities and challenges, that the issue of internationalization of education, especially telematic, faces in general and particularly for the Latin American region, which is our concern. There is thus the need to cultivate and increase awareness and knowledge to recognize and enhance opportunities in order to alleviate limitations of regional and international projection. This is evident with regardto the consideration of certain issues such as equitable access and use of connectivity to join networks, associations, and regional and international programs, and the promotion of national and regional policies to achieve international cooperation sustained over time.

Discrepancies and deep debates are imposed between the pragmatic visions and the consequent fear of loss of a sense of development of social identity and cultural awareness in the midst of competitive transnational businesses. The quest for integration and cooperation in a relevant and equitable higher virtual education, with regional and international transparency, is at an early stage of development in Latin America. There is no wealth of examples, save the progress made in the European Union, Bologna, but almost none within the framework of theMercosur. Therefore, the internationalization of higher education in general and virtual in particular, in Latin America, focuses largely abroad and is basically an importer of higher learning. The internationalization of curricula and the teaching and learning processes still is not among the priorities of the higher education sector.

The internationalization of higher education should respond to the impact of mundialization at the same time ensuring respect for the individuality of each nation (Knight, 1997), within the international global flow of technology, economy, knowledge, individuals, groups, values, ideas that cross borders and that affect each country differently, in its history, traditions, culture, priorities, and projects for the future.

## SOME RISKS AND ALTERNATIVE PROPOSALS

Any technological advancement generates resistance and inequality, especially since all complex phenomena -such as socio-cultural and technological developments that we are analyzing- has or sets a different speed of change and innovation to the whole social unit: ICT, networks, and the Internet are not the exception. The gaps, isolation, and fragmentation, barriers, and precariousness in communication are some of the risks that ICT establish in the regional and local context inserted in transnationality.

While some evaluation/accreditation systems for conventional and virtual higher education programs and institutions are at the beginning and others show medium progress, the process of articulation and convergence of directions and modalities of the programs in international higher education lies in development and maturation. The vast heterogeneity that characterizes the curricular designs of educational programs with ICT and virtualprograms with regard to academic criteria selected for the confrontation of programs, materials, projects, and tutorial actions, depending on parameters for their conception, design, implementation, and evaluation, are in discussion with regard to goals in continuous reformulation.

What generally happens is that technology is incorporated –from the technological myth- without discerning the educational models- consequential to underlying epistemological and sociopolitical choices- and whichhave traditionally marked the dilemmas of higher education institutions. With this, it is evident that what is considered first is the "how" of the program, rather than the "why" and "what for".

The transnational financial capital has rapidly seen the growth in this formative demand and the need for increasing coverage of new groups and social strata, as well as the global weight of the value of knowledge. The market acumen points to uncontrolled trade, with succulent profits, of massifying disciplining electronic educational programs, close to social control.

So, while today virtual higher education is growing, it tends to be international and global by definition, imports and exports technology and educational services from the central points of knowledge production, in courses and programs of formal and non-formal education, although not always of educational quality contrasted in local contexts or within frameworks that respect multilateral work. Therefore, we must be alert on two issues that can affect the profile and intent of international, conventional and virtual higher education programs, with negative consequences especially for developing countries: their marketing, especially with academically unreliable suppliers operating online and who regard education as a commodity (just another good within the World Trade Organisation); and, in particular, the disciplining of autonomy, through rigid highly structured telematic educational systems, of zero quality and transnational accreditation.

Both sides operate in a ubiquitous way in local telematic headquarters and interconnectstudents in their quest for equivalence, credits, and continuity of their training in different countries. The challenge, therefore, is to move forward in the regulation of these exchanges increased by free trade and the limitation of monopolies, above all through control systems of thecultural industries, with their publishers of print material and electronic-virtual services.

From a socioeducational analysis, there are serious issues to consider from sociopolitical, organizational-administrative. and academic reflections which seek quality through international higher education programs for local contexts. In these issues, what is highlighted is the need to:

- Understand internationalizing should mean deepening democracy, today reduced or subordinated to polar or commercial, and even fundamentalist, interests to overcome the "single thought or mentality". Educating for democracy (Dewey, Giroux, and other thinkers) means regarding it as an ethical event that involves educating towards values according to "procedure principles" (Carr, 1999), in order to counter the material and symbolic violence existing through indiscriminate cultural transfers
- Alert against the dangers of uniformity that technological mediation may produce within the internationalization of processes and products of higher distance and / or virtual education programs with ICT, given by a subjection to sociopedagogical and technological-communicational, unidirectional and linear models, depending oncentral programming, or ignorance, or epistemological silence with regard to the approaches chosen to carry out the convergence of the educational programs, or the lack of respect for multiculturalism and the difference, resulting in the inability to teach at a distance in a critical way
- Further studies of cultural hybridization -within a reformulation of the social sciences in general-, considering the issues of identity, differences, interculturalism, authenticity, miscegenation, and others.

The challenge is to overcome the instance of production and distribution of single thought, mainly in universities -undergraduate and graduate levels-, to allow ir to regain its central role of producer of socially useful knowledge, taking advantage of the shared generation of new knowledge in educational, intercultural, and open projects and programs. Today, due to the opportunities offered by ICT, equity, democracy, and global values of justice and solidarity can be realized by allowing the existence of virtual communities of learning, practice and research, provided they are "chosen".

Thus would international higher distance education be characterized, valuing the difference, which must permeate the design and development of programs and materials, within a convergence, to highlight specific situations and contexts, cultural and linguistic frameworks, needs and peculiarities of participation, and knowledge on the part of various countries, areas, users.

Along this line of deconstructiva criticism of the conventional or industrial technological-educational model of distance education (Fainholc, 1999), now with ICT of massive international distribution (or delivery), the goal is to strengthen very expensive elements of the educational task par excellence: disciplinary content to be transmitted and the deployment of the higher thought functions of students, the provocation and development of critical thinking and solidarity, through the various processings and didactic activities in participatory designs, etc.. to transfer them to broader social situations and strengthen the spirit and sustenance of democracy. This will be achieved with:

- the deepening the epistemological specificity of the disciplines and logical structuring of their contents, in the desire to build transdisciplinary, located, and holistic approaches;
- the need to respect the complexity of the educational situation and the construction ofknowledge, and to teach to think in a complex manner, considering the many interdependentvariables that should appear in the design and development of distance education programs and materials;
- the central value held by the subject and groups as re-creators/producers of knowledge andcontinuous resignification of the meanings carried out at a distance, in telematic interaction with what they have learned: emphasizing the role of students and groups as centers of educational action makes us rethink situations from the user who reconstructs knowledge, organizes and processes information, recreates and questions, implements and transfers to individual and social environments;
- the identification of supposed self-reliant and highly structured materials, hindering the practice of the deconstructive and researching concept of knowledge through theoretical-practical confrontation and vice versa;
- the increasingly stronger incorporation of the social and cultural nature of the processes in the development of higher psychological functions and the symbolic language of the learnerwithin interactive dialogue.

Within the referred framework of resemantization of global projects, which even presents the reality of hyperuniversities, education must be acknowledged as a cultural process that integrates differences and is deeply humanizing. This implies that scholars and administrators, tutors and researchers, should review their frameworks of thought and action, not only to complete their educational work efficiently and effectively in the broadest sense, but also in a relevant and situated way in terms of a “glocal” synthesis: configuring and consolidating essential values such as those that emphasize equal opportunities for the production of knowledge in local and global sociocultural articulation, in a shared, distributed and perfectible way. Thus, the higher distance education processes mediated by ICT and the Internet will play a key role in the knowledge society.

## Internationalization / Transnationalization of Distance Education Programs within the New Settings for Higher Education

According to the Global Alliance for Transnational Education (GATE), the new settings for educational transnationalization (Aranovich, Carrizo, and others, 2000) point to any teaching and/or learning activity where students are in a country different from the one the institution which provides the educational program is located. Transnational virtual education is also understood as a new opportunity to diversify sources of funding for students from/in other countries, who obtain a degree from a foreign university, because they do not have the opportunity to study abroad due to labour, family, or financial problems. It is understood as "training over the Internet" due to the application of specific instructional and sociocognitive design, either using the Internet, LMS, constructive, collaborative, and distributive environments. It does not only entail publishing information for students using the attributes of the Internet: it involves creating technological-educational, semiological, and communicational mediations, for environments of autonomous management and collaborative learning (with or without technological platforms or systems).

This is possible because ICT for virtual higher education:

- Support the transmission, sharing, re-creation, and validation of accurate and valuable knowledge distributed in networks;
- Provide flexibility and adaptation with transparency of information that comes and goes to and from the university, the local community, global society;
- Need media skills: sociocognitive skills to manage information, read critically on screen, and so on. to create and express knowledge on the part of learners and groups.

Thus, GATE describes some possible ways to pursue transnational higher education, which generally point to distance education programs: a) distance education; b) locally supported distance education; c) twins programs in institutions in two different countries; d) local branches of foreign institutions; and e) franchise agreements. While these proposals have high expectations of transformation and improvement of the educational system, we must not forget that, in a virtual modality (Silvio, 1998), within the information society, they are found in a particular context marked by their development with a strong massification in terms of their access, reduction of public funding, and of high competition among different universities in the world, within the regional/global market.

The transnationalization of higher education has resulted in both positive and negative elements (Garcia de Fanelli, 1999). Among the former, we see the training of individuals and groups with a high degree of cultural hybridization in situations of social interaction; among the latter, we see competition of educational offers within the free market, where fraudulent practices and the granting of university degrees without sufficient guarantees of quality may prevail. To avoid this, there are government agencies responsible for assessing the quality of higher education training proposals, although such regulations may settle on inflexible forms of social control and lead to a standardization of the various educational proposals.

# QUALITY

It is necessary to address the concept of quality in the contexts we are describing : a socio- historical-cultural construction, depending on ideologies, interests, and pressure groups -many of these from an elite- existing within a social unit, be it a distance education organization/ program, or outwards with regard to its sociocultural regional and international, and specific occupational, current and/or future integration. Therefore, it is a part of the *habitus* of the current existing cultures.

The concept of quality refers to the ability or suitability for use of a process, product, or service that is optimal for a social segment, today with particular emphasis regarding market, according to the perception that is held and demanded of the same. From a socioeducational-electronic point of view, the concept of quality presupposes the integration in the educational product or service of subprocesses that proved successful because they are useful, valuable, viable, precise, realistic, clear, prudent, ethical, and have been incorporated into the hardware, software, and mindware of the educational practice, in our case mediated from the technological- educational point of view and ICT.

It is believed that a product or service has quality when it meets the needs and expectations of the user according to parameters such as: the stability and security that the product or service gives the client; reliability or ability to perform the functions of teaching, guidance, and support, without errors and for a specified period. However, this is not a "route" defined unilaterally, but rather is suited to the circumstances and structural and cyclical possibilities. In other words, there is a close relationship between quality and context, from a sociological and cultural-historical point of view. With regard to the topic at hand, the state has an inescapable role, which takes flight by itself in this area of regulation, accreditation, and quality assessment, of the supply of educational proposals for transnational virtual higher education.

One consequence of the above-mentioned is the need to have and offer a quality, effective, valid, and valuable higher educational training, to prepare new professionals, according to national and regional social demands, posed by globalization today. This is a challenge to consider university education alternatives supported in ICT.

A virtual higher education program that provides a service of quality face-to-face, or semi-face-to-face, distance, pure e-learning or blended learning, should contemplate most of the elements presented in the following record –by no means comprehensive-:

a) Development and review of strategic plans for intelligent short, medium and long-term organizational development of the social unity in which it is inscribed.
b) Generation, distribution, re-creation, and appropriation of socially useful knowledge, depending on hierarchical sociocultural and economic needs.
c) Incorporation and updating of technology and ICT in management, teaching, learning, evaluation, documentation and research center processes.
d) Professional and comprehensive continuous training of teaching, technical, and administrative staff with proper wages, coverage, and incentives.
e) Fair wages for instructors/tutors, which while representing a high incidence (Marsh and others, 2003) in the cost of education, should have the same weight as they make up the image of the program, as well as materials used. Therefore, it is necessary to

be very critical when it comes to initiating electronic distance programs, because they often respond directly to the goal of reducing costs.

f) Participation in processes of local, regional, national, and international community development to strengthen the training of an emerging global citizenry thanks to ICT, through quality educational services along with other universities and research centers in the world.
g) Self-assessment and permanent adjustments.

As we may see, the issue of the transnationalization of virtual higher education programs in constructive quality frameworks is often marked by standards ranging inside the contradiction of control versus social change. Achieving a regulation/modulation of virtual training projects (sometimes led by public universities with public funds) is difficult, without falling into social control, generally meant to preserve social inequities within a late hypercapitalism, or displaying the higher profitability produced by the educational activities planned. The economistic criterion is often accompanied by low-quality educational proposals, without real concern in training the ability to continue learning, solving social problems, building and/or strengthening the cultural identity of the region or social unit in question.

## REFLECTIONS ON QUALITY IN VIRTUAL EDUCATION

Consistent with the current historical cultural times, the learning objectives, the agencies which produce knowledge and practice mediated by technological resources, sophisticated administrative structures for various efforts, etc.. are diversified, which today rely on networks and the Internet as the main resources.

As a result, the outcome of university virtualization is a virtual campus consisting of various digital spaces, where various functions, not only administrative but sociocultural, are performed: teaching, learning, group discussion, information exchange, research, management and so on. (Silvio, 2000). The rise of virtual education programs not only generates demands for accreditation proposals, but also continuous improvement of users and their social inclusion.

Faced with the emergence of different proposals from organizations, teaching environments, and guidance of learning with more autonomous mediations, the choice is to list minimum quality standards systems to achieve suitable educational telematic products and processes in national and international contexts. They are not intended as a utopian adequacy as a "must" of the educational task of virtual interaction to be confronted with the real service in question -under construction and constant reformulation-, but rather as an inscription within a framework of specific sociocultural and technological-educational relevance and preparation/ testing of mechanisms that produce monitoring and analysis cuts (as a kind of"state of the art") so that at any time during implementation of the online program (or course), we may know the status of its development; in other words, to know what levels are being achieved, within what socio-recursive process of development it is found, at which point the process of quality assurance is, and so on.

The suggestions made regarding the quality of virtual education are not isolated events. They are the product of the confluence of a number of historical-cultural, socioeducational,and technological factors that led to the creation of a new paradigm for sociocultural understanding for a different kind of academic work in national and transnational higher education. In other words, they are related to principles, techniques, and practices closely linked to the evolution of an information society towards a knowledge society.

Any new paradigm seeks to address old and new problems while it faces others. In general, the goal is to train people and younger generations, and provide them with the necessary tools to live as fully as possible in a society with dignity and not just success. To that end, a set of conditions, tools, and methodologies is provided in different places and times (with teachers, peers, knowledge, and devices, materials and resources) which will facilitate the acquisition of knowledge –in a shared way, through communication and exchange – and which they need to rebuild and re-signify their knowledge. Knowledge can be stored in different places: conventional resources, mixed universities (physical and digital), a network of information and research centers, libraries distributed throughout the world, and so on.

Problems that may arise within the mentioned training processes of higher level are not new. What is new is the revisit taking place of the underlying paradigms in terms of the rethinking of the classic directive, communicable, and unilineal proposals of face-to-face learning. The training processes are mediated today by "artefactuales" technologies, of instructional design, which are based on languages, artifacts and artifices, procedures and strategies of a sociotechnologically mediated pedagogical communication (or computer communication: CMC).

What are the implications of this new paradigm -media technology and strategies-, for the quality of virtual education distance? The emergence of new controls, some more authentic and/or bureaucratic than others, takes place with standards,parameters, concepts of quality within the proposal and within the social framework of internationalization, which expand alternatives to traditional face-to-face education with assessment methodologies and systems to ensure their management, maintenance, and continuous improvement.

Interest in the quality of international virtual higher education and the proliferation of proposals to evaluate it correspond to the line of work of an "education managed within a managed society", no longer falls within "quiet and calm" frameworks ofbut rather operates with organizational control in turbulent and competitive arenas (Silvio, 1999), within a new knowledge "market".

The quality control mechanisms are embodied in the global framework of the Global Alliance for Transnational Education (GATE) and the Accrediting Council for Independent Colleges and Schools (ACICS), for educational organizations exporting from the USA, UK, and Australia, and the framework recently developed by Israel due to the progress of transnational education in this country. In other words, times indicate that international virtual higher education is moving in hegemonic media, of quality assurance, and also attentive to the promotion of freedom, flexibility, and intercultural diversity.

It is time to draw up proposals for a design of regulatory policies of international virtual higher education. The goal is to generate a framework for assessing and managing the quality of education with respect for sociocultural diversity, regulation, and hegemonic non-control of local academic, cultural, and socio-economic forces, acting on culture and not just on the market by combining the new variables.

Future proposals should include some of the guidelines that are listed, such as legislating specifically for the case of foreign universities in order to subject them to authorization procedures to allow them operate within national territories, with the same rights and obligations of the rest the local higher education organizations. This authorization should clarify the scope and use of the term "university" in these proposals, and not imply that the degrees offered are officially valid with automatic revalidation.

This will seek to eradicate the uniform delivery of information in the pedagogical framework virtually mediated by a university, a transnational educational program,and an instructor who, in addition, in the new paradigms, must overcome being transmitter in order to become facilitator/creator of sociocultural conditions to produce learning, and with a student who instead ofrecipient becomes a participatory agent and builder of his/her own knowledge within a complex relationship mediated with technology.

## INTERCULTURAL VIRTUAL HIGHER DISTANCE EDUCATION

There are various problems that require attention in the management of virtual higher distance education with integration and diversity management, in other words, within a socio and intercultural approach. The goal is to clarify the interuniversity collaboration frameworks in different social units in the various possible alliances with local agencies, industries, NGOs, colleges, and so on. For example:

- Making sociocultural profiles compatible with values so they are reflected in the curriculum and assessment/accreditation, and taking advantage of differences depending on audiences; it is a challenge in terms of decisions and design.
- Revising local practices and customs, values and beliefs, that underlie credits systems (Barajas Frutos, 2003) ; their ability to adapt and transfer is another challenge.
- Analyzing and prioritizing language problems (if it is understood that language in itself can reduce the sense of isolation among participants and help create a sense of community) characteristic of regions and groups of course users, may reduce negative effects and capitalize on the positive ones in the use of virtual learning environments and networks of cooperation and research, and contribute to a deeper intercultural appreciation.

The learning materials created in a single language should be adaptable not only for their use in other languages at low cost but also to become auxilliaries to bring together people from different cultures to interact in a common language through various learning experiences. The goal is to imagine valuable resources to reduce prejudice, promote understanding, respect, cooperation and solidarity among various cultures.

Hence, the different languages that are intermingled with the different technological narratives of ICT and the institutionalization of the most diverse channels of communication should not be considered as barriers between communities and nations but rather privileged channels of integration between the cultural profiles and individual and collective autonomy. The languages, although somewhat pre-existing and even standardized due to the use of the printing press, are complemented by the "new" technologies that are beginning to play a central role in the culture of internationalization and in the restructuring of societies through the institutionalization of information and communication technology, and which should be investigated in terms of its social impact.

Since the cultural and training problems of the citizenry for global coexistence, from an open, virtual, and distance learning, are not minor issues (Van den Branden and Lambert, 1999), it will be necessary to recognize and rank each area of human activity, of every nation, every social group (local, national, regional, multinational), economic or religious group or other, including subcultural virtual ties. Culture represents a complex issue that engages the attention of anyone from politicians to entrepreneurs, educators and philosophers, artists and athletes, and the whole citizenry. Everyone, together with the theorists, perceives the systematic element of the evolution of historical progress, in order to interpret that communities have been "imagined", built, established, and resignified in an inescapable way in this evolution.

## THE VIRTUAL UNIVERSITIES, MUNDIALIZATION AND THEIR IMPACT ON CULTURE

Communication mediated by ICT provides enormous opportunities for international and transnational collaboration within and between conventional and virtual universities allowing them to expand all of their proposals for knowledge production. These include teaching proposals with the creation of learning communities (Slavin, 1990; Harasim, 2000), or scientific research and action-research communities (associated with virtual communities of knowledge production) and investigative evaluation communities, enable in turn, an internationalization of curricula, the exchange and mobility of students within multilateral agreements with local agencies so they may obtain undergraduate and postgraduate degrees or complete courses, with different concrete possibilities to develop sociocognitive and technological skills in users/students, according to the various training-cultural proposals in the table of international interaction.

A central aspect to discover and inquire about in terms of the possibilities of global virtual universities (or hyperuniversities), established through ICT, is their ability to communicate to articulate tasks and programs, which constitute a challenge to streamline the management and administrative-social regulation of the structures that compose it.In any case, international ventures should be characterized by and take into account, as goals, the relaxation of these administrative, organizational, and management structures, of the curriculum proposals, the attitudes, values, and cultural attitudes, and of the socioeducational and learning models, of communication and collaborative production, of research and evaluation/accreditation, not only to establish channels of legal approval but also socioeducational interaction to overcome rigidities in programs and projects aimed at flexibility and respect for intercultural diversity.

## CULTURAL INDUSTRIES

Today the telematic educational proposals shape national and regional identities and cultures, saturated with trans-national references. Many of the electronic training programs belong to the *cultural industry*, understood as the productions of for profit institutions and companies, by way of social programs and practices of a country, region or organization, distributed on a large scale as personal and collective cultural expressions.

The term *cultural industry* was coined by Enzensberger (1970), although his predecessors are Horkheimer, Adorno, Marcuse and Benjamin, of the Frankfurt School. Today it defines the production and distribution, given by international trade agreements, the meanings as symbolic and material goods from the creative expressions. Its contents and forms impact in shaping the individual and social consciousness, as reflections of the historical and social product of a time. It covers the production and distribution of books, records, films, TV shows, software, theater productions, musicals, and other items associated with training, culture, recreation, and entertainment. It increasingly influences –by means of complementation agreements- on investment, trade among businesses and the participation of countries tending to change habits and transforming social relations. With a strong presence in non-traditional exports of countries, it makes visible the contribution of local cultural products in international circulation, whose impact is beginning to overcome its inviolability.

Then, the nomenclature of *cultural industry* is not current: it dates back to the movement emigrant German theoreticians who in 1932 developed the proposal for a "critical theory" that disassembles the oppression enforced by the capitalist society of the time with the production of material and symbolic goods and distributes in a variety of industrial formats in an hegemonic way. That is, it produces a mental saturation within a communicational and psychosocial framework of cultural totalitarianism with social alienation. The mentioned movement inspired other responses of social contestation (such as the French May of 1968) to shape what is now recognized as the "cultural Marxism", embodied in the historic figures of H. Marcuse and A. Gramsci.

Moreover, the transnational presence of cultural industry in general and of productions of ideas, today, electronic goods and services in formal telematic educational programs, contains some contradictions: at the same time as symbolic products are distributed calling on the knowledge and exchange of a creative diversity of ideas from existing cultures, there may be the risk of sectarianism in the selection and dissemination of products (some authors are not considered), by way of a single disciplining and unrepresentative thought. Garcia Canclini (2002) argues that the current culture is a hodgepodge -or hybridization- produced by the impact of accelerated interaction of fast ICT within a multi-ethnic and intercultural interdependence.

The electronic production formative mediated by ICT -starting to play an increasing role in the distribution and circulation of international circuits- should be analyzed from a theoretical-critical point of view, from the historical guidelines of the Frankfurt School and others (including Morin, Eco, Mattelart, etc..), so as to reveal ideologisms within the businesses on the rise, the growth, and participation of "canned symbolic products" that make up the cultural industry and that move in international circuits.

Cultural industries are industries without chimneys that start working in the twentieth century with print, radio, and television and its derivatives, which are increasingly articulated with computer and electronic products, of huge storage capacities and fast distribution, never before imagined. The emergence of cyber proposals of art, literature, music, and other communicative services resize culture on a worldwide scale within a virtual marketplace that also includes educational programs, at any level and modality, as recreation and entertainment products.

Recreational offers for online games and courses of various contents and purposes (history, geography, cuisine, astronomy, languages, etc.) flood the daily lives of shopping centers and homes, as well as educational media centers at real and virtual universities, and instructional resources used by companies. These practices mounted on telematic discourse of technological convergence have expanded and changed the culture and interaction with strong modeling impact of the "cognitive toolbox" (Bruner, 1999) of individuals and social organizations.

The concept of cultural industry, related to online distance learning offers, needs, then, to be viewed from a "critical sociology".There is evidence that behind the appearance of commercial freedom, encouragement of creativity, and support to solidarity, there are complex sociopolitical mechanisms that shape and pluridetermine individual and collective, not always democratic mentalities and social processes.

By extending the concept of reason, perception, and sensitivity, critical sociology analyzes evidence and suggests overcoming -once again- the instrumental reason geared toward technical mastery, now of monopolistic international circulation, which does not reflect the interests of the subjects and groups but rather coopts them as historically determined or constituted subjects.

There continue being lags and crisis of meaning as a result of these situations, because not everything can be explained and understood from an "instrumental rationality of the means/ends logic" that characterizes the ICT, applied to the cultural industry in general and electronic distance education programs in particular. Its deconstruction is central to a possible discernment and sociocultural understanding.

One could argue that the massive and industrial online electronic educational proposals, are becoming part of the cultural industries, of regressive effect, powerful appearance in late capitalism, as they take the shape of a "managed education", inscribed in the single thought represented by a "society of control", considered by other theorists (Foucault, Virilio) as our immediate future due to the capitalism of overproduction and technological concentration that sells products and services.

Hence the need to practice a critical socio-educational theory explaining trends and setting limits, to analyze the traits of internal constitution and modes of operation (and cloaking), through historical and dialectic contrast between the personal and the collective, of processes and products presented in the "package" of technological platforms where educational, social, and cultural programs are installed.

Thus, it is related to the epistemological demystifying trend that contributes to knowing how, today, personal *subjectivity* and social *identity* are shaped as fluid -not fixed- secondments generated from an interaction framed and associated to the current globalized development.

Accordingly, while there is as much applause as criticisms regarding cultural industries where global-electronic educational achievements take place, these are in progress, although their projections of homogeneity and uniformity may be anticipated, we remain at the level of conjectural prophecies. Only the social future will tell whether these efforts have been or not conducive to the development of consciousness and solidarity as socializing ways to improve the overall quality of life.

Fractal times of uncertainty with cultural times of fuzzy logic, rapid changes that transport processes and products by ICT, and which are submitted in new narratives, texts, and contexts characterize these sociotechnological practices that transformed and intersect all of theeveryday and specialized human relations, without knowing yet where they are headed and how they are taking shape.

"Enhanced intellectual creativity, a plethora of systematized and available knowledge, along with other inputs, are still achievements in outline, besieged by the dystopian fantasies of police control, the negative aspects of globalization, the technologization of power and politics, the exacerbation of individualism and racism, the existence of marked imbalances in the international arena and the other ghosts of the undesirable that seem relative, against the expected or predicted from the more optimistic wing of the gurus and experts mentioned, the image of a future democratic, pluralistic, humanized, and distributive society."(Rivera, 2002).

## The Telematic Construction of the Social and Cultural Identity Provokes Crisis

The construction of otherness or personal and social identity mediated by ICT represents a novel anthropological and epistemological issue for the evolutionary development of social relations, showing various tensions between the notions of individual and culture.

Identity is defined as the reason by which two elements - subject or phenomena-that appear as different are the same thing in reality. The identity derives from an intrinsic quality of these elements, built from reason, identifying similarities but which are different in nature.

From the constructivist line of social sciences, it is established that identity (inscribed within the educational field in general and electronic distance field in particular) is not a fixed entity but is artificially constructed through social interaction, today mediated by technology, and with a complex weave of discourses and virtual, local, and international institutions.

It is also acknowledged that ICT are a central part of the current digital culture, despite the existing socioeconomic and cultural inequalities, particularly in the southern hemisphere, where cyberspace has become part of the everyday routine to the point of questioning the relevance of interaction with computers in shaping identity.

The interactive possibility and, above all, of simulation, of ICT establishes fuzzy personal and social boundaries, that affects how to perceive and understand the world in a diffuse way (such as in the interplay of characters). The framework for the collaborative role-playing computer provided by computers help the opportunities to setup fluid identities. The user, as he/she situates and redefines him/herself, lives at the same time several and varied backgrounds, experiences an intense contact with ideas, people, and feelings shared -close and far- if placed in discussion with unintended consequences.

The creation of a mixed and glocal identity takes place, thus, in factual and virtual, global and local, hybrid contexts,a result of an alternative socialization relative to these frameworks of synthesis between the settings mentioned, of virtual interaction.

The issues mentioned are the concerns and debates that are recovered from the viewpoint of a critical sociology of education; they addresses the problems of the "difference" and also the "we" in the collaborative contexts of virtual interaction,valuable inputs for the organization of identity in digital times.

With globalization and the crisis of physical places and conventional symbolic codes, there is a loss of the inscription of local social ties in tangible territories, while there is also the inauguration of the era of non-places, where history becomes another piece of information.Identities in constant motion, instability, and ambivalence appear, even to the point of the impossibility of being named in shared languages, as many suddenly disappear from the network. This requires a deeper understanding of the training phenomenon of individuals and groups in their social relations in transnational telematic times.

ICT, as technology in general, are developing faster than language, which contributes, through intersubjective communication, to name and delimit the phenomena, to build - although today in fluid way-the identity or subjectivity of individuals and groups. This is consistent because when referring to technology is not the only conceived as equipment or devices but by the cultural heritage where values, beliefs, and ways of doing/re-creating/anticipating the proposals or styles of production and social use of knowledge are anchored. Thus, technology is related to the implicit or tacit knowledge that together with the conceptual and procedural, attitudes, beliefs, and values, are part of the new narratives that are processed, transported, and distributed by ICT.

Against this backdrop of global, digital, and virtual contexts, cultural industries produce fragmentation and uncertain consequences in the formation of personal and social identities. These are shaped from the models provided by the global technological-hegemonic practices, of interactive egalitarian claim, although in the reality of sociocultural satellitezation and standardization, beyond the possible and welcome re-creation the players at local venues are able to carry out to overcome monopolies and sociocognitive dissonance through the usual industrialized practices and mediations.

We are witnessing the need for the emergence and development of another *habitus* (Bourdieu, 1991), because linear systems give way to complex and recursive technological proposals of flows. Just as the printed text must be articulated with hypertext, which establishes another kind of reading through interactive navigation, global cultural industries will be appropriated according to the regional/local records and for the benefit of their users in a reflective way, to become provoking hybrid contexts and bearers of criticism, now through ICT and the Internet.

## Some Open Socioeducational Proposals and some Warnings

The centrality of education –face-to-face and virtual- today is seen in *situated and distributed* settings and programs (Brown, Collins and Duguid, 1994), in computer mediated communication connected with the necessary appropriation of ICT. Within this table, respect for the diverse is another input that replaces the concept of fixed and stable identities for changing and perhaps ephemeral ones. However, they may also be instituted as the ones to overcome rigidities, anachronisms, and stereotypes which deserve to be "revisited for a deeper understanding of the technological mediation produced.

Thus, within a sociological reflection of a virtual distance education, it is argued that:

a) The articulation and use of technology in educational processes does not automatically lead to better representation of actors so that they are successful. It represents a strategic opportunity at the mercy of decisions made about the social control or change, if it comes to anticipating and managing possible futures.
b) It requires placing higher education in its international distance alternatives within a cultural process of permanent change to adapt to the demands of the information and communication society that produces electronic knowledge with quality, equity, and relevance.
c) Online distance education of pure or mixed proposals integrating ICT leads to reviewing sociohistorical-cultural inscriptions where the organization, administration, and curriculum will be the useful and necessary innovation to accompany a broader sociotechnological change, but without total assurances of achieving, through the generation of knowledge, the overcoming of various social inequalities and inequities.
d) There is a need for strategic planning of technological change to create relevant virtual environments of e-learning or blended learning. This requires very careful monitoring of subprocesses and products within the creation of a higher training framework in the style of a virtual hyperuniversity with the convergence of technological services, although it is not a full guarantee of socioeducational effectiveness, satisfaction of social needs, and incentive to learn for users.
e) Assuming a proactive leadership in the roles of managers, designers, faculty, and students in these sociovirtual environments, contributes permanently to protagonism and reflection of the innovation process of mediations (Barbero, 1986) with ICT for a contextualized and distributed learning through networks, within a "glocal" setting inscribed within an appropriate and critical educational technology (Fainholc, 2002).
f) The virtual education model is a socioformative paradigm amending protagonism and competencies as well as the organization and management of the programs, curriculum, teaching and learning, to move from a linear space and time to a virtual recursive context. Knowledge is no longer focused on time and space but is shared and open; it requires trained facilitators, powerful educational materials, organizational styles and cohesive internationally decentralized management, which should synthesize the local cultural identity with the global world identity, in an interrelationship and integration with other cultures, for a creative enrichment in diversity.

From this critical socioformative cultural position, facing the complexity and possible typical fractures situations of the situations of ambiguity –where trans/international collaboration and convergence are recognized as valuable and necessary-, the approach of hermeneutic rigorous, ethical, and unique work, supplementary to the systemic holistic and recursive approach, are inputs to review and further new paradigms.

The interaction within the mediations with ICT, in turn inscribed in the virtual learning culture, will increasingly tend to shape teaching and learning situations with users who must become reflective hyperreaders (Burbules and Callister, 2001). Invigorating cognitive and metacognitive strategies not only of higher thought functions, but also for the practice of deconstruction of totalitarian ideological configurations, towards a cultural change of respect for diversity and difference, by means of critical reading in electronic supports (Fainholc, 2004) and virtual collaborative interaction, must be unavoidable subjects.

Near and remote participatory collaboration, made possible by a synchronous and asynchronous communication in the virtual realities, bearing in shaping another subjectivity and identity where sociocognitive residue of the interaction with and of technology (Solomon, 1992) to occur within electronic virtual educational programs.

"The sociotechnical study of the mechanisms of control now in its beginnings, should be a study able to describe […] after the corresponding adjustments […]some mechanisms taken from the ancient societies of sovereignty[…] how to make way for new forms of resistance against the societies of control? Is it possible to find an outline of future forms capable of countering the joys of marketing? Isn´t it strange that so many young people call for a "motivation", which requires training and lifelong learning? It is they who must discover what such things will be useful for […]"(Deleuze, 1999).

The alternative counterhegemonic trends embodied in socioformative national and international agents and agencies should take over all the symbolic codes of the media, mediators, and mediations in technological convergence, take advantage of the information stored and distributed by ICT to fortify the sociopolitical empowerment of individuals and groups. Therefore, the participation and creation of mediated communicative environments for the shaping of "other identities", although we still cannot know which they would be, should strengthen a "digital humanism" required by the current times.

The centrality of higher virtual educational programs of global scope, as we have seen, are characterized by uncertainty, movement, change, unprecedented expression ... which is why we should strengthen thinking strategies, collaborative action and solidarity, democratic, independent, interdependent, joint search for meaning at regional and international levels. Accordingly, the generation of alternative or counterhegemonic thinking will encourage critical-reflective minds and actions with different protagonisms, inscribed within a a new virtual morphology of the logic of social global networks. This time they should be visualized as valuable devices for another kind of *knowledge management* from the equitable and relevant access and use of ICT and information, while recognizing that it is located at the level of utopia, because half or more than half the globe is still electronically excluded, enough reason for a proposal of change without delay.

*Chapter 6*

# THE VIRTUAL STUDENT IN DISTANCE EDUCATION

This chapter presents a proposal for descriptive and explanatory phenomenological re-construction, from the viewpoint of a critical sociology of education, from the perspective of the student enrolled in distance education programs. The aim is to bring some elements to this knowledge to overcome the usual interpretive reductionism of this profile from the lines of functionalist, Marxist, and empiricist thought, in order to give another meaning to the configuration of the distance student's role in electronic programs as we acknowledge their inscription in the structure of the programs in question and these within the sociocultural settings in the current capitalism.

To this end, some critical-structural considerations are presented and paths leading to online educational programs are described, which students of this modality would have to adopt in facing training needs. Existing obstacles are also described in situations of social interaction and technological-educational interactivity mediated in these program with the use ofICT, to propose sociocultural alternatives that will discover issues to be improved and illustrate these realities in a more relevant way.

The sociological analysis that we are dealing with describes the vicissitudes of the educational proposals articulated with ICT, which organize symbolic spaces for the student being trained online at a distance, to be able to learn more comprehensively and interact with greater autonomy and social collaboration when facing the great challenges of educational processes in general, which are not always addressed and met. This will be the result of complex processes that will interrelate the educational proposal designed for specific settings and users in the framework of the mediated interactive complex within a specific online program and inside the sociocultural context in question.

It is useful to bear in mind that technology and ICT do not determine, but rather shape and mold society (Castells, 1999) on several fronts, including online educational programs; although they take charge of this telematic proposal, they are not wholly responsible for it.

Many and various gaps and asynchronies cling to a technical-instrumental logic and prevent or discard alternative choices, which could actually give these proposals profiles genuinely related to the intended educational change with equity and relevance.

Therefore, the level of knowledge and skills that a student acquires in an interactive educational distance program is less crucial than the weight of social values and attitudes prevailing in society as a whole, shifting towards an information and knowledge society relevant to the twenty-first century.

A theoretical-practical proposal for sociological analysis from the standpoint of the distance student should take up the parameters that characterize science (Kuhn, 1971) in its central features:

1) It should be an *empirically accurate* theory, with the necessary and sufficient evidence for the observation and recording of quantitative and qualitative data: in the case of sociology, as it does not necessarily achieve universal and definitive generalizations, it should rescue the positive features of specific analysis about what is being studied (in this case, the student's role in online programs) at a specific time and space, to advance in the production, extraction, and sharing of contextualized insights with other similar situations.

   With regard to the methodology used to delineate and interpret the collection of quantitative and qualitative data to feed such theories (not general but of medium scope), we refer to a systematic and reflective study -coherent from the logical point of view- which in sociology corresponds to the methodological design of a qualitative action research (Giddens, 1997), backed by a theoretical framework that provides such data its significance.
2) It should be *consistent with other theories accepted in thefield*: the sociological perspective of analysis today lies at a frontier of knowledge, understood as the intersection and synthesis of multiple determinations to achieve a unity of understanding from the diverse and the multidisciplinary.
3) It should be *simple*, in other words, comprehensible in its formulation, which makes it extendable not only to a level of professional *training,* but also to the general public, since the topics covered deal with and include the training of individuals and groups.
4) I should be *fruitful* for research via direct, current and later action, where the *horizons are expanded* allowing us to increase understanding of the phenomenon to be explained. We recall Popper's position when he argues that everything in science is tentative, subject to correction and replacement (Popper, 1965).

The distance student with ICT, like it or not, is immersed in the globalization of the fluid and open network society (Castells, 1999); they will have a real chance to be involved as a result of undergoing the process of developing and implementing their skills and abilities to complete activities and interact in real-time and on a planetary scale.

Within this continent of globalization, the student is connected in order to navegate and surf, which typifies the emergence of a new mentality: surfing is faster than swimming, and there is no need to plunge into a depth, in other words, there is a more *superficial* contact with the substance or reality in which a person moves. This illustrates what distance students do at the beginning in the electronic programs they choose.

Relationships that are only "skin-deep", encouraged and allowed by ICT connections, although useful to link people (and build social ties), are also easily dismantled (because they are ephemeral); among other sociological traits, they will characterize the telematic training interactions, or differentiate "those who are connected from those who are disconnected" in a world of unequal distribution of opportunities.

## SOCIALIZATION IN THE STUDENT'S ROLE IN DISTANCE EDUCATION PROGRAMS

In the process of socialization (Torres and Gonzalez Rivera, 1994) (Hess, 1969) that interests us, the following elements may be seen: an environmental or institutional structure; a set of beliefs, values, attitudes, etc..; designated agents of socialization; objects of socialization; a more or less formal teaching and learning process that makes this possible, in our electronic distance case; a product in terms of achievement that will be regulated or adjusted in actual practice.

In this context, it is understood that the socialization process is not neutral in a context that shapes social consensus, namely regarding the goals sought and the means to achieve them (Clausen, 1968). With regard to education, it is explicitly assumed that its main social function is to become an agent with social and labor roles, to be played based on consensus(Durkheim, 1965).

The concept of *habitus* (Bourdieu, 1997) closely linked to socialization, is defined as systems of durable provisions; structures formed and predisposed to function as structuring proposals, in other words, as principles of generation and configuration of practices and representations that may objectively be *regulated and be regulators*, that is, objectively be adapted to an end without supposing a conscious proposal of it nor the operations necessary to achieve them.

The *habitus* allows us to reflect both on the internalization of exteriority, to the extent to which it is the product of objective conditions, and the externalization of interiority, to the extent to which it organizes practices and thus contributes to the re- productive continuity of the structures.

This *mediating* concept makes it possible to restore to human practice its ingredients of *freedom and necessity*. Any practice, therefore, may be understood by articulating two always present dimensions: one which is a ritual, that is, mechanical, predictable, regular and regulated, and the other a strategic dimension, that is, conscious, free, improvised, original (Bourdieu, 1988).

Practices will no longer be mechanical reactions, forced and directed at the constraints of "structures" or historical, socioeconomic models, as explained in general in Marxist interpretations. They are mediated by the provisions of the social agents and operate as highly varied and diversified practice organizers that suggest a multiplicity of explanatory models, which, in turn, act as stimuli and catalysts for action.

However, this apparent, even chaotic, diversity in social practices, cannot be explained as a resource of the free subject and spontaneous creator, because the necessary practice, although relatively autonomous in relation to the specific situation under consideration, it is the product of the dialectical relationship between a situation and a *habitus* as a system of durable and transferable provisions. This takes place through the existence of transfers of mental schemes that allow problem solving by integrating past experiences, in order to function at any given moment as a matrix of perceptions, appraisals, and actions. This enables the completion of tasks, thanks to corrections or the monitoring that takes place depending on the results (Bourdieu, 1988). The habitus relates to a system of rules, principles which generate and organize practices and performances collectively orchestrated (Bourdieu, 1991), which, as a socialized body, is incorporated by individuals as part of the world and which structure perception and action.

Thus, for example, *habitus* developed within the family preside over the structuring of the subsequent school experiences and/or those that could sustain studies in the form of distance education in adulthood. In turn, *habitus* resulting from formal schooling function as a matrix for the structuring of work and professional experience, and so on. Therefore, any pedagogical action establishes -if not imposes- meanings as legitimate, which are maintained -if not perpetuated- in shaping schemes and provisions of thought and action in individuals and groups.

There are two typical ways to form *habitus*: learning from spontaneous and implicit familiarization, which accounts for practical knowledge, and pedagogical rational, planned, artificial, institutionalized work, which aims to learn provisions that are not natural but arbitrary cultural creations, formalized as precepts that are transmitted in practice (Bourdieu, 1979). This, as is perceived, is applicable to the proposals which, in mediated electronic contexts, would shape the profiles of students in distance education.

## THE LEGITIMIZATION OF DISTANCE EDUCATION PROGRAMS

Accordingly, an electronic educational program with ICT (as any other educational expression) legitimizes a pre-existing pattern of knowledge and values of the elder society, which then is reflected in the process of educating and training individuals and groups. This society may present, in turn, socioeconomic and cultural fractures and fragmentation, a cause and product of various kinds of inequality and, therefore, of the educational kind. It is worthwhile, then to recognize that these inequalities will have to be sought *outside* the education system and then are manifested within it in all its forms.

The implementation of distance education programs and the emergence of the social category of "virtual student" could be explained as a response to the failure of liberal policies based on the proposal of distance education programs to compensate for educational inequality, often resorting to proposals mediated by ICT to solve existing problems, especially in the peripheral countries.

Also, the development of late capitalism and the hypertechnologization of the digital society has sophisticated and ranked the occupational structure of transnational level. Faced with this new reality, it could be argued that the electronic-telematic distance education programs have emerged as manpower training proposals that attenuate drastic changes presented in the relationship between capital and labor, with the emergence of great contradictions in the new society.

In fact, the training proposals in general, and specially manpower training at a distance, although they historically arise as part of a quest for the democratization of knowledge, now, more than contributing to social equality or equity, satisfy the demands of economic enterprises (transnational organizations) to form a workforce tailored to the overall sociocultural conditions of the global society, via tele-educational proposals.

One could argue that the environment and telematic social relationships that distance students learn and develop through ICT, give or take a feature, support the characteristics of the current digital culture and especially prepare for the working conditions of global social organizations and/or telework, where several users are socialized and adapt to new realities, first as telestudents, and then as teleworkers.

Electronic distance education is a way to accompany the late capitalist structural economic development of the twenty-first century. Therefore, while it is important for the development of sociotechnological and central cognitive skills, the development of certain socioemotional features that contribute to certain forms of awareness relevant to new situations is more significant. Beyond agreeing with the new features, it should be acknowledged that they are required under the new digital societal frameworks. A high motivation, proactive behavior, positive predisposition and self-mastery or self-discipline, the quest for greater attention and necessary mental concentration, abilities to organize time and develop independent study habits and/or with a virtual group, quick and efficient adoption of new uses of new languages and artifacts (tiny and/or nanotechnology), change the sociocommunicational habits of individuals and groups.

From this perspective, distance students who adopt and adapt to the mentioned profiles will be successful,beyond deploying their abilities and traits consistent with their “multiple” intelligences. To this we add the rules that underpin mediated interaction with various technological-telematic support, since all of this would be part of the *hidden curriculum* within a socialization that shapes the consciousness and subjectivity of a telestudent.

It can also be explained along the lines of the *correspondence principle*, as evidenced by the similarities to certain features of the current digital social system, although it has received enormous criticism for its resonance to functionalist and/or reproductivist theories (Althusser). Said principle may explain the integration of young students in education systems through a structural correspondence between social relationships and the productive economic system, where education is regarded as a means to achieve this end, to contribute to success, and indirectly, to legitimize the existing (neoliberal)social order.

Thinking of alternative, anticipating modes, re-creating forms of electronic distance education and the role of the telestudent may serve to overcome the existing social order and promote the construction of a more equitable society where education plays a variable intervening role. This idea will be explored in the last chapter.

## The Socialization of the Student in an Online Distance Education Program

The positions concerning the overall process of socialization in a broad sense within which the subjectivities of the individuals are produced –members of a society from the relationships that they exchange with the environment- are enriched when said process is regarded not as unidirectional but as a bi/multidirectional process between agent and socializing instance. This occurs within a distance education program where the student's role is understood by his protagonism within the specificity in each proposal.

Thus, interdependent, contradictory, relationships of domination and search for balance of power, are presented in the mentioned telematic reciprocity, primarily through the virtual triad student-tutor-distant group.

However, it is within the larger sociocultural process where the subjectivities, in general, are shaped. From a macrosocial point of view, this means that people are born, develop, migrate, are uprooted (many becoming nomads, like "wasted" residue within globalization) (Bauman, 1999), as projections of new phenomena related to hybrid socialization of overlapping subcultures.

In the primary socialization of an individual (characterized by the first flows of family life), there are, now, juxtaposed social norms and interwoven values that enable this person to adapt to new situations (cities, employment, if found) and to broader social horizons where he/she self-regulates his/her behaviour and is able to survive.

These are not easy times, because people generally appear as separate and nameless results in the middle of everyday social destructuring/restructuring. There theyinternalize and re-create patterns of behaviour and contradictory values, if not opposed, which at the same time allow them -not without conflicts- to survive.

This process of socialization becomes *secondary* socialization, as a result of a social systemic spillover given by the incorporation of social, cultural and organizational formal norms and customs, existing within the current digital society.

The emergence of a tele-education program with ICT does not constitute a linear training proposal, as a disciplining social process, but refines and specializes the various requirements related to those areas and sectors that make up a social unit in crisis.

Thus, electronic online educational efforts are intermingled with traditional educational proposals, given today by blended learning options.

The above-mentioned positively enriched the analysis of the social integration of the student into the online educational program, according to numerous studies of the critical sociological perspective (Apple and Beane, 1997; Fernández Enguita, 1990; Giroux, 1990, and others) including the already mentioned "hidden curriculum".

In fact, we are dealing with the context in which online telestudents are inscribed – through a sociohistorical construction-, and where they acquire and demonstrate knowledge, not always explicit in telematic interactions, which cover academic, organizational, administrative and ethical contexts. The student´s varied performances are inferred through the ethnographic observation of everyday socioeducational virtual practices of distance education programs: most of it as "naturalized" behaviour. Thus, organizational climates appear as passive and reveal a high acceptance from the telestudents enrolled, of the conditions and rules established by the programs.

There is thus a logical structuring and regulation of distance learning, progress and performance parameters that the telestudent must carry out and demonstrate. However, there is a lack of explicit critical analysis regarding these frameworks, multi-directional communication and mediated activities that compose the pedagogical proposal.

This is worrisome in general, and even more so, if the users of the proposal are, for example, professionals and/or teachers in training; we should investigate whether these student users simply abide by the terms of the program. This aims to identify how they experience and learn to develop and exercise their rights and responsibilities with regard to personal and group participation and expression within said programs.

Accordingly, it would seem that a certain "model or profile" is to be expected from a distance student, which does not necessarily "institute new subjectivities and relationships." So, it is important to study and identify what characteristics are required of a student for each context and program.

In turn, we should acknowledge that "learning to be a distance student" might involve a certain degree of "symbolic violence" (Bourdieu, 1979) and that there would be other alternative forms that could be designed and expected for the performance of telematic students. The generation of some features would be a consequence of *learning contracts* that are designed and established by each program. This matters, not as traits of a secondary socialization in -doctorates, masters and non-formal distance learning offers of courses in businesses and corporations, of continuous learning (or *lifelong learning*) -, but as a proposal for development of communicative actions that are interwoven within and in interdependence with the specific context.

Parallel to the formal academic curriculum (given by the official content and methodological structure, educational materials, the instructions provided through tutorial communications, etc.), the reason why a person enrolls in a program, the hidden curriculum, full of symbolic relations, discourses, norms and values of the dominant subculture, with its countermessages, unofficial signals, conflicts, etc.. also has a high socializing power for the virtual student, especially when one considers thesocial control exercised in the program in question. As an example: on electronic networks through educational chats and forums as scheduled educational activities within the formative proposals, we see how in everyday collaborative exchanges of telestudents, in the re-created language -from a particular slang - , in the icons used, the jokes and music shared, etc.., one "learns" to be a student at a distance. The interaction in the program, its link with tutors, sharing recreational space or informal talks provided under the many technological platforms, allowing an individual to feel they belong (or not) to a certain gender or ethnic community, etc., forms a special subculture - given by the pervasive and permanent mediated interactions.

## MULTILINGUALISM AND INTERCULTURALISM

These are times of cultural and socio-economic globalization with the internationalization of markets and capital, cultural industries and hegemonies, monopolies of values and norms, which produce uniformity through control practices. These are times of new organization models given by the technological revolution, which mark serious mutations in the anthropological dimension of culture and society, from language to the ways of living to changes in the modes of production and circulation of knowledge, today increasingly digital/virtual.

The cultural space is fragmented by the presence of multicultures, multilanguages, and multireligions, in the face of which resistance to what is different may appear, or may even lead to violent and insecure climates; there could be mistrust of the distant, foreign or migrant group and lead to an aggressiveness and externalization of prejudice. Often, ethnic or religious minorities are perceived in sharp and irreconcilable opposition and these thoughts, feelings and actions do not escape people from various walks of life, including educational proposals in all of their manifestations, modes and media.

The new multicultural field explores identities and shapes other communities and cultures. Mediations with new technologies create a new heterogeneous subject connected in a complex way to a multiple environment: immediate and virtual, selective and massive, local and global, positional and nomad at the same time. To consider the subject in the information network, the notion of *interface* may be the key, understood (Bateson, 1986) as interaction between systems that are not entirely closed, as a space for trade,of transcoding and transubjectivity.We should consider the proposals of virtual distance interaction suggested by the electronic systems of education from this standpoint.

In this digital or electronic age, faced with this new mode of construction of the self, one might ask who are those who are "connected" and interact in this system and how the new cultural profiles under construction affect nomadism and transience, instantaneity and interculture, and thus the configuration of subjectivity.

Education, like culture, may be considered a somewhat agglutinative (or even proselytizing) activity because it seeks to convince, convert or socialize individuals and groups to abandon their old habits and replace them with other new or different, supposedly better ones.

The complex interrelationship between what is established and what is foreign, alien or different explains many of the conflicts between groups not only within the larger culture - national and transnational- but also within an educational program, in our case online distance program, where codes, standards and habits are diverse; often there appear bad behavior or prejudices through misunderstandings, which can result in marginalization and stigmatization, and thus cause a dropout of virtual students.

The term "multicultural"-as descriptive of the reality of today's societies where different cultures coexist and live together- is the key, like the term "intercultural", in a normative way, refers to the process of communicative exchange and interaction desirable in today's societies.

Understanding interculturalism from a sociological viewpoint requires including and considering, in all formal and informal socialization, the cultural code of the concerning society or group. This involves facets of an explanation that provides theoretical and practical elements to interpret knowledge verifiable in reality across multiple acts and ideas. So, today identity is configured in a multicultural society as a transparent dialectical relationship between the "I" and the "other", or between "we" and the "others" because "there is no identity without the existence of the "other".

Methodologically, in this context, ICT should serve to:

- produce, store, distribute and consume narratives and retranslation of different meanings,
- demonstrate perspective with critical views, of introspective and social confrontation;
- foster empathy, as the ability to feel mentally, emotionally and solidarily identified with the position and state of mind of another individual or group and their way of seeing the world;
- develop self-evaluation as the ability to recognize one's own ignorance in the analyses conducted and how one´s own patterns of thought and action shape (or not) the understanding that is achieved;
- use knowledge verified in an effective way to understand other social events in new situations and different contexts.

The intercultural paradigm is founded on understanding and dialogue between different cultures and identities, without falling into a superficial relativism, as it deals with cultural diversity within a *relational* framework, with dialogue between the common points in order to reach consensus. Proposing a relational universalism is relevant to the idea of emerging citizenry, with multiple loyalties, rather than a "universal" supranational or global citizenry.

Somehow it comes to creating a counterculture or alternative culture of synthesis –not a simple task-, which pursues and distinguishes the collective and creative use of discourses, meanings, materials, group processes and practices, in order to explore, understand and balance positions in a particular social setting.

The importance of multicultural and/or intercultural education is acknowledged in each educational program to equalize educational opportunities, with presence and representation of culturally distinct students. This is even more necessary when it comes to people with cultural disadvantages, which requires a rigorous and wise management in dealing with differences in order to alleviate the "dark side of globalization", subject to the rule or the opinions of the global market that generates serious dissociations and unresolved paradoxes.

Knowledge, now also with ICT, is culturally decentralized from its prevailing axis of the dominant culture in the formal education system with the book as the central force in the last five centuries of history. Other cultures and languages are discovered and triggered through unconventional ways, such as the online educational programs which from the standpoint of their electronic support prevail and clump together in various languages.

Interculturalism presents one of the greatest contradictions: on the one hand, other knowledge is produced and circulated beyond the prevailing control and reproduction and, on the other hand, as a frequent reaction, strong sociocultural standardization occur (in general and due to ICT ), which comes to threaten the freedom and re-creative expression of said groups through the coyuntural cyclical exercise of dominant or hegemonic groups. Such events require a lot of attention for further research on the production of sociocultural knowledge beyond the existing one, still marginal with regard to technologically mediated actions.

The presentation of cases and practice situations across different media and technological procedures of everyday use in these programs, to discuss the communities represented in virtual classes, promotes an awareness of linguistic variations, the alternative resources used, sociocultural interaction styles, etc.., that virtual students bring from families and different cultural communities and may contribute to the program (Area Moreira, 2003).

## A Sociotechnological Contribution for an Intercultural Education of the Citizenry

Online distance education constitutes fertile ground, not only to explore the theoretical and methodological aspects relating to the field of intercultural education for the training of the citizenry, from moral and political philosophy, but also to articulate and appropriate the tools and languages of ICT, concrete practices of interactive mediations, elimination of ethnocentrism and development of respect for diversity from a moral point of view.

The goal is, from this perspective, to overcome the reductionist sociological approaches, which have generally characterized the field of conventional educational technology, dedicated only to considering distance education as the application of resources or media in education, without considering the bases that support it.

Sociocultural settings are essential to understand paradigm shifts and their impact on society, culture, education and the citizenry of our time, but also recognizing their strong, transversal and ubiquitous presence, makes the consideration of an appropriate and critical educational technology proposal interesting for intercultural education for the citizenry, which increasingly will have greater weight in virtual distance learning.

Regarding technology and ICT from a substantive and not instrumental viewpoint, not only configures another rationality, new ways of thinking and acting, but also presupposes a critical view of sociology and technology, both inextricably linked to the digital culture of the global society.

Intercultural education consists of the generation, consolidation and sustaining respect for diversity in an emerging citizenry within the current world setting. This involves the great challenge, determination and commitment from governments, public and private organizations to train citizens through organizational and community projects of formal and non-formal, classroom-based and distance education.

Interculturality refers to interdependence, reciprocity, appreciation and practice, from the citizenry, in terms of respect for the difference of cultures. It involves critical and self-critical dialogue with intercommunication between different social and cultural groups. It supposes, within the communication held in educational programs in general and distance learning with ICT in particular, confronting and working towards the elimination of ethnocentrism and cultural stereotypes, which in turn involves the relativization of their own culture, the discovery and understanding of alternative values regarded as valid and preferable for choosing.

Therefore, the goal is to achieve maximum levels of development and maturation of sociocognitive, ethical, communicative and expressive-emotional skills which provoke various and varied fundamental epistemological and desirable ruptures in the interpretation and sociocultural practice of virtual interaction.

The practice of this intercultural education, which concomitantly works for peace entails and involves a profound transformation of social structures and organizations, and attitudes of all those involved in distance programs, including virtual students. It points to a statute that allows said users to exercise civic, political and socioeconomic rights and duties, and participate in public life with egalitarian exercise of diversified skills.

It is and will be necessary to co-exist in very different cultures and subcultures and deepen the individual´s training of *autonomous moral judgement* (Piaget, 1968), which requires *designing rich and powerful learning environments* (Perkins, 1995) mediated by processes, products and services –and centrally by teaching materials- distributed equitably by ICT or online, as multiple opportunities for communication so telestudents may build citizen understanding and respect. Learning to talk, making decisions based on consensus and working together in solving problems, playing different roles, learning languages, reflecting on situational contradictions, paradoxes and dilemmas strengthens the moral and sociocultural content seen in the values of liberty, equality, justice, peace, solidarity, responsibility and participation.

## The Path to Becoming a Virtual Student of an Electronic Distance Program

Any distance education program with ICT provides some context for development and exercise of basic and specific skills depending on the content and procedures that characterize it. It should offer, for each student, a satisfactory level to maintain their motivation and develop it further. This will depend on how the proposal is designed and how it is articulated, not only in the broader sociocultural context, but consistent with the provenance of the student to achieve an optimum point of interaction (and potential sociocognitive anchor) which may be articulated with the level of development reached thus far.The program should be characterized by a high degree of *socialcohesion*, containing and guiding its users/students by providing guidance and support in said context, which in terms of educational administration marks a strong and coherent proposal.

From the standpoint of a sociology of education, it should aim for the social modulation that said social unit exercises in its users. Students must internalize institutional rules, as well as work and communication routines according to time frames set by the organization, with answers depending on the demands given in the organizational charts they receive.

Furthermore, if this is an educational effort, it should propose and provoke challenges to understand and implement, in a demystified way, as well as revisit and create new and different ideas and concepts. This means that in addition to inscribing, disseminating and re-creating disciplinary content that characterize the proposal inserted within the broader cultural heritage, it should remove anachronisms and be the engine for sociocultural change, or at least its criticism and reformulation. This will be facilitated by the existing possibility of an internalization of a set of flexible rules and values that should characterize the online program in question: it is what constitutes its philosophy and wealth.

The socialization process will allow the idiosyncratic, adaptive and re-creative incorporation of an educational proposal by a subject who becomes not only a profitable online distance student, but also a person in full training, and later trained, according to the requirements of today's knowledge society. This process takes time: cultural objects that constitute an online program with their knowledge, values and procedures, shape and modulate the thinking and transfer into action as a result of several factors, including the interaction of technological supports selected for this program, the dominant hegemonic practices, forms of representation contributing to a reconstruction of society, subjectivities and their cultural context.

According to the disciplinary contents of each tele-education project, there should be a certain balance between maintaining, enhancing and reformulating the domains of symbolic capital for which the student approaches a tele-education proposal in cyberspace. The ultimate goal aims to promote and develop the training of the citizenry which faces the new era of the knowledge society with the formation of a technological mindset. The intelligent and relevant use of ICT with the preparation, evaluation and implementation of tools to shape said mentality, awareness and transform information into knowledge, in turbulent frameworks, is what characterizes the sociohistorical times we live in the twenty-first century.

The above-mentioned, however, is not without obstacles. Just to name a few:

1. Every society and culture (and subcultures) create their own emotional coordinates. The emotional formulas are cultural conventions that enable individuals and groups to build a world of interests, desires and expectations depending on the frame of reference of the particular time and context in which the individual/student interacts and socializes. In this setting there are powers, representations, misconceptions, prejudices and so on, which intersect. "Ambition and desire for fame are an example of the close relationship between emotions and the forms of expression of a culture" (Odeina and Halevi, 2004). Thus, the attraction felt by someone anonymous for

someone famous reveals something like an illusion of what was not experienced and is desired. One is famous for reasons that are not substantive, not as a result of the implementation of an action of significance. For example, you can become famous for enrolling in an expensive online educational program offered by a foreign university, although the student is not dedicated and cannot prove to have achieved prior learning merits.

2. The global virtual network society tends to create polarized and highly heterogeneous societies. From the viewpoint of users as students of distance programs of various kinds, and from a sociological analysis, there are problems of exclusion and marginalization-recognised as part of the current digital divide, namely: barriers to communication- due to a lack of infrastructure and connectivity-; ethical issues –due to the great diversity of languages and cultures not always acknowledged and respected; problems caused by the preponderance of English (another problem of exclusion), considered "lingua franca"; and the overabundance of not always valuable and useful information, without an entirely reflective reception by the user.
3. A student who wishes to join a distance education program should internalize a series of work routines, conduct patterns, institutional and subcultural rules typical of the organization (technical and administrative arrangements, guidelines and limits for communication, quality standards, etc.) or course he/she is enrolled in. He/she must become an active and reflective participant and/or member of an interactive learning environment mediated by ICT. This technology-mediated situation that characterizes socialization is not the result of the intrinsic property of technological devices used at a distance and online, but rather the composition and the attribution of meaning given by the various sources of the program.

   The virtual students who are successful in these new and complex situations of interaction with ICT are those who have possessed, managed or been able to develop a system of powerful predispositions to interact and decide in facing uncertainty, maintaining their basic assurance despite radical changes in all external circumstances.
4. Descriptivelly, other *obstacles facing the virtual student* may be: little motivation and little willingness; abundance of reading materials (print, audiovisual and telematic through the Internet); demands of work; concerns, etc.., all of which distract them; not having an incorporated pace, self-discipline and methodology of autonomous study at a distance; years without formal schooling; limited social contacts which are transferred to classmates and teachers; etcetera. Some of the ways to work towards integration might include: providing free access to technology in connectivity and offering the necessary technological literacy to operate equipment and understand instructions regarding the tools and symbolic languages with sustained tutorial guidance.
5. Among other difficulties, there is the need to learn and practice a comprehensive reading of digital text, and a critical reading on the reliability of the site/program on the Internet in order to demystify ideologies and "isms" in general.

   Here we point to not only the intelligent use of ICT, but also the optimization of the conditions of the work-study process carried out by the person enrolled in an online tele-education course, to achieve a virtual learning. Everyone knows the value of evaluations prior to entering the program, which provide knowledge to those responsible of the general and specific characteristics of entrants, and which is useful for the user´s (metacognitive) self-awareness so that he/she may become a protagonist of the proposal.

The program as a responsibility should explicitly teach (Fainholc, 2004), a minimum requirement of the hypermedial symbolic language of the Internet, as well as a methodological *expertise* to conduct analysis of online texts. Learning to criticise and deconstruct semiological components, the ideology of the text submitted, seeking the credibility of the same, and so on. is highly productive and unavoidable; it is necessary to train expert hyperreaders (Burbules and Callister, 2001) and reflective navigators, as well as optimizers of all digital resources of virtual communication and virtualization tools (weblogs. Wikies, simulations, etc.) offered by an online educational program.

6. Other elements of the virtual student role seek to strengthen their prosumption (Drucker, 1994), which involves not only using the program, now with a clear and exploratory reading of concepts and relationships, but the individual and group production of knowledge as the information provided is resignified. Information management skills, with the development of information organizers in semantic maps, will enable a "virtual sociopedagogy" for the understanding (Perkins, 1995) and the empowerment of various human intelligences (Gardner, H. 1982 ) through the symbolic codes presented by the virtual learning environments with ICT and the Internet.

The skills to be developed -described below- will allow the telestudent to recognize and respect the technical and administrative rules established by the tele-education program for his/her enrollment and integration into the system, with the consensus-based acceptance of the management patterns that are expected to be used in learning.Friendly communication, with feedback, with tutors, respectful coexistence with colleagues to carry out collaborative work and participation in forums, weblogs or others, are part of the socialization process that every student should undertake in order to become an effective and studious participant within the organizational and virtual culture which characterize the distance education program he/she is enrolled in.

Thus, the critical socioeducational theory helps to consider and highlight various flaws and shortcomings of the distance education systems and how they affect the specific contextual inclusion of telestudents, since they are necessarily involved in a virtual social construction, with its inherent features, trends and limits. In other words, it is necessary to recognize the conditions and obstacles that appear in shaping the roles of telestudents in distance education programs with ICT.

## The Use of ICT, the Conventional Student and the Virtual Student

If the goal is to outline the virtual distance student, one could say that they are young adults of both sexes between the ages of 28 and 45, married or living with a partner, with specific work and place of residence, with some or medium level of socialization in the use of

ICT and who wish to improve their standard of living. This is why they enroll in higher training electronic distance courses, because they possess greater flexibility than traditional courses, although all the training received thus far has been from traditional attendance.

In fact, the difference with conventional students is that they present a willingness for interaction with ICT and do not have as much time available as face-to-face students, who happen to reside near the university campus or have moved there because of the good technological and telecommunications infrastructure in classrooms.

Virtual students may present two types of behaviour: a higher degree of virtualization, more autonomy and expertise in habits and implementing various procedures for specialized content, a willingness to concentrate, read and study, with good organization of their scarce free time (which gives them less time to rest) and self-discipline; whereas another type of virtual student presents a low level of cognitive flexibility, less independence despite having a hard personal and work schedule (they work, are married, etc.).

They should all maximize the limited time they have, so after their everyday job, or at night, they enter the virtual campus with their customized passwords. They surf around the course and around the world almost every day, without leaving their homes, have discussions with classmates guided by their tutor, thousands of miles away and without having met face-to-face. They ask classmates out to cybercafes because they possess a virtual warm –although not deep- relationship, to talk about different topics related to their study and, perhaps, others.

These students generally benefit in comparison to face-to-face students; they only need to connect to the Internet and can stroll through the campus or do the required exercises to be sent to the tutor in order to pass the course.

In all cases, we are referring to an urban middle class student, from a family with complete schooling, medium/high sociocultural level and economic availability to pay the tuition for the virtual training course.

But there are problems, as well as the obstacles mentioned, which a distance student faces… online users come from societies in constant turmoil and transformation, and face very different socialization situations, which have presided the the shaping of their subjectivities: people from rural areas who must adjust to urban codes, women prepared to be homemakers who now work, students who come to institutions and programs which are organized in a way that is very different to what they are accustomed to, and so on.

There is very likely a mismatch between the *habitus* possessed and the interaction conditions in a new electronic educational setting. The result may be a person divided, beset by contradictions and in a process of restructuring when facing the unknown.

In this situation of ubiquitous social ambivalence and anomie, a critical sociology of distance education should inquire about the specific social conditions that promote, in the best way possible, intercultural processes and responses, which are solidary and integrated at the same time, within a social whole that must contain and transcend them. At the same time, it should be recognized that distance education programs, even more so those with ICT and for Latin America in particular, should have another meaning, introducing other dimensions and social expectations to help develop complementary but central capabilities for conventional educational proposals.

While an online distance education program via the Internet can be, in theory, the option of equitable distribution and democratization of information through student access, it often becomes a barrier to overcome: a lack of tools preventing the student from establishing horizontal and transparent communication relationships; a lack of cognitive strategies, which leave him unable to exploit the more abstract functions of thought; an absence of individual and institutional facilities, among others, have excluded peoples and regions from digital development.

There are, thus, abysmal distances -and not just physical- which should be acknowledged and settled and overcome before installing distance education systems. Feasibility studies and various sociopolitical decisions contextualized with reflection, of a strategic nature, should cover key social groups to settle old (and new) forms of social, informational, digital exclusion. Otherwise, the construction of subjectivity -relational reality and changing interactive product- will lead to poor, fragmented, and uneven tele-training proposals.

For the generation and consolidation of a proper socialization of the virtual student in electronic educational proposals, it should be understood that artifactual means -with their symbolic language and specific properties-, while helping to structure mediated interaction processes, need the allotment of flexible time and space to appropriate the corresponding tools for the respective technological environment. Thus, the subject is identified and performs according to the expectations and profiles of certain social roles and communicative actions depending on the particular technological environment and linked to what it means to study online, which is possibly connected to his/her future work, occupation or profession in the network society.

The respectful intersubjective and interactive dialogue with other students, immersed in the same subculture of online distance education, contributes to the acquisition of the capacity to act according to models of social relevance characteristic of the virtual times.

The artifactual mastery needed by the virtual student is becoming increasingly important in these educational programs. Cell phones, wireless personal networks, peer to peer file sharing, digital video capture and editing, and all possibilities of interactive telematic work (mobile computing and communication) increase the flexibility which is typical of online educational programs, complementing (and sometimes replacing) the possibilities virtualization attaches to existing conventional educational programs.

Not all virtual students enrolled in a program are equally successful. Sometimes it is argued that with minimal socialization there would be a similar adjustment to sociocurricular proposals, without considering that there are factors of socioeconomic differentiation and belonging to various subcultures that should not be disregarded or hidden due to their great influence on favorable educational processes and outcomes. If there are or occur problems of adaptation, socialization and integration into the conventional face-to-face educational proposals -at all levels of schooling and throughout the world-, we mustn´t think that online educational programs are exempt from or have overcome these issues, even more so in Latin America. The differences in habits, skills and attitudes, as already indicated, are significantly associated to the socioeconomic and cultural origins of the students enrolled and affect their student work-study process, their completion of the program in the desired time, their ability of retention and possible outcomes.

These variables are "anchored" (or not) on a pre-existing framework which favors (or not) a know-how, an everyday knowledge, with routines and an atmosphere of social interactions that reference the virtual student, even more so if it comes to university degree and postgraduate educational levels. At these levels there are several "inherited" characteristics which are put into practice by their prior socialization and sociocultural affiliation (Bourdieu, Chamboredon and Passeron, 2002) and which promote an evident academic productivity and profitability, depending on the socioeconomic level of the user/student.

While there may be scholarships that favor students with a poor pre-existing virtual educational and technological repertoire, the issue is not resolved only with financial aid. The quality and the floor for interactions are not only refocused because there is more money to provide income and other requirements established in a higher education program. Nor with only a few a reforms in the curriculum or the mere incorporation of technology in distance programs, since these would only superficially attack some traits that do not contribute to true equity and the improvement of student yields with all the consequences that this entails. The sociological analysis that demystifies the social factors of cultural inequality should be implemented with concrete measures, which require specific socioeducational mediations, for example, the reformulation of inequities with the guidance of tutors, who with relevant strategies ofsocial compensation and "corrective teaching" encourage virtual students so as to enable the modification or "change in the social heritage".

Educational programs with ICT of pure online or blended learning, due to their flexibility, could adopt some of these measures and incorporate them into their instructional design.However, large scale industrial proposals rule, which operate with supposedly neutral instructions, of a general pretension, which become "more obvious" to those students who come from more equipped social sectors.A lot of knowledge cannot be handled nor mastered because it cannot be possessed, in spite of the individual willingness and effort placed on it on the part of students who come from poor levels, ethnic groups, or women.

This is why, all programs must provide, by way of compensation, the necessary elements so individuals may interact in non-traditional frameworks and promote the acquisition of skills and attitudes that will enable authentic intellectual work and social integration.

## OBSERVATIONS ON DROPOUT RATES IN DISTANCE EDUCATION PROGRAMS

*We refer to "dropout" when a student in general, and especially, a virtual one, interrupts in a premature way a study proposal (or course) and, consequently, gives up his/her responsibilities of follow-up, completion, and delivery of the respective practice work and examinations.*

The dropout rate is calculated, each year, by dividing the number of studentswho withdraw from a course without having sent any practice work or having taken any exams, by the total number students who enrolledand started the course.One problem arises: where do we include or count those who interrupt the course, and then some time later, return to complete it? It is necessary to differentiate them from those who completely abandon a course. It is an important aspect, since the number of students who interrupt a course is considerable (more than 60% in less developed countries).

Dropping out or deserting a distance program, from the virtual student's point of view, could also involve a feeling of failure, the frustration ofa hope he/she had at the beginning of the course and/or giving up something that had been deemed important in their lives.From the university's point of view, dropouts could also be considered a failure, if not a damage, since students withdraw from training proposals and courses which had been prepared with great care, money, and work.

The causes of dropout could be related to adult age, the genre and type of work carried out by students; also a lack of background information; a low socioeconomic level, with a lack of independent study habits; low academic level; lack of self-control and self-confidence, as well as professional ambition; low commitment levels for an integration into the program and the group with other students through collaborative work and a reluctance to turn to instructors/tutors for guidance and orientation.

## DIFFERENCES BETWEEN THE CAUSES OF DROPOUT IN DISTANCE PROGRAMS AND THE CAUSES OF DROPOUT IN CLASSROOM-BASED PROGRAMS

While in this modality some of the causes of dropout could be a lack of motivation and interest, with the feeling that the course is not contributing anything new, or a rejection to the way of teaching –beyond scarce economic and technical means-, it may be argued that most of the adult student dropouts –even those possessing their own economic and technical means- occur due to communication problems (Mercer, 2001), above all in collaborative group work.

In distance education, in order to foresee and counteract possible dropouts, it is essential to give attention to the structuring of not only the content to be transmitted in order to generate significant learning in students, but also frame rich situations of support through mediated communication and interactions.

From a sociological point of view, dropout could be analyzed as a conflict between the student and the educational program; also a possible cause of the withdrawal is the need to work and care for a family with a reduction of availability, with high fixed costs and low variable costs (contrary to classroom-based university courses). This evidence points to the fact that the road that leads to the decision to study at a distance and remain in a program is paved with doubts and difficulties which call for not only greater reflection and investigation, but also require a case-by-case analysis.

Among some of the strategies that may be used to address distance student dropout, we should identify those with a higher risk of dropping out, so as to offer them specific aid opportunities, and consider that dropout is inversely proportional to socioeconomic level and educational background of the virtual students, in general, before their enrollment, which leads to more refined economic analysis within these programs.

Can distance student dropout be studied with the same concepts and instruments with which face-to-face education is studied?Can student dropout in traditional programs be studied with the same concepts and instruments with which electronic educational programs with ICT and Internet are analyzed? Can student dropout in electronic educational programs in central countries be studied with the same concepts and instruments with which these proposals are analyzed in peripheral countries and regions? Are we dealing with the same causes of dropout or a lack of social and academic integration?There is still an absence of socioeducational studies to deepen the theoretical-practical field of distance education with the use of ICT.

# Student Intercommunication in Online Distance Education Programs

*Are distance students more communicated or increasingly isolated? Since the last decade of the twentieth-century, a contribution has been perceived towards a great transformation in communication relationships, which are technologically manifested in the global telecommunication networkTherefore, another epistemology arises and is established, which involves a tremendous discontinuity in cultural, as well as generational and epochal changes.*

The Internet, chat, SMS, Instant Messaging (IM), I-pod, YouTube, weblogs, Second Life, among others, amplify and influence the exchange, mediated communication and socialization processes, to shape new technological environments confirming an enormous impact of ICT in shaping subjectivity through the learning environments of distance education.

The involvement and multi-million dollar investment of large computer and telecommunications companies play an important role in the process described. These companies donate equipment (computer and printing, communications, audio-visual editing, etc..) and grant economic contributions for the testing, development and implementation of technological innovations, such as those in mobile technologies and wireless infrastructure which later reach the education sector, which in turn pushes for their (not always relevant) transformation.Various adjustments are thus planned and redesigned to incorporate mobile devices (laptops, interactive simulations, digital cameras, etc.).

In cyberculture, the semiological-sociological relationships given by -synchronous and asynchronous virtual mediations- gain strength in comparison to physical face-to-face relationships, which lose strength, but fortunately do not disappear. The feeling of overcoming geographical and time barriers to participate in "something magical", such as capturing what seems to be remote and elusive, or perhaps the anonymity that characterizes many electronic communications, stimulates a lack of inhibition, and communications by e-mail, chat, blogs, and text messages on mobile phones grow in different social settings.

While access and use of mobile communications spread from the sociocultural point of view, due to the low level of discrimination presented in their interaction, it is still difficult to get individuals and groups to join the larger society without exclusions. Moreover, although the beliefs more entrenched in the current social imaginary on emerging technologies indicate that ICT homogenize social groups, promote equality between its members and democratize culture, digital divides are enormous and continuing (with the exception of the referred use of mobile phones): ICT conceal serious inequalities and produce significant generational and educational inequities. Many adolescent/young adult users (between 12 and 29) distance themselves from their elders, which in turn, among other considerations, tends to perpetuate the myth that new technologies are just for young people as part of a generational rite.

Generational gaps are also detected among young people themselves: the younger ones, for example, use technologies that the others do not know about or do not make the most of, which ultimately makes them "in or "out", belong or be excluded;for many young people this involves social and cultural connotations of great weight because they are excluded from certain social relationships and/or lose opportunities in communications, work and others in terms of social belonging.

Virtual students incorporate and use communication devices in everyday relationships and interactions demanded by distance education programs for the completion of pedagogical tasks, tutorials, exchange among peers, etc.., through cell phone text messages (SMS), which are dynamically different from regular asynchronous messages through e-mail and/or weblogs.

Accordingly, and in relation to the above mentioned, it can be argued that the use and handling of new technology influences and is influenced decisively by social class, gender, ethnic origin, cultural and technological environment in which thestudent has grown (whether or not there is a computer at home, connected friends, etc.). and the institutional environment at the schools he has attended previously and currently attends. It is not only related to the existing predisposition in the participants and their availability to talk, nor with the different size of the technical devices used: while the cell phone is small and possesses an "uncomfortable" alphanumeric keypad, the computer has a large enough keyboard and screen to fully capture the attention. Nor is it related to the possibility that the user student has to make "stable contact lists", and that these lists are extended and modified in the chats. Structural factors and interdependent multicausal reasons, in terms of social, economic, cultural and organizational status, exist and characterize the broader societal situation where the electronic educational program in question is inscribed.

Along with the features of instantaneity, spontaneity, speed, etc.., which characterize and encourage these mediated operations there are, concomitantly, various risks that must be acknowledged. The cell phone, text messaging and weblogs, as new means for remote communication, deserve to be studied in relation to the profiles of social, economic and psychological contexts users belong to within the prevailing digital culture. Depending on the technological-educational design, they will be more or less inserted as the principal or auxilliary means within electronic training proposals where educational telematic interactions are developed (Rheingold, 2004).

Some theorists claim that "the presentation of self" the way in which each person and group communicates for a typical communicative action is chosen, in other words depending on the specific audience addressed and vocabulary used (Goffman, 1959).

The groups virtual students belong to possess the conception that these individuals have of themselves. This is manifested in the mobile communication supports and media selected:text messages (SMS and others) as well as the choice of recipients or reply procedures are substantially used by young users, whose characteristic of versatility and speed intervene in modeling their individual and group identity within social networks.

Beyond the obvious explanation of the key role of adolescents and youths in the spread of mobile phones and messaging, the fact remains that this contributes to a non-accessory role in distance education, in versatile communications with their tutors, in addition to those informal communications they engage in with their course mates, in a more egalitarian way.

But being more communicated does not mean that the stages of loneliness and isolation that characterize contemporary cyberspace and even mediated interaction have been overcome. As they are very communicated with shrunk vocabulary, without sharing a lot of content or information of little significance, in the midst of restricted human relationships and covered with "technological sadness", people choose virtual worlds as substitutes for real experiences because, in spite of it all, they provide social positioning and prestige.

The option is to not only overcome the instrumental logic and linear artefactual rationality which become, in these coordinates, an end in itself, but rather frame these actions within an expressive-communicative recursive media rationality, inscribed within another epistemology, in other sociocultural relationships and within another ethic, to strengthen core values which are in crisis and require several re-thinkings.

## THE SUCCESS OF A DISTANCE STUDENT

Although we do not agree that the quest and achievement of success in terms of academic results is what characterizes the good performance of a distance student, today the consideration of the results obtained prevails, within the society of ephemeral cyberconsumerism, rather than the training processes experienced by various protagonists.

One could argue what an online distance student requires is associated with the mechanisms underlying the "learning by doing", through the help of others (Vigotsky and PDZ in Moll, 1992). This provides the framework for trial and error, and reflecting on the various sides that make up the individual and shared tasks. There is also the ability to confront achievements in terms of goals and timetables pursued in a meaningful way (or intrinsic motivation), in an environment where they feel safe and esteemed, a risk-free environment where the work carried out possesses the appearance of real work, which encourages commitment, reasoned experimentation and decision-making to live its consequences in a manner applied to action. The motivational and socio-cultural affiliation factor with personal recognition/guidance constitute central variables for the successful study and performance of distance students.

Such success would depend on the development of some skills in telestudents-and by extension, all people in general of the information society- namely:

1. for information management (IMS);
2. media, expression and communication;
3. critical reading on the Internet.

1. The challenge of developing Information Management Skills to assist in the search, evaluation, organization and use of information gathered from various electronic sources and not always rich in content, has deep projections for designers and managers of distance education programs, as well as for the conventional educational system. Such is the case of weblogs, where anyone can post whatever they want on the Internet, in an easy and inexpensive way, without any control or verification of quality.

    IMS involves being able to clearly define a topic or content and research area; select keywords to facilitate the search, expressing the concept; formulate a search strategy that includes the various sources of information and understand the ways in which it is organized. One must be trained to analyse the data collected in order to assess its relevance, quality and convenience to process information and turn it into knowledge. The IMS, beyond developing competency in managing computer tools, requires a deep knowledge of how information systems operate and of the dynamic link between the required information and sources used to satisfy any need for the same. This aspect undoubtedly will be a prime requirement for students who want to "learn to learn", in general, and in distance education systems in particular, within a "lifelong learning" proposal.

Perhaps somewhat excessive expectations are placed on these training proposals of telematic communications that ICTs are intended to promote: connecting students with each other and with their instructors/tutors, as well as these with their peers, forming educational communities and producing knowledge from action-research, as a central trigger for distance education programs.

The key issue remains whether computers are truly effective and relevant in the training process of an individual (the conclusions of numerous studies about whether computers improve the actual process of learning are categorically unconvincing). The findings, still under revision, lean towards a combined selection of mediations and media, depending on users, social settings, sociocultural and educational objectives and content to be managed and distributed.

It is true that the potential is inmense, but "maximizing" is not synonymous of success in terms of learning processes and teaching products. The use of simulators enabled by computers helps distance collaborative work, as well as instructors/tutors and students to process useful information, but do not have the last word: doubts and confusion abound.

Just to mention and illustrate the above-mentioned with only one statistic, we know that U.S. students are placed, at the international level, in the 12th to 18th position in the areas of mathematics and physics, while Asian students are in the first positions. The American students have much more access to computers than other students. What do Asian educators, for example, do that Americans and others should emulate? Learning depends crucially on what some teachers do best: *light a flame in the hearst of studenst, guide them, care for them, and be a model for them.* None of these attributes is communicated easily through the information market.

2. *Communication skills* may be defined as the complex set of knowledge (concepts, procedures, attitudes, values, etc.). implemented in reflective and verified practice in a situation of mediated communication, where players can critically deploy their expression within a situation designed with a rich and balanced distribution of opportunities to choose from and implement communicative acts. It is also where the exchange of emitters/receivers (EMIREC) becomes apparent in two-way dialogue. It contributes, thus, in an equitable, representative and assertive way, to appeal to all audiovisual and electronic symbolic codes, to form various possible, expressive and creative communication paricipations, within a framework of trust and good faith between partners in a social group. The structuring of educational content and activities would thus be carried out through technological supports of horizontal proposal within a circular communicative pattern.

   *Media skills* are understood as the expressed capacity for analysis and production of expressive and communicative possibilities, with cognitive and sociocultural appropriation of the different types of languages –today in technological convergence on the Internet- in order to assess and complement their wealth and limitations, their differences and similarities –intersected by the variables of gender, age, religion, ethnicity, geography, culture, etc. The hypertrophy of persuasive consumeristic messages (hyperconsumption, contents of social, racial, sexual discrimination, etc.). within a global marketplace, appearing today in all mass media and ICT and the

Internet, should be offset by the development of reflective and deconstructive awareness previous to their selection and adoption.

3. Together with the new virtual communication matrices -ICT not only as another means of sharing information, but of communication and expression-, there is the need for their explicit teaching and thus, learning the practice of a *critical reading on the Internet.* Reading, in general, is the situated process of activation of sociocognitive frameworks in an individual interacting with a text (print, visual, auditory, computer, etc..), where he/she employs and recreates cognitive and metacognitive strategies to configure different packages of information. In other words, reading on the Internet helps to understand near and distant significant sociocultural discourses through the dominance and the application of the symbolic code of the telematic networks where the text is encoded.

   The Internet coding process takes place in a connective, hypertextual, and interactive way.This is whythe Internet points to a sociocognitive and perceptual activity where, by means of sociocultural mediations and appropriations and in interaction with other resources, the individual and collective imaginary is recreated through telematic paths towards a reconstruction of knowledge (Fainholc, 2004).

   If the goal is to develop the participation of a telestudent in a virtual community, it is recommendable to study the conditions and frameworks where the interaction is materialized, beyond the tools that every environment should offer.The new sociocultural imaginary of the twenty-first century, in which online educational programs and their virtual students are inscribed, should be concerned with other realities, such as technoscience, democracy with expanded representation, and theemergence of a digital citizenry participating in the Internet, among other issues.Therefore, the values that would constitute the basis for these programs could well become topics to work on so as to demystify the hegemonic socioeducational realities presented in the virtual learning environments of a massive industrial type.

## STUDENT INTERCOMMUNICATION IN ONLINE DISTANCE EDUCATION PROGRAMS

The interaction that occurs in a virtual learning environment is different from the one that occurs in a face-to-face or classroom-based environment, because its specific characteristics in the forms of relationship and interaction are different, in other words different mediations occur. Current studies which refer to the interactions mentioned are still deficient in their ability to provide more comprehensive interpretations about the sociocultural profiles -except those related to statistical descriptions that most of the e-learning platforms provide with quantitative and automatic information. Information concerning the number of interventions on the part of students, their duration and distribution, among other things, are useful to obtain a first approximation on the interactions produced in virtual space, but are insufficient for the investigation of sociocultural processes that are generated. Therefore, we must define objects of study and combine analysis methodologies to account for new communication processes configured from social interaction and educational technological interactivity in order to overcome myths and/or prejudices given by the actions resulting from numerical participations in the various programs in question.

The phenomena and processes related to social interaction and virtual educational-technological interactivity -which should be deepened, not only jeopardize the achievement of mediated learning based on the reception (passive learning) and/or activities of discovery, simulation, problem solving and implementation in the field (learning by doing), but constitute the core of the configuration of subjectivities through the communicative exchanges between students and tutors, in learning communities or others. Based on the existing incentives, a student becomes a good virtual student and an increasingly skillful thinker, where he/she reconfigures his/her "situated subjectivity".

While the raison d'être of these electronic online systems consists of fluid exchange between individuals and groups, it does not always take place. For several reasons: while interaction, mediations and communication are central, more than once, educational institutions or organizations use technological forms and tools which are not developed through the intervention of individuals and/or specialized educational design teams who recreated proposals, and there were few suggestions from direct users, namely, the students and tutors of said online educational programs.

In interaction with ICT, presented in a curricular, communicative and interactive online proposal, there is not always true awareness of the implication of the nature of the "processes, phenomena, and actions of interaction" -as so many others- requested during the distance learning and which require much expertise on the part of those involved. Recognizing the new interactive virtual roles that are expected and required from the distance student involves, from the standpoint of a socioeducational analysis, asking ourselves about the characteristics of this interaction, describing positive and negative traits within the specificity of each project, its obstacles, potential conflicts, power relationships, etc.., which are different from those expected, and underscore a reality that requires further analysis both for the classroom-based student as well as the distance student using conventional means. This does not mean that the same study categories or variables are not being used for the analysis of the didactic or psychosocial interaction, from theories and tools hitherto known in the social sciences.

It is necessary to consider and recognize how little is known about each element that makes up the interactive educational process mediated by ICT faced by the virtual student on a daily basis. In the current state of development of these programs -as in other spheres of the greater social reality-, there is much to be explored and deepened in terms of the causes, problems and conflicts, difficulties and frustrations involved in human communication, more so in these cases with electronic interaction rules, with deadlines for interaction patterns, with correction parameters, etc.. typical of the formal educational programs.

## What does an Online Student Need and Expect

1. *Technical-administrative, sociopedagogical, and cultural support services* to aid interpersonal communication systems, with immediate feedback, which any distance education program must possess. It involves providing all the elements necessary to meet the demands of the virtual student, before, during, and after his/her integration into the educational program in question. It involves receiving, online, any guidance and socioeducational support,as well as the entire content, the work methodology and

technical operation, didactic and assessment activities, bibliography and webliography corresponding to the content, with their respective assignments to be completed and sent for correction, communicating the criteria and parameters for this. Moreover, it involves receiving instructions in order to communicate, depending on demands and needs, with his/her tutor, receiving a list of email addresses of all the individuals who will be attending the course or class in order to establish work, exchange, research groups and communities and so on.

They must also be attuned to and aware of all of the services provided by the program, for example, library service to lend bibliography, links to other websites, media library where they may request/receive CDs, videos, etc.. , timetables for teleconferencing, updated dates for chats as well as various kinds of assessment, instructions to interact in forums, participation in more informal logs (diaries), etc.., registration of assessment service for consultation and self-control of learning, cafeteria, and so on.

Moreover, they must manage the accreditation of their learning process, validated by the authorities of the program, of the national and international agencies for evaluation, certification and accreditation, in terms of the quality of education offered.

2. *Assistance in strengthening their autonomy and independence*, which will depend not only on the amount of dialogue proposed by the program in its design and held in a concrete way in the everyday reality of study, but also on the degree of *transactional distance* proposed by the program in terms of the structuring of activities that the student must carry out, by *the quality of the underlying values and attitudes* and the co-responsibility that stems from the mediated synchronous and asynchronous communication and interactions planned by the program.

   Feelings of belonging, expressed identifications, underlying displeasure, disagreements, misunderstandings in synchronous or asynchronous circumstances, and so on. may appear in technologically mediated conversations, which will demonstrate the level of cohesion with high or low productivity and sociopedagogical and cultural integration through the (real or potential) existence of inevitable conflict and an awareness of these, the willingness to recognize them, accept them, manage them and solve them.

3. *Motivational strengthening* through specific emotional incentives which promote the attachment of the virtual student to the program, with increased productivity in learning, independent and voluntary overcoming of (personal and group) difficulties and conflicts and a greater commitment to their studies, avoiding a possible dropout from the program. In other words: the student needs to palliate his/her different types of flaws, often economic, infinite flaws of a sociocultural nature, and increasingly of an educational nature, which require a multiple motivational strengthening.

   There may also appear diverse linguistic and cultural clashes related to degraded study habits, poor concentration in the completion of activities, little commitment in the organization of time in a fruitful manner for a responsible kind of work, etc.., which are some of the behaviors displayed by virtual students as they enter the system. These are behaviors that may still be evident once the course has started and which cause the student situations of delay, fear, shame of ridicule, dropout, and so on. and due to the same, not consulting the tutor -of paramount importance to his/her role- or his/her peers.

The salient features of a conduct expected from a virtual distance student from the socioeducational point of view, relates to: demanding contact and seeking satisfaction through a tutor´s guidance, for example, when there is a lack of comprehension of the content or inconsistencies in some text received, the corrections made of the activities in response to e-mails and so on.

That is, the goal is to expect, verify, and gain access to guidance and advice through all the avenues made available by theprogram, with regard to the work-study to be carried out, the delivery of exercises and evaluations, and so on.; the goal is to seek attention to meet specific needs, above all, strengthen listening and guidance through social interaction.

*Chapter 7*

# The Sociocultural Analysis of Tutorial Actions in Distance Education with ICT

In today's world and society, crisscrossed by telematic networks in transit and/or with shifting paradigms, the systems of positions and social roles expected in institutions and organizations are in crisis and moving towards others, not fully defined yet. While they are under review and reconfiguration, we can say that educators will no longer be able to teach the same content with the same methodology, tutors working on distance education programs (now in online connective articulation) will have to adopt and constantly recreate new roles within different educational proposals, even more so if the analysis framework is concerned about mediations that frame objectives and actions within a critical-reflective revisit of history, society and the organization where the educational effort is developed.

In times of structural ambiguity and uncertainty, there is blindness in knowledge given by error and illusion; deceptive everyday visions emerge, which lead to practices, in this case, wrong tutorial actions as they omit or fail to recognize central features. The establishment, definition, and comparison in practice of the roles to be played by tutors as they carry out their actions, will be achieved by deciphering the underlying concepts within the framework of the "new sociology of education." Its pillars are social phenomenology, ethnomethodology, and symbolic interactionism, among others, which emphasize the idea that reality is constructed by the subjects in negotiation processes.

The theoretical, methodological and comprehension problems of the above-mentioned processes occur because studies often remain linked to a "spontaneous epistemology", affirmed in a functionalist and intuitional positivism characteristic of an intellectual activity of a previous sociological reflection (Bourdieu, Chamboredon and Passeron, 1975) or not relevant to a more comprehensive integration required today.

The sociology of education can not wander –although it continues to do so- between the enunciation of a/some social theory/ies with no contrasting and empirical data with no theoretical basis, at the risk of falling into poor and reduced depictions of their socioeducational and cultural explanations and hence failing to contribute towards furthering knowledge, disciplinary research, improvement of practices and so on.

In our opinion, this is what has happened and still happens in the study of distance and online programs and with the role of the tutor and tutorial actions to be carried out in general, and especially with ICT. While descriptions of innovations or "best practices" abound,they are in general testimonies which remain in the descriptive stage. Often these interpretations are likely to be transferred to various cases and fall into several transpositions: technological, of semiological formats, didactic, and so on.

The approaches of sociology –so they may be useful and valuable in epistemological and authentically disciplinary terms- should overcome the classic opposition between rationalism and empiricism in order to advance the theoretical and practical knowledge in a consistent and at the same time reliable manner (Bourdieu, Chamboredon and Passeron, 1975). This task should be part of the role of tutors andtheir actions in electronic online distance education.

Within these processes, the actors create “objectivations” as elements of common sense that serve to understand the behavior of others and allowing them to explain their worlds with meanings that may often be inferred. Examples of such objectivations may be the variables of intelligence and its various types, social classes, ethnic groups, styles of organizations, etc.. Their background is distance learning which is conceived as the product of negotiations on these meanings given among students, between each of them and the tutor, with materials designed to structure the disciplinary content, and so on.

The challenge of the tutors and their actions in online tele-education systems, as educational counselors at a distance, will be in deciding whether they will “perform” not only to promote a facilitation in student learning, but also contribute to a social control or change from said online programs, what intentional social influence they will exert (can, should, or choose to exert…) to strengthen (or not) the prescriptive purposes of an organization within a current axiological framework.

The tutors should provoke a deepening and reinterpretation of the historical, geographical, philosophical, political, sociological, economic and cultural contents of the program, which provides the context-framework where their action takes place in interaction with students. This challenge seeks to overcome existing “official stories”, if the goal is to understand the weave of -explicit and implicit- social relationships present. As an example of the tutorial role of distance education programs, it is recommended to get acquainted with and revise the geographic subcultural maps of the places students come from, from those with high income to others who have been “uprooted” by migratory movements, economic crises in their countries of origin, individuals who have regrouped in search for political asylum, remnants of migrant groups resulting from natural disasters or environmental degradation, etc.. ,who may decide to update their knowledge, study and interact at a distance.

Then the instructor-tutor is bound to not only to study the contents of the subject matter, but also recognize the living material presented by the global hypersociology to which we have referred. Today the world is represented by new groups: ethnic, fundamentalist, religious, among others, who are new users/students of these educational systems; their members decide to enroll to become trained and updated in new specialties, in general of an economist nature, which emerge as a consequence of the global commercial demands connected from remote realities from and which interact through ICT. Knowing the new identities and understanding the beliefs, values and attitudes of these diverse backgrounds will be not only useful but also necessary to carry out their functions.

Therefore, from a holistic sociological reflection, it seems that the overall quality of the model of society where an online educational program operates is more important than the quality of the tutorial actions of said program; however, they mustn’t be ignored. Within this framework, program designers and tutors of must study, analyze and understand the dynamics of the tutorial actions which- together with the online didactic materials- are the visible face of the projects in question. In this regard, the current discussions concerning the quality of these programs are about which offer the best results(Garcia Aretio, 2004).

One possible contribution to broaden this perspective aimed at enhancing the social sustainability and governance is the approach of "science, technology and society" (STS), which represents and involves both the equity and democratization of science and technology articulated with ICT to enhance awareness and criticism within the programs in question as regards the artificial scientific and technological world with its unpredictable consequences and risks.

## Keys to Understanding the Tutor´s Role in a Virtual Educational Program from a Sociological Point of View

We understand electronic tutoring as the pedagogical activity articulated with virtualization tools, whose purpose is to guide and support students during their training process through various proposals and various formats. In the case of distance education programs, tutorials are a social space for essential communication and coordination, mediated by technology, from the simplest (telephone, mail, etc.). to the most complex (from e-mail to Learning Content Management Systems (LCMS). In this context, the tutor should be the actual interpreter oflearning needs and student demands. The tutor´s performance should be based on empowering these capabilities in situations of specific action within independent, collaborative, and interdisciplinary work. There are several tutorial proposals to achieve the above-stated: individual, group or collaborative; classroom-based or distance; electronic, telephone, audio-visual, etc..; mandatory or optional, with all the possible combinations.

Moreover, there are different sociological perspectives for the analysis of the tutor:

- Regarding the *prescription of the tutor's role*, we may see: a) the one who accompanies participating students in a personalized way during a classroom-based or distance learning process, in all its forms, b) the person responsible for the continuous follow-up of the achievements and difficulties presented c) the one who clears up doubts and queries (academic, administrative, etc.). about the operation of the training program on a daily basis.
- Regarding the *functions* that must be carried out by virtual tutors, these may be grouped into three categories:
  - academic function, as they guide the work of the participants, support their self-learning process, guiding the completion of pedagogical activities and contributing to the understanding/application of the basic concepts;
  - function of nexus or key link between the participant and the educational program (from the school and/or the university in question), which is why the tutor will remain in permanent contact with both to assist in the management, implementation, and follow-up of all the actions or efforts that are required;
  - role of continuous guidance and support of the participant in the search for a comprehensive and personalized training, building a communicative and

motivating relationship with responsibility for his/her actions and his work group.

- Regarding what the tutor *should be*, from the disciplinary, organizational, and sociocommunicational point of view, it is expected that the tutor's functions should seek to:
  - generate a solid educational background;
  - provide a source of information about the mission and objectives of the organization;
  - provide guidelines for a philosophy on the professional development of individuals;
  - be adviser and counselor in terms of specific skills and competencies to be developed;
  - provide feedback on the performances observed;
  - accompany or coach in activities designed to develop skills and experience;
  - help students to develop their educational journey (or career plan in an organization);
  - maintain honest communication with the student;
  - skillfully master the infotelematic and communication tools with adequate experience in virtual environments.

*Which involves developing and implementing the following skills:*

- Optimum mediation of materials, with provision for reading and conceptual and methodological comprehension of the respective content field while guiding and strengthening participant's self-learning.
- Ensuring a motivation to generate dialogue and reflection on the individual student and the group.
- Avoiding the anxieties of learning, a product of the mediations and the distance of participants.
- Creating a permanent interaction by appealing to innovative resources such as educational weblogs and virtual workshops, resource production, social forums (cybercafé and others), exchange of experiences, and so on.
- Permanently placing themselves in students′ shoes in order to understand their readiness when facing a set of materials or a screen to develop an activity far from the physical presence of the instructor/advisor.
- Urging the formation of interactive groups, either for the collaborative completion of practical work, through face-to-face or electronic chat sessions and discussion forums, weblogs, mailing lists, among other tools.
- Promoting interest in research and the deepening of knowledge.
- Adapting to the difficulties or situations that may arise while carrying out the activities proposed and others that might arise in the process.
- Maintaining a friendly relationship with the participant: being attentive while communicating and patient in the "virtual listening", keeping in mind that elaboration times and processes are not the same for all students: respecting the learning pace and styles of each student, different values, and so on.

- Reflectively knowing the virtual environment where they perform tasks so as to share it and transmit it to their learning group.
- Explaining the content, practical activities and applicative field work to be done, as well as sharing and sending in the established or opportune times.
- Permanently offering their help and making their communication presence known.
- Encouraging students to be independent and to take risks in the development of various activities: they are anticipators, explorers, creators.

*In order to comply with these features of the tutor's role and the role of tutorial actions and the, the following conditions should be considered:*

- Reviewing the personal characteristics of those who assume this task, in terms of personality, communicative ability, motivation and empathy.
- Designing a careful selection, timely training/education and a real supervision of performance for its improvement.
- Develop and implement a formative proposal to enable the tutor to experience in actual practice, the experiences a participant will later undergo in a virtual education course. A high level commitment from an academic point of view, with experience in using and applying ICT tools, a stimulus for the development of students′ cognitive and metacognitive skills, to strengthen the self-management of their processes, of intercultural and multilinguistic contextualization, of understanding of the organizational characteristics of virtual education programs, among others, are central skills in tutorial actions.

## Keys to Analyzing Tutorial Actions in Virtual Education Programs

The role of the tutor is manifested in tutorial actions that make up a sociovirtual space of unavoidable communication and coordination in distance education and/or electronic programs. This space can be configured as a place of values or as a sea of uncontrollable anxieties. It is necessary to exploit this ambivalent space so, beyond the differences, we may promote intercultural respect and understanding through the movement or flow of ideas.

When discussing the tutorial actions (Fainholc, 1999), we should recall that distance in sociocultural and educational interactivity is not only geographical distance in distance education, but the probable "psychosocial and cultural distance" presented by the respective program in its design and implementation. Therefore, the inclusion and consideration of the various practices and tutorial supports, anything that might fit into a framework of interculturality, will tend towards the strengthening of respect and enhancing the quality offered by the program in question, which will be operationallyevident by the strengthening of self-mastery and autonomy in terms of the products developed by the educational program.

Tutorial actions should be in accord with an interdisciplinary approach represented by the psychosociology and sociology of distance education, and we must be aware that in these actions of pedagogical guidance, as in other factors, the previously rigid boundaries between face-to-face and electronic education, today are increasingly blurred, precisely because of the increased technological emphasis on the mediations which favour uninterrupted dialogue and interactivity, at least from the standpoint of the proposals of ICT, which help cover key aspects.

Tutorial actions are defined by the goal that characterizes them: boosting in a contextualized, distributed and guided way the autonomous of the individual and group learning of the student, inserted within a virtual community of learning and knowledge production. This is a communication process in a continuum that can range from the most distant electronic or virtual to the closest, including the real face to face relationship or by videoconferencing.

## Tutorial Actions

They involve roles of administrative-communicative and pedagogical guidance and facilitation, among others, formed within a teletraining program, course or activity, distance teaching or training; they involve studying and/or learning with ICT or in an"electronic" way that complements the remote, open, virtual aspects mediated by the computer, Internet-based and telematic, to propose and secure distributed and collaborative activities, in a flexible manner, within the new environments or virtual learning environments in the information society and the knowledge society.

Tutorial actions tend to provide guidance for the learning of students through intersubjective dialogue mediated by ICT, which extends the possibilities of multidirectional communication in unsuspected ways. It is expected that the profile of the tutor to come from and become inscribed within the framework of appropriate and critical educational technology with a strong command of the disciplinary area, to guide the student and at the same time be a facilitator of learning with deployment of didactic aids within the proximal development zone (PDZ), established by the sociopedagogical framework of the program in question.

For these tutorial functions, it is necessary to(Fainholc, 1999):

1. Select tutors keeping in mind the disciplinary area they come from and their experience in unconventional teaching systems or their genuine willingness to join something new.
2. Train them so they may fit the profiles of the roles expected and in the deconstruction not only of social and pedagogical representations moderately in force, but also in the exercise of roles for so these may be verified in practice and in a shared way with those responsible for the program.
3. Create awareness about the need to monitor and self-evaluate their performance on an ongoing basis, in contrast with the users/students, where possible through workshops where they reflect on the performance of their duties.

It appears that there is within the online training programs a number of determining or delimiting conditions, which have already been mentioned. Thus, the challenge points to educating and training tutors in such mediations, strategies and techniques for a quality distance teaching, as it is known that a very high success rate of these training actions lies in the figure of the tutor within a sociopedagogical process of negotiation of meanings. Also, willingness, high motivation and the efficient and critical use of the technological media, depending on each situation of telematic guidance, are central variables.

Therefore, although the sociopedagogical proposal may be more or less structured depending on the program, the advantages of solitary or individual learning should be harmonized with the collaborative learning or teamwork, in order to consolidate learning situations that strengthen the development of autonomy and independence, with the combination of digital technologies and study materials in formats best suited to each specific situation.

The tutorial actions to be deployed in their relationship with ICT in online distance education remind us that we are not dealing with what is the opposite of or contrary to face-to-face education, nor its extension. It is an educational strategy in its own right, which in the historical-cultural times ofextreme interrogation, perplexity,and ambiguity that characterize the twenty-first century, requires serious contrasted research in the field with regard to the best combination of resources for pure e-learning or blended learning (with the appropriate use of technology).

Among the myriad topics to be considered in tutorial actions, social representations that act as filters within the same have special relevance; they are carried by students when they enroll in a distance education program with ICT, referring to the possible performances of the roles of tutor. These representations are a concept located at the intersection of psychology and sociology, together with the chapter on the management of the programs, in our case online programs, which seek to rescue the system of beliefs, opinions, mental maps, social cognitions, etc., in existing students as well astutors in a sociocultural and didactic dialogue.

Why do social representations in the roles that are played in online distance education interest us? Because they are organizing principles of the positions taken on the symbolic relationships between the social actors in question, positions that are inserted, in turn, into concrete social relationships that take place in a mediated way in these educational programs. Social representations are often linked to what tutors have heard when students refer to "long-distance education", or when faced with the practical work to be carried out, users say, "Ah, I didn´t know they had to be completed and handed in", or in reference to the attached bibliography they must consult or download from the Internet, it appears that it is often read, cut and pasted, if they have to submit a brief essay. This refers to the sociocultural and educational anchors which in terms of prior learning have helped to build the concepts held by people when faced with unheard of educational situations. These are objectivations carried out by the students of the realization of certain expectations of the tutors´ roles with abstract concepts previously internalized in the interaction. This is essential when it comes to deepening the didactic dialogue mediated by ICT. And, moreover, it is connected to the sociocultural academic and management task that should be present in the training of distance education tutors.

The contributions of cognitive psychology inscribed within a sociohistoricalstructural approach (Vigotsky, and his "proximal development zone") (Moll, 1994) also provide elements to enrich the understanding and practice of tutorial actions, marked by negotiation and technological-educational mediations in the virtual construction of meanings, saturated not only with social representations but also stereotypes. Many of these sociocultural prejudices have prevented even historically the deployment of the strategic role of distance education, configured as a rather rigid reality and resistant to innovation, filtered by social representations sometimes rooted in authoritarian regimes opposed to a democratization in the construction of knowledge in a virtual way.

It is due to the existence of these rigidities and social representations with such ambivalence, that in cyberspace the socioemotional approximations of computer mediated communication, among other traits, appears with the feeling of loss of self-control, which makes many individulas adopt strange or different behaviors (disguising themselves, using pseudonyms or virtual names, or resorting to avatars or artificial characters, and so on.), of which the tutor should be cautious. In other words, there is still a large deficit of rational elaborations to approach to the socioemotional knowledge that contributes to a more complete understanding of knowledge.

From the sociocultural viewpoint of tutors′ and students′ expectations mediated by technology, and as a consequence, these may be reduced or magnified into prejudice, stereotypes, the wrong attitudes and values, and so on. Often, so that contents and messages may generally fit into the limits, established by the Learning Content Management Systems (LCMS), as interventions and communications, the communication style is determined in the instructional design, sometimes even the number of words and the concepts that must be included so they may be displayed on screen.

Hence, the expected behavior of the tutor is often constrained to their reflective and critical capabilities in reference to technical questions related to design. Just to illustrate this: the quality of the cyberdiscussion, even with Web 2.0, should not be conditioned by the technologies that are used or predetermined to communicate in a project, since this would lead to behaviour that would disable the ability to discuss and share ideas, but they abound when it comes to publishing news of doubtful authorship, sending messages in response to exercises, or pseudoparticipating in forums and chat rooms, etc.. The ever popular principle of least effort can also be limited in these environments by the stimulation or scantiness of the tutorial actions within the various communication exchanges, with their consequent risks of lack ofquality and low motivation to develop the communication skills that should prevail in cyberspace.

## How Does One Become a Tutor?

In some ways the goal is to take up again old discussions about the role of the educator and contextualize it light of the new digital environments and frameworks of educational programs mediated by technology. The goal is to also work out if it is a trade, a semiprofession, a profession, an analysis which belongs to the field of new occupations in the organizations of the information society. Asking ourselves whether ithelps set up or strengthen a profession, a semiprofession, or trade (of high turnover, in the case of tutors as it is being analyzed) responds to concerns associated with the exercise of their role. It is expected that this will affect the characteristics of the role, in the deployment of their skills, development of mastery and professional self-regulation within an educational program of telematic interaction.

The characteristics of occupational *competency, vocation, license, independence and self-regulation* should be considered as variables that, while in other contexts awarded educational qualifications of a social recognition of the teacher, are or would be the characteristics of a tutor in these unconventional educational programs.

In the features of the transformation processes, the etymological meaning of the teacher trade should be analyzed (Lerena, 1982), which has much to do -as well as the tutorial actions in these electronic programs- with practical knowledge. *Trade* (oficio, in Spanish) comes from *opus* (work) and *facio* (do), this is why a trade is learned by doing, practicing, while we reach a profession through academic qualifications. It is a well-known fact that “a teacher (maestro in Spanish), and we may as well add tutor, is someone who knows, someone who masters an art, not only someone who earns a living by teaching” (Lerena, 1982), we may add in our case “virtual” teaching. On the other hand, professor/professional –from the Latin *fateo* (recognize, admit), in the same Indo-European root as *fari* (speak, say) - is not the one who knows but rather the one who *professes*, the one who recognizes certain principles and doctrines, so that the teaching and tutorial professional could be the one who meekly professes an area.

It is necessary to address a “sociology of professions” in connection with the profile of tutors linked to the socio-educational discourse of ICT, as specific knowledge to justify special skills from a university education which, we believe, is the only thing that ensures legitimate knowledge. We should take up again in the sociology of professions, what is related to the before-mentioned *competency, vocation, license, independence, and self-regulation,* which point to the socio-pedagogical discourse as theoretical-practical knowledge as to justify a respective license and competency, from a university education, which is the only thing, we believe, that ensures legitimate knowledge.

## Playing the Role of Tutor in a Virtual Program

The functions and characteristics of the tutors are defined according to criteria adopted by the electronic programs in which they are inscribed, since an interdisciplinary contextualization articulated with everyday experience is the best team to inspire and adapt the tutorial guidelines required by an educational program with features like the ones which are being analyzed. Among the more representative criteria that should characterize it, it is useful towards achieving the above-mentioned, to highlight today the shift from a standpoint of multiculturalism toward interculturalism, as the framework where the tutor will carry out tasks in these programs. In the first framework, the tutor coexists with different cultures within the same real, media, or virtual space, because it is the typical pluralistic situation of existing cultural communities within the program with distinct identities -including learning communities or knowledge creation communities which may form within them-. In the second, within the framework of interculturalism, the tutor attends the set of relationships between these different cultures, namely, observes and take cares of the dynamics between the cultural communities.

Any reality is multicultural, pluralistic, and diverse, and being respectful of this, in other words, trying to be intercultural, points to the development of specific pragmatic communication devices contrary to multiculturalism which as a trait, characterizes all contemporary societies. Put in a different, interculturalism may be defined as a construction that favors the understanding of social and educational problems in relation to cultural diversity, whereas multiculturalism is limited to recognizing the multiplicity of existing groups without needing to achieve educational goals (which involve greater understanding).

Accordingly, tutorials are a space of coordinated intercultural aid, founded on actions to guide and facilitate e-learning, and routing actions to strengthen, individually or collectively – in a virtual or face-to-face way-, the capabilities of students in situations of specific action such as the achievement of a cooperative learning and/or interdisciplinary work within the organization and the planning of each program.

The purported performance is related to:

- *An academic function* or one aimed at supporting the self-learning process of theparticipant as regards the content.
- *A function of relational connection* and communication which is fundamental between the student/s and the educational program, to obtain a permanent contact and facilitate the required communication and administrative sub-processes.
- *A function of psychosocioeducational guidance*, to direct the search and find information, and offer advice on activities which intensively implement functions of thought.
- *A technological function*, to become – with sociotechnological, psycho-communicative, and methodological skills- a deep connoisseur of ICT, and the interactive possibilities of combining technologies selected depending on the program in question.

However, questions arise about the tutor, in general, and online training, in particular: Does the tutor play roles *on line* different from those played in conventional teaching? If so, what is the training they should receive?, Which skills should be developed and demonstrated in their performance?; keeping in mind that the quality of tutorials within the service of the program is the most important aspect, beyond the content and the development of the technological platform,what would be its defining characteristics?

Although, obviously, the contents make the difference in any training program, beyond the design and technological applications, what matters the most in virtual training is the dedication and encouragement in the care of student services, to develop not only their participation and understanding of the issues, but also their maturity as an autonomous person. Again, the before-mentioned defies the training, performance, and evaluation of tutors over time, as well as challenges us to assume the new technological challenges.

## Expectations as Regards Roles in the Tutorial Electronic EducatIonal Communication. Conflicts and Misunderstandings in Terms of Roles

The expectations regarding the role of the instructor-tutor in electronic educational programs on the rise in the information society are challenged by ICT ; these technical resources should be considered as elements useful to not only send, receive and distribute information, but also to enable creative expression or, in other words, recognize their socio-semiological-communicational determinants and their economic-political and sociocultural assumptions for the (re)creation depending on the proposal and the various contexts.

Besides mastering the technical procedures, the tutor should possess the necessary disciplinary knowledge to rescue and research in an interdisciplinary way their key concepts and confront them in their practice mediated by ICT. In addition to this many times a guardian must teach a comprehensive conceptual and critical reading of the content in these media so students may demistify them, appropriate them, and use them to express themselves creatively in the language and codes that characterize them.

The tasks involved range from promoting a critical understanding of the meanings distributed by technological convergence to the opportunity to observe their strengths and limitations when it comes to confronting them with reality, when it comes to solving various problems depending on the contents administered. Therefore, the tutor must know all the technological and pedagogical resources (simple or sophisticated) to select them, combine them, and apply them in designing mediated learning contexts through the formulation of objectives, content, implementation and evaluation activities in the context of various organizational and administrative requirements, so it may be truly useful to the distance student being guided.

The new experiences that are presented to a tutor as an instructor in a context of learning mediated by ICT -in pure e-learning or blended learning- are challenging: on the one hand, rewarding and motivating, on the other hand, they may be cause for concern and anxiety. With an appropriate professional development and sustained support given by the organization and the program in question, it is hoped that the concerns and anxieties of the tutors will decrease, self-confidence will grow, and reflective practice of sociopedagogical and technological skills will increase.

The consideration of the conflicts in the roles mentioned seeks to think about power relationships within tutorial actions, which constitutes a contribution to deepen the prospect of a sociology of distance education. If the concern of the sociological perspective is to develop discernment through critical thinking, identifying verifiable evidence, we should promote the search for the bases of what is presented as a given or natural in tutorial actions, rejecting assertions and generalizations without verifiable arguments and pursuing reasons different from the ones already established.

In this practice of a sociological view, it is inescapable to link the concept of power. It is understood as a network that produces meaning that penetrates the whole social body and in our case, the discourses prepared and distributed in distance education programs, which appear as visible and invisible, hidden and present, manifested by the components of a program, among these tutorial actions.

The goal is, thus, to perceive, analyze, and dismantle the social-political and technological conditions of production, distribution, and reception/use of the discursive practices proposed. In turn, we must also unveil the sociopolitical micromechanics of power so that, in a given tutorial situation, a user (or reader or navigator or student) may recognize their participation as authorized and/or condoned, encouraged, inhibited and/ or subjugated. In other words, it is important to recognize which voices compose and from which positions held discourses arise, as knowledge produced within a socioeducational strategic and contextualized relationship that originates, links and mobilizes the various roles and functions that make up the tutorial actions of an educational program.

In this regard, Foucault points out, the "truth of science at a given moment in history lies in its consistency with other knowledge." A main task of the researcher and scholar of social sciences is to discover what are the rules and order under which scientific-technological discourses are originated, considering that said methodological order has been so strong throughout history that concepts of great thinkers like Plato, Socrates, Kant, Rousseau or

Piaget have crossed the boundaries of time to form the various fields of culture at a given time.

All these codes are ordered and form discursive fields, basis of the common social discourse, from which specialized discourses stem (in our case, distance education), which are institutionalized and remain dominant in society and social organizations which offer online educational programs. This is what Foucault (1977) calls "genealogy" or alliance of scholarly knowledge and local memories that make up the knowledge to be presented as true or legitimate by an elite of power. In order to oppose this, some possible alternatives of knowledge may be installed, which also leads to dichotomies (and misunderstandings) between knowledge and power, and/or discourse and power.

As e may see, it is important to conduct a sociological and strategic analysis "power" variable within a technological educational program or system within the complexity that involves all social interaction with different negotiation options regarding power. This is not a personal attribute, but an inherent property to social relationships that may be (or not necessarily) asymmetrical, which will depend on the negotiations that are engaged within it.

Then, the starting point is the process of social interaction, the main unit of sociological analysis, referring to the interrelationship between social actors in an environment where there is an exchange, modification, and enforcement of ideas, thoughts, feelings, beliefs, etc.. Social interaction is enabled by the existence of a normative and axiological framework, which is established and shared, a product of a prior socialization in the culture which it is a part of,and subcultural, referring to the electronic educational program in question.

These are actions that take various interactive forms, that can mean as much solidarity and consensus –which lead to social cohesion and integration- as lead to a confrontation, rivalry and open conflict. These actions often appear as redundancies, misunderstandings, disputes, restrictions, etc.. between the various positions and powers existing within and outside an organization or a program, and influence the field of decisions taken.

Conducting a sociostrategic analysis of power involves acknowledging within the mentioned social interplay, the existing and available resources or the ones to be obtained, useful for achieving the goals of the system or program in question, which although they are formulated, in practice they may be contradictory or uncertain. The above-mentioned may be applied to understand, from another angle, the tutorial role and relationships.

Electronic learning requires that electronic teachers or tutors possess certain beliefs and attitudes: they must be convinced that the use of ICT has the potential to contribute to students′ distance learning. This in turn influences positively on the beliefs and attitudes of their students in relation to e-learning. However, tutors should unconditionally accept the virtual environments of ICT as given, unquestionable and established by the scientific-technological power elite. Tutors thus struggle to adapt to these new environments that technologically change all the time, often a little or not flexible to the demands of student learning, and that should become a subject of discussion with instructional designers and, consequently, by the tutorial actions that tutors carry out as facilitators when facing strait-jacket (highly structured) sources of information. All of which is not free from conflicts and misinterpretations.

The electronic tutors or instructors need to reflect on their tutorial practices to identify those that most effectively contribute to learning or suggest technological-educational adjustments or also design teaching materials beyond unnecessary technological sophistication. A series of questions arise again from everyday practice: Are we taking advantage of the strengths of each electronic distance format and overcoming the deficiencies and weaknesses of each?, Are we offering a face-to-face or virtual teaching that actually adjusts or support technologies?, Is e-learning a complement to face-to-face training or tutorial interactions or are these a complement to e-learning?, What are the roads to a full or quality virtual teaching, with tutorial actions that make sense on their own?

To better understand tutorial actions in the absence of longitudinal socioeducational studies in the long term, verified in the heterogeneity of programs, and rigorous research in the area, which articulate and at the same time deconstruct theoretical and practical –oftentimes routine models-, it is often argued that the tutorial roles of distance education programs should not be defined by the use of technologies nor by an amount of presence or distance, but by what their pedagogical models and designs grant in significance to the proper use of resources, both for training orientation and for the production of materials and a significant socioeducational tutorial communication of relevance.

Thus, the interesting thing to demystify, and which leads to a timely and relevant socio-cultural reflection of the modality in question, is to reassess in each context all of the components of each program, and hence the requirements of the tutorial roles, their expectations contrasting what is done in practice and what should be done for their timely improvement.

## Conflicts and Contradictions Facing the Role of the Tutor or a Critical Theory of his/her Role

There are a number of conflicts regarding the expectations of the role of the tutor which can make it difficult for him/her to carry out his/her functions. There are multiple causes: from their training and/or education (if they come from other areas that are not formative) in comparison to what they can actually do in practice, what they should do, and what they might carry out in the situations in which they will have to perform/work.

Conflicts in the expectations and perceptions of the role of the tutor lead to contradictions and paradoxes which deserve a critical analysis that will contribute to awareness and the search for possible solutions. Therefore:

1. It is expected tutors be trained professionals, specialized and updated to perform roles and functions, namely:

*Academic*: to guide students in their self-learning, strengthening their cognitive and metacognitive, technological, socioemotional, and technological-communicative skills through the use of content, didactic activities and interactive exchanges; motivating, generating trust, promoting self-esteem; supporting the student, monitoring their tasks, providing information about their achievements and problems, offering incentives to participate in contributing to the production of useful and socially valuable knowledge.

Creating awareness of the sociocultural context in which they will perform, in order to guide the student in the search for answers and solutions to the various situations and problems that may arise and which may only be face with the ability to listen, accept, respect, and communicate in multidirectional ways.

Managerial, to handle technical, administrative, etc.. situations, with horizontal leadership concerning the project and the learning, not only from a personal and group but also organizational point of view.

Some problems are perceived here:

1. Not all tutors have access to systematic training/education due to economic difficulties, or lack of opportunities. Thus, there are tutors who can not or do not know how to talk with plain language and adapted to the students′ level of representation; some times they are professionals who are so specialized that they can not adapt to that level either.
   - Many of the training proposals remain at the theoretical level and do not include in their designs practice or internships, where the tutor is placed in real or simulated situations of distance teaching and learning to implement skills and knowledge.
   - Many times the guidelines for the future tutor are partial, because only technological aspects are considered and not those related to the program design, the structure and development of content, the types of leadership for project implementation and evaluation of distance programs.
   - The rule in these contexts is still a lack of continuous training in the field of tutorial actions covering the pedagogical aspects, the use of ICT, the review of theoretical frameworks, the acquisition of new skills, and so on.
2. It is expected that the tutors carry out multifunctions. This involves finding supplements to the didactic materials, which often are not updated due to a lack ofinstitutional budgetary possibilities or other reasons, acting as didactic designers and developers of educational materials, in addition to carrying out tutorial actions and being responsible for energizing the forums. Many tasks in poor institutional conditions or a lack of material resources, an absence of clarity in the educational criteria, a lack of responses to demands for support and institutional backing, weaken the performance of the everyday tutorial task.
3. Other limitations: the technological kind, through the interaction with the virtual platform, on which mediated teaching and learning process is mounted, which may lead to rigid situations in the proposals of the Learning Content Management Systems (LCMS), which often restrict or limit the explanations and conceptual, methodological, dissidence and so on. Even the existing constraints on electronic educational programs (with technological platforms, implementing quality standards of various kinds, for example, SCORM) carry certain weight. This does not mean we must be against the existence of regulations and/or quality standards but that we should advocate for the consideration of their assumptions, so we may then revise them in light of the teaching and learning processes, the main reason for their existence.
4. It is esxpected that tutors conduct a personalized follow-up for each student, to encourage and monitor their progress, so that the tutor may become invested in their progress or their problems and ensure that they are working at an appropriate pace. But in most cases the work load prevents this from happening: they are constantly hurrying to complete time consuming tasks; or the number of students is high and

they cannot assist all of them, leading to feelings of isolation and loneliness in the student and possible dropout.

5. The tutor should lead a mediated empathetic-emotional relationship, but since his/her role is that of a distance education guidance professional, a neutral emotional cordiality is expected, as well as a functional specificity, among other characteristics, which can cause conflict between the socioemotional and technological-educational areas.
6. It is expected that the tutor participate in a full and frank communication with the program by exercising leadership, but on the other hand, although they could make their "assessments" from contrasts in the field, they are not encouraged nor taken up. Often dissidence is not accepted with regard to reference and ideological conceptual frameworks, which are neutralized.
7. It is also expected that they promote in the student body the production of knowledge through collaborative and reflective learning. This is not easy when facing limitations, weakness, or absence, increasingly so, of thinking skills in students just starting these programs, which prevents them from dealing with instructions and other complex tasks. This requires the tutor to, in more than one occasion, to provide compensatory education, which consumes a great deal of what little time they have.The same is true regarding the low motivation present in many students –when they are "sent" to take courses-, who complete the didactic activities and evaluation in a mechanical way, and do not submit their work within the deadlines set forth.
8. It is expected that tutors include in their educational proposals ethnic, social, and cultural diversity. However, online education systems do not generally recognize the linguistic pluralism, nor interculturalism. An intercultural education i snot included, one that would promotes equal representation and expressive opportunities, why is why a cultural enrichment does not take place.
9. It is expected that the tutor participate and exercise leadership in the community, especially in rural or poor areas, but on the other hand is not accepted that theyopenly intervene, for example, in political events. In other words, their intervention in community areas is accepted and valued, as long as it does not give rise to controversy.
10. They are encouraged to include updates or specializations in the content and methodology used by the program, in other words, they possess autonomy for the structuring of learning experiences. However, there are controls on these aspects and it would seem that the tutor is not entirely free to choose or update content and they way to teach it.

So, with reagard to conflicts in the expectations and perceptions of the tutor's role, often the negotiation of these situations, although satisfactory in the short term, do not solve the main issue: proposing alternatives from a critical theory of virtual tutorial role which include, contrast, and reformulate a wide range of expectations and perceptions of tutorial actions, which consider conflicts, contradictions, and paradoxes within the organizational complexity and intercultural hybridity of these online education programs.

All distance education projects should include an analysis of the context of knowledge production and tutorial practices that enable or disable it in terms of possible actions and critical nodes requiring the construction of alternatives for improvement. As this is generally disregarded, the exercise of tutorial actions presents, in addition to those mentioned, other conflicting situations, in general labor issues, such as:

- Work overload, because they generally must assist a very large and heterogeneous number of students, making them resort to answer with generic messages or usefragments of text copied and pasted without due care, leaving aside those students who do not insist or ignoring aspects not considered important.
- Also, as support for the student, "low cost" tutors are selected, in other words, those who are recently graduated, with no teaching experience, or professionals who agree to work for low pay, which means that the tutorial action suffers.
- Use of linear low-cost learning materials or those found in Internet databases or sites of dubious update in electronic format, requiring little human intervention and sidelining the production of flexible materials. In fact, it only involves the transmission of information in virtual form, scrimping in reflective academic-conceptualdiscussions during a telematic teaching.
- Specialists or prestigious authors are called to prepare the materials. In other cases, they are authors who master the content but are not socialized in the spirit of distance education and even less so in the format of Internet browsing, which represents another way to write, read and interact. The same thing happens when marketing actions are multiplied in the programs or only aspects of graphic design and navigation in the digital environment are covered, omitting psychosocial and educational variables.
- Other hidden aspects of the socialization of the tutorial role: professional skills are developed from a curriculum with social-philosophical leanings set in training conventional classroom-based teachers, with underlying concepts and values, which although need renewal, updating, do not correspond to the electronic distance education frameworks. Or excessive "feminization" in the calls for tutorial roles. In addition, men, pressured by a higher social prestige and better economic conditions, dismiss these job positions, holding out, as always, for bureaucratic and administrative roles, both in supervison as well as management of the educational work.

## PERFORMANCE IN THE PRACTICE OF THE ROLE TUTORIAL

The virtual spaces of teaching and learning posed by ICT tend to substantially change the practices of each of the actors of education in general and especially in these programs. The management ofinformation and construction of knowledge in these environments poses new roles for interaction between students and teachers/tutors, where the technological mediations impose practices and new relationships which must be adapted to specific educational situations, not to mention other more conventional means which have been used in distance education.

Online education opens doors and expands horizons, while modifying human and education relationships. It is desirable to provide a high level of content in these valuable opportunities for interaction.

The tutor's role is, therefore, essential and will depend not only on the disciplinary content to be taught, but also the sociocultural context in which they'll be working within the electronic education program, the profile of the student who will beinteracting with them, and their cultural heritage and provenance, their proactive or resistant attitudes, the degree of technological literacy, and so on.

## Recommendations Affecting the Development of the Tutorial Roles to Take into Account with the Use of ICT

From what has already been pointed out, emotional factors can be identified, factors of professional development,of methodologies for facilitating learning through the use of technologies, of design of educational material, and of technological difficulties and resistance, all of which affect the development of the tutor's role in electronic educational programs. Here are some recommendations designed to help both new tutors and administrators of online education programs for an effective implementation of distance or blended e-learning.

The emotional factor assumes a significant place in the adaptation, learning, and implementation of electronic learning; it requires time is from the new future tutors or teachers. Resistance to what's new may cause stress and anxiety. Initially, tutors may lack a clear understanding of what is required of them; they taking much of their time learning how to use different technologies and adapt the content creating educational materials with little or no knowledge oftheir design depending on different electronic media. This must be articulated with the knowledge of teaching practices, which are not always known, which may cause a little effective implementation and lead to frustrations.

Anxiety is particularly significant, especially with regard to the use of technological programs (or authoring software) in general, because there isn't always training and assistance in this area. The anxiety would be less if there were a stage of socialization and learning for training and experimentation as well acknowledging that, with reference to technology, it is impossible to know it all, and that not everything can be achieved and the best way, in initial stages (From Moll , 2001).

Reading and debating with colleagues books and journal articles, participating in conferences, as well as interacting with the various software, and specifically knowing the goals they want to achieve with electronic learning -tasks that require time and attention to a small number of students-, will contribute not only to develop patience and mastery in the tutor, but also the skills needed to carry out this role. It also requires realistic budgetary policies sustained within the distance education program. It is necessary to propose and provide professional development for tutors, with resources and tools necessary for their performance, and thus successfully achieve the objectives specified. For the success of an online education program, it is necessary to provide a planned program of professional development to contribute more effectively to the acquisition and exercise of skills and attitudes that the tutor needs.

Educational institutions should design systematic plans for the introduction of online learning (Inglis, Ling and Joosten, 2000) to provide guidelines to help prospective tutors/teachers in this implementation. The analysis of all pedagogical and technological aspects required by tutorial actions is also part of a proposal for professional development.

The joint development by all those involved in the electronic program in question, of a manual or note book refered to the educational and technological aspects related to the characteristics of distance education in this format would help its effective implementation.

## THE SOCIOLOGICAL COMPETENCIES OF THE TUTOR TO WITHIN AN ONLINE DISTANCE EDUCATION PROGRAM OR ORGANIZATION. REFLECTING IN AND FOR TUTORIAL ACTION

It is interesting to distinguish, from a linguistic point of view (Chomsky, 1971), the concepts of *competence* or general ability applicable in multiple occasions and *performance* or skill required to solve a specific situation.

In the professional field, being competent involves demonstrating the ability to perform a job or function. Some define competence as the body of knowledge and skills that allows a person to exercise professional activity according to the requirements of any production within a job. However, although by its etymology, it originates from the root word *competere*, or *petere*, aspire, go to meet (compete in an event), from the same root we have the Spanish verb "competer", which means "be the responsibility of , be the obligation of" (which may have other connotations), for example, if applied to one who is vested with authority for certain matters, and especially one who operates effectively within a specific domain of human activity. In education, the term expresses a certain ability or potential to act effectively in a context. The different meanings of the term have been clearly stated.

According to Perrenoud (1999), the formation of a competence allows people to deploy and put into motion, implement and integrate the knowledge and skills gained in various complex and unpredictable situations. This is why, they are defined as the abilities for effective performance in a specified number of situations, based on knowledge but not limited to them.

Weinert (2001) states that "competence is interpreted as a more or less specialized system of abilities or skills that are necessary and sufficient to achieve a specific objective." It would be that overall ability based on knowledge, experience, values, and rules that a person has developed through his/her commitment in practice.

In general, we plave ourselves within the framework ofholistic, dynamic, and functional competencies, which in turn relate to specific sociocultural demands. Hence, they are also defined as the abilities to respond to the demands and perform adequately. In other words, they arise from a combination of practical skills, knowledge (including, in turn, tacit knowledge), motivation, ethical values, attitudes, emotions, and the various social and cultural components that are mobilized together to achieve effective action.

## Core or Key Competencies

While there is no universal meaning of the term "core competence", there is unanimity about its differential characteristics which lie in an applicative "know-howand which could accommodate a variety of pertinent contexts and fields. It has the characteristic of being inclusive, so that each competence covers knowledge, procedures, and attitudes which, because they are core, are essential, fundamental or basic, in other words necessary and beneficial to any person, group, organization, or society as a whole, beyond the social, cultural condition, gender and family environment of the individual who exercises it.

In all national and international reports relating to the subject matter, certain core competencies are emphasized, which are inevitable, and which a citizen in the twenty-first century should possess, develop, and improve. These skills will be the process and product of training proposals increasingly mediated by ICT, in which tutorial roles are central. We are dealing with the mastery of comprehensive and critical reading in a variety of media supports, the writing and calculation, the interaction with ICT in mediated communication, foreign languages, problem solving, reflective thinking, leadership, creativity, motivation, social and interpersonal relationships, teamwork, skills in facilitating economic integration and the ability to learn, and metacognitive competence (as the ability to understand and control their own thinking, etc.). within learning processes given as prerequisites for ensuring a quality electronic learning.

It is worth recalling that many of the competencies listed are *genericcompetencies* or transversal, in other words, competencies independent of the courses they relate to, all of which are applicable to distance education. According to B. Rey (1996), the term "transversal" does not refer to the common elements of various specific skills, but to complementary and independent aspects of the disciplines that may be used in other fields. Just as the general competencies are better developed with the help of many disciplines, the specific ones occur within a particular discipline.

Other organizations have expressed their views in this regard, such as the European Council in Lisbon (2000), which defined "the new basic learning skills throughout life", listing as examples information technology, foreign languages, technological culture, entrepreneurship, and social skills, including: communication in the mother tongue as well as in foreign languages; mastery of ICT, the application of calculations and mathematical skills, science and technology; entrepreneurship; interpersonal and civic competencies; learning to learn, and interculturalism.

Also the European Council in Barcelona (2002) reiterates the competencies set forth in the study conducted by the Programme for International Student Assessment (PISA) in the year 2000 on the school factors related to quality and equity (Organisation for Economic Co-operation and Development -OECD). Thus are categorized three main levels of key competencies: 1) the ability to interact in socially heterogeneous groups; 2) autonomous behavior, and 3) the ability to use technological tools in an interactive way.

In England and Wales they are known as *key skills*, in Scotland, as *core skills,* and in Portugal, as "essential general competencies".Some of those considered relevant to the tutor´s role in the electronic programs in cuestion are listed as follows:

1. Implementing cultural, scientific, and technological knowledge to understand reality and deal with situations, solve problems, and make decisions in everyday life.
2. Using the language of different fields -cultural, scientific and technological- ofknowledge to express themselves in an effective manner.
3. Using the local language to correctly communicate and structure thinking, as well as foreign languages to communicate adequately in intercultural situations of everyday life, work, and process information.
4. Adopt personalized and collaborative working and learning methodologies independently, responsibly, and creatively, aimed at the implementation of actions to achieve goals set forth in tasks and projects.
5. Evaluate, investigate, identify, and organize information in order to transform it into knowledge that can be used and transferred to other realities.
6. Promote a harmonious relationship between individuals, groups, and organizations in (real or virtual) space through a personal and interpersonal approach to improve co-existence and quality of life.

From a sociocultural perspective, among the competencies of greater relevance to the professional performance of tutorial roles and actions, the *sociological*, *communication*, and *media* skills stand out.

1. *The sociological skills* point to the training/education for the development of a contextualized and collaborative teaching project mediated by technology and ICT, respecting the diversity of social groups.
   - This involves acquiring, developing,and implementing skills and methodologies to shape collective workshop proposals, or classroom-based or distance workshops for the search and analysis of data to enable the design of educational projects mediate by ICT: use of statistical data, demographic sources on the environment (census, etc..), local and territorial sources of information, databases of social services, etc.., techniques for the inclusion of ethnic minorities, and the use of existing resources in the environment (parents, associations, production companies, etc..), development of tools for collecting quantitative and qualitative data (surveys, interviews, discussion groups, etc.).
   - Training in promoting change in the social and cultural context of users and students for the reality they will have to live in, with the application of techniques for removing attitudinal rigidities and identifying existing cultural norms respecting students´ expectations.
   - There are certain competencies related to sociological knowledge required for the performance of future tutors, basically linked to the various articulations that may take education as a social fact from the perspective of public policies -including its distinctions of gender, religion, ethnicity, ruralness, etc.-, within the framework of the knowledge society, globalization, and internationalization, with its problems of economic polarization, social inequality, and various segmentations. For example, understanding the phenomenon of immigration and behavior of communities, habitats, and fostering social networks; raising awareness of content and formats for all media and ICT; understanding the

phenomenon of social change and theresistance to it in adopting new roles in organizations and their leaders, students and faculty.

2. *The communication skills* include language skills, although they go beyond this, because they involve learning and exercising the active skills of listening, speaking, reading, and writing in different mediums and codes, exercising -developing maturity and wisdom- the dialogue of confrontation of ideas, expressing concerns, questions, dissidence, answers, images, agreements, disagreements, enthusiasm, and so on. It involves skills of respect in the participation in communications.

   We are dealing with those skills that ensure adequate openness to others and a fruitful relationship with others, as we understand different viewpoints. These are skills where effective procedures for communication in general and telematic, in particular, are applied, with proactive and assertive attitudes for expression and understanding. Knowing how to work with other people in acommunicative and constructive way, with a group-centered behavior and on interpersonal understanding, promotes self-learning, self-assessment, and fluid reasoning for a reading, interaction, and browsing on the Internet.

   Hence the importance of the possibility of expression (Habermas, 1989) which includes the potential emancipation of individuals and groups, as they appropriate the symbolic codes of all the technological means that exist today and which appear in technological convergence. It is worthwhile to mention the socioemotional side of thecommunication skills, which tend to improve the social and cultural dimension of the individual, his/her ability to interact with others.

3. *The media skills* involve the comprehensive and critical reading (Fainholc, 2004)–the essential prerequisite of writing- in various media in the information and knowledge society. Its development tends to strengthen communication and expressive possibilities of various kinds of languages, verbal, nonverbal, audiovisual and telematic, based on the analysis of their differences and similarities. They focus on a situated criticality according to different social groups, subcultures, age, gender, ethnicity, religion, etc.., to overcome any social, racial, generic, age, language, etc.. discrimination, displayed and distributed in the productions in question.

As a result, a competency (Spector and De La Teja, 2001) points to the ability recognized and verified by a community that practices it, as it isproven in a relevant way. However, this is not something universal, since performances may vary from onelearning or practice community to another, even within a single virtual community.

Notwithstanding the enormous changes that ICT impose for electronic educational programs and for the tutor´s role, which requires continuous technological-educational development and training for their career, the most important thing is the ability to empower them for an opportune, valuable, and worthwhile performance, in the tutorial accompanying of students.

By the same token, in the scale of assessment the ethical effort of the tutor´s role in their tutorial actions should be taken into account (Kushner, 2000) on all tracks pointing to their public legitimacy as a form of performance and research in action to secure agreements on possible dilemmas that the existence of the new roles involves. This refers to the subject of values and ideas of justice in any assessment, which aims at achieving in a representative way consensus and agreements on the principles and procedures governing the confidentiality of information and guidance of the student.

The deepening of these and other components of electronic educational programs will help the maturation of the field of sociology of distance education.

## VIRTUAL TUTORS FOR ONLINE COURSES

Their presence and insertion involve a new "interpretation" or view of the conceptions established in general by the tutorial roles and actions for distance education programs. The virtual resignification proposes new directions within the many technological resources and potentialities, which tutors may appeal to today, to promote effective telematic communication and interaction with the student.

The goal would be, thus, to create, consolidate into action, and implement a *critical theory of the virtual tutorial role*, as a commitment to the program and students, which will defy its technological overdetermination and conceptual overstructuring towards the practice of mediations that better release authentic meanings of social interaction.

The sociocultural and educational relevance that characterize these efforts liesbeyond digital artifacts and languages: it is found in the environments and processes that the tutor creates along with the students and the rest of the components of the educational program under way. The challenge is to establish the formative scope of such resources, since not everything that is technologically feasible is educationally relevant *per se*, because it requires the option of guiding,appropriate, critical, andnecessary pedagogical dimension regarding relevant tutorial actions.

The tutor's role in learning in virtual contexts points to an educator, a communicator, or content specialist who has been professionalized for this educational position, where the weight of their actions is the mediated guidance, the guiding help electronically connected to the telematic guide of the student's learning process, respecting their idiosyncratic characteristics, multiple intelligences, and cognitive styles within a mediated process with several resources (telematic or not) to obtain a quality educational product (Fainholc, 2006) in the online or blended learning course, within an institution or organization.

It would be worth mentioning, thus, some recommendations for the tutor'srole in the planning and implementation of their tutorial actions in a virtual course (Berge, 1996), which would cover several areas:

- pedagogical, with the use of educational and discursive resources to facilitate learning;
- social, by encouraging human relationships among members of a group or community;
- managerial, by establishing general procedures for handling program information, communication in discussion forums, etc.
- technological, for an appropriate relationship between the system, the software, and the interface designed; and
- of continuous tutorial training to manage online courses, moderate asynchronous discussions and guide synchronous discussions; integrate different teaching and

learning styles in courses; actively interact with students and give them constant feedback with respect for cultural differences and others.

Thus, tutorial actions have no reason to exist if not understood within a virtual educational network, which involves guiding, listening, and facilitating the remote learning of students within a system of mutual expectations in an online technological educational program.

A sociotechnological educational program calls for, so it may be understood, its inscription within:

- *The symbolic sciences*, which focus on the unique ability an individual possesses to come up with, use, and transmit symbols, and therefore, instead of understanding behavior as "given facts", handles the interactive exchanges and negotiations which take place in the most diverse social situations, and through which users (tutors and students) mutually define their expectations of which behaviors are appropriate, accepted, and valued.
- *The critical sciences*. The critical or emancipatory interest arises as a result of the goal of the critical social science that seeks to provide means for educating people on how its objectives and purposes may have been distorted or suppressed, in order to denature it, specify them, and eradicate them to enable the search for genuine goals.
- *The practical sciences,* as the application of scientific knowledge or organized in terms of the specific tasks of programs and actions in their integrated dimensions: a) the organizational aspect, which relates the facets of the administration and organization with decisions and activities of designers, managers, technicians, tutors, students, and users; b) the technical aspect, which involves devices, software, systems, and procedures for their operation; and c) the ideological or cultural aspect, which refers to the values, ideas, and re-creating activity established by any technological-educational practice monitored by theoretical reason and controlled by practical reason.
- *The theory of power*, which considers and analyzes the symbolic means by which certain individuals and groups can dominate others, promote, and achieve their own goals and interests even though they may be opposed by resistance. This refers to the sources, media, and relationships of domination, control, and subordination that may arise in tutorial situations within historically specific social processes such as electronic educational programs in question. Power may be coercive, in other words, directly use punitive force to impose and maintain the control, or it may be the result of underlying inequalities which establish a differential access and unequal distribution of the key societal resources (today, information, connectivity, technological, material, or symbolic resources). Although power is generally considered as circumscribed to the public domain of politics, in its institutional and organizational forms, it is present in all situations and social relationships and in all moments of interaction, because it limits and structures interrelationships between individuals and groups. It is thus the interpretive context in which all constructs discussed acquire - or are given- a full concrete meaning.

The critical theory of the tutorial role aims to provide elements to better understand and anticipate this organizational behavior within the virtual social systems in terms of the performances of a tutor. For a better understanding, within a proposal of redesign of tutor training, we should appeal to the aforementioned guidelines within the "umbrella" of the concept of "mutual expectations" existing in a particular program, where the particular interactive profile would help to determine what kind of "interpretation" the enforcement that each tutorial action will have.

The way we virtually teach or guide telematic learning requires a change in the underlying educational paradigm; these processes focus on the interrelationship between the tutor and student, student and student, student and knowledge, and student and interface. Notions of interdependence and autonomy, involvement and responsibility for learning, make up the new educational paradigm, which aims to establish good electronically mediated educational practices and centered on the student. Therefore, the teaching style adopted by the tutor (Lévy, 1999) is more important than the tools used in electronic distance education, when it encourages the "collective intelligence" of student groups, guides the virtual learning process, and fosters the spirit to investigate, select, and organize information, manage resources in a timely fashion, and build knowledge in an autonomous way.

It seems appropriate that tutors be able to advise and manage (Salinas, 1999) the learning environment in a flexible manner, so that the students use the technological- educational resources in the development of collaborative experiences, with a monitoring of student progress, provide feedback to support their work, and offer real opportunities for growth.

## THE TUTOR'S ROLE IN THE FUTURE

The tutor is one of the key pieces of an educational program with ICT. Therefore, he/she should strengthen this virtual context from various aspects and especially in terms of a sociocultural viewpoint, as they inscribe within it a rich mediated socioeducational dialogue, where the learning and interactive and reflective implementation will take place.

The tutorials are a territory where the various trends are in conflict, as in any socioeducational situation. They represent tensions between the maintenance and reproduction of traditional patterns of valuation, thought, and organization, and the introduction of innovations and changes related to the same.

If the socioeducational trend is the deformalization of the educational processes and relationships a they are replaced by flexible and diversified, open, personalized, and democratic models (Fullan, 2002), the configuration and the continuous review of the tutorial actions in general and within the non-conventional and electronic educational systems in particular will present major challenges and dilemmas.

Among the characteristics of sociohistorical and technological acceleration, with the rapid production, accumulation, and rethinking of scientific-technological knowledge, learning is projected with increasing force as a process continued throughout life. This is why, it will be necessary to not only improve technological skills in the tutorial roles,but also consider core aspects of their training related reflective decision-making, of apractical and interdisciplinary nature.

By adhering to critical theory, which rejects the neutrality of technology and instead argues that the technological rationality has become a political rationality, it is understood that the social conflict of an online technological distance education system must be addressed, for its understanding and fair projection from a pluridisciplinary, explanatory, and predictive perspective. Critical theory shows how, in a way unseen, values and interests are sedimented through rules and procedures, tools and artifacts to describe, explain, and thus revise the, very, little, or un-representative forces in the pursuit of power and the advantages that characterize a dominant hegemony, as a single thought.

In any technological-educational program we should keep in mind that technology is not a destination, but a setting of conflict in the power struggle and, finally, where many of the options or civilizing alternatives are debated.

*Chapter 8*

# WHICH ELECTRONIC DISTANCE EDUCATION IS APPROPRIATE FOR AN ALTERNATIVE KNOWLEDGE SOCIETY? ANTICIPATING THE FUTURE

> "Sooner or later, served daily with the evidence of our interdependence, we will have to realize that no one can claim the earth, nor any part of it… What is in our hands is to decide whether our common destiny will end in mutual destruction or generate solidarity of views, goals and actions. Beyond our diverse religious or political beliefs, often very different, and sometimes fiercely opposing, we all want to live with dignity and without fear, with no humiliation, and to be allowed to pursue happiness. This is a common ground so firm and broad enough on which to begin building solidarity of action and conception."
>
> Zygmunt Bauman

What a great social, cultural, and moral challenge for education in the knowledge society and in the context of globalization, which seems to lack the "ethical compass" to rescue the notion of education in itself and in all the forms and formats it appears in our contemporary society!

Effective responses must be global and depend on the generation and development of sociopolitical scenes of training forces, of *creative synthesis*, which invigorate committed social interaction and participation –which defines the maturity of a society- to overcome difficulties which are still unknown or unimagined. These questions must be backed up in their resolution, as a central goal, by the educational processes.

What does an education that will produce a *creative synthesis* involve? It involves thinking that the model of incommensurability, seeking explanations for the shift to new paradigms, is theoretically weak and counterproductive from a practical point of view. We must recognize that the dimensions of analysis are neither stable nor universal nor uniform; that there is a need for interdependence and complex overlapping of categories, concepts and methodologies to resort to, so as to enable the epistemological and sociological analysis.

This would mean that the phenomenon of cultural fragmentation mentioned throughout this work, would not necessarily be painful but could be, contradictorily, liberating. Or, when referring to the *hybridism* of electronic educational programs, although we recognize that they reflect a certain "impurity", the convergence of a *mix* or technological juxtaposition, it is noteworthy that these proposals re-create and appropriate -from a broader cultural context- of phenomena and relationships existing in current social and discursive structures.

Visualizing *diversity* does not suppress but stress the need to integrate, through the capitalization of strengths, various proposals enriched from the formulation of values and criteria, which in turn should serve as a framework for mediations for the consideration and respect for the "social and cultural differences".

It would seem that pragmatic fertility in these analysis -in our case referred to a sociology and prospective of distance education-, regarding the relevance of the discourse, rather than the ontological purity would be a viable basis to come up with creative synthesis, and thus, which electronic distance education is needed, for which knowledge society.

A course must be found, anticipated, and charted, to enter the twenty-first century, which will be impossible without recognizing that knowledge -and this points to all human actions- is shaped from rhetorical, political, and ethical acts, which emphasize some characteristics and properties and obscure others, affirm the contingency of its value and the need to understand and appropriate it, even more so in today's world where knowledge is privileged as a central processing resource. In other words, it takes a lot of education to ask unprecedented questions and create synthesis.

## Which Kind of Education for which Knowledge Society?

There are good electronic news and also contradictory and problematic aspects in thinking and developing training proposals for the new cultural-historical times, in an egalitarian way and "lifelong learning", calling on ICT as media and languages that are quickly and constantly renewed.

Contents and forms of knowledge such as the existing technologies have an expiration date. The state of insecurity appears in the constant search in various facets of life: this reality is intersected not only by Internet, but also by the manufacture of products, the mobility of travel, health care, communication with others, recreation, research, and the development of scientific and technological knowledge.

Learning occurs and is renewed in the course of a lifetime, which is why all knowledge should be flexible, because it is constant renewal and reconstruction. The world has changed a lot and will continue to change: education does not only entail passing subjects nor doe sit only take place within the walls of a school. The knowledge needed to survive in today's world of knowledge is, above all, tacit; it intersects daily practice; it is obtained in factual and virtual interaction; it is confronted in a shared experience, without much awareness of the fact that it is acquired, improved, re-created … This experiential knowledge should be combined with the theoretical and abstract to provide tools to children and young adults and adults to face,with relative guarantees, the problem-solving opportunities that life presents to them.

The production and distribution of knowledge has a cultural, social and cognitive, as well as economic cost , for countries and for individuals and groups. Without a commitment in these areas, as well as a sustained financial support, no education and research center of the country will be able to respond to the challenges posed by the emergence of the knowledge society. However, before this can take place, a change is needed in the *why* and *what for* it is learned, in *what* is taught and *how* it is taught, which would redefine the mission of the learning and therefore reconsider its meaning in the context of progressive "creative synthesis". Moreover, everything is reformulated, including, the roles of the teachers, students, and content: Einstein –an example of a bad student, said that the important thing is to askourselves questions, to which we add: inthe exchange with others (or collaborative work and virtual learning communities), the synergistic possibilities of problem-solving are increased.

## WHICH IS THE ALTERNATIVE KNOWLEDGE SOCIETY?

This question arises in reference to the new and ubiquitous technological paradigm of a knowledge society, where the "innovative capacity", in terms of the symbolic capital perceived as relevant and effective value, should overcome stages of inequity in many regions and sectors of the world regarding what is offered by hegemonic societies as a "model to be adopted" for a knowledge society.

To make lifelong learning a reality, with and for the full training of the emerging citizenry in the network society of information flows, the digital culture of the twenty-first century and knowledge, it is necessary to overcome the limits to access and "infoexclusion" ofindividuals, groups, and organizations, which as "lost, not considered, or wasted attributes" should be socially recovered or restored, through conscious efforts, sociopolitical decisions, and a practice of formative experiences, today mediated by ICT.

The question is *which is, what kind of knowledge society is being built, are we shifting towards or leading to*; a question needed to clarify several points: what kind of knowledge was there before, is there now, and which is the desired/required knowledge to configure the society that the current times call for. Among other features, this will depend on various factors, including: recognizing the symbolic language and technological formats of ICT and the socioelectronic networks, the economic and social needs of the context and the reasons for which they are on the rise and develop (or not), and the political-cultural decisions of the organizational settings that contribute (or not) to a scientific and technological development of the medium in question, its support, and consolidation.

Referring to an alternative knowledge society involves considering different variables in interdependence for its configuration. Honest and realistic decisions should be made to ensure, through sociopolitical goodwill based on consensus and strategic planning, self-sustaining future projections. An alternative knowledge society aims at equal sociocultural and economic-formative opportunities of an entire population. This will require investment in education at all levels, in science and technology, research and development, just to name the most prominent areas.

Online distance education with ICT could become a proposal of choice. It involves a proposal that combines an interdiscipline for the study-work in this field -as pointed out- and at the same time, a strengthened agreement of committed sectoral policies (with the least possible amount of double meanings, ambivalence, and contradictions) in an articulation ofsystemic-holistic "creative synthesis" in response to local present and future deficits and needs within a glocal framework.

Distance education is part of the continuum which today involves the training of individuals, groups, and organizations, for which it will be necessary to establish guidelines for safe investments in technological infrastructure and telecommunications, which cannot be delayed, in order to achieve an equal coverage and access for both remote or urban areas, with low costs. This will contribute to the slow work of creating awareness about what socio-technological mediations involve for education, especially with an appropriation of ICT.

Changes in the information and knowledge society make a genuine democratization with equity and quality an unavoidable issue. The horizontal and mutable structure of the Internet stirs up issues and intellectuals authorities in an anonymous, "glocal" (global + local), fast, non-hierarchical and temporary way in its results, unlike the past knowledge, originating from qualified universities, of universal pretensions, given by a vertical andhierarchical accumulation of knowledge that reached those who accessed it in a stratified way to its precincts.

With ICT and the Internet processes and products have appeared which correspond to other productions, that shape other ideas, which, among other factors, not only have more to do with trial and error but with the breakdown of the stiff scholar of intellectual authority, with new ways of exercising knowledge, and, above all, with other opportunities for participation.

Referring to an alternative knowledge society means that the appropriation of ICT servesto enhance awareness and personal and group democratic expression, as well as inscribing efforts in the sociopolitical and discoursive sphere through an articulation and application of ICT in lifelong learning, as a synergistic, open, and utopian concept.

Building an *alternative knowledge society of adigital culture* would require:

- A *viable and sustainable* development, as an open and continuous process of adaptation to different articulations ("creative synthesis") and successive and unpredictable changes, which should emerge from the cultural force and specificity through dialogue -not imitation- with other cultures;
- A *discussion of multidisciplinary approach* on the global and local social reality, about what is cybersociocultural;
- A *critical and ethical* perspective for a transversal dialogue, with unprecedented questions, towards a reflection, analysis, and reprocessing of alternative proposals.

Within a macro view, it is insisted(Carr, 1993) that these searches be formed as ethical activities that lead to social transformation. Therefore, we are dealing with the field of *sociotechnological action-research*, which must enquire about the society that we want to build. With this responsibility, there is a tendency towards the redirection of the current scientific and technological research as a central constructive element and as a strategy whichresponds in a meaningful way to a new or different information and knowledge society.

The alternative knowledge society is the society of *equity ethics* in the creation, distribution, and use of resources within an intragenerational and intergenerational sustainable balance. It is the society of *lifelong learning*, as the current times call for, which stimulates and strengthens the expression of identity, which should not be separated from a culture of dialogue and criticism of ethnocentrism and xenophobia. The challenge is a proposal for broad representation with equal access to achieve an infoinclusión and expression of all existing social practices beyond those who have produced them; in other words, those who designed and assisted in their preparation.

The alternative knowledge society is inscribed, therefore, within a *communicative-rationality* (Habermas, 1989) so as to allow the symbolic resignificación of all languages, technological supports and formats, which are today in digital convergence with ICT and the material appropriation of all media and mediators in the interaction and navigation, to absorb and synthesize the intercultural differences in "glocal" contexts.

In addition to the previous question about what kind of knowledge society, another question arises: Is the knowledge society a political-economic tool, a construct, or simply an empty concept? As we are dealing with sociological practices to dismantle the established global power in its dealings with cultural programs, as well as online distance education, it is necessary for the new profile:

- To recognize the diversity of cultures and people with different interests, their practices, ideas, values, social meanings, which that have led them to *coexist* (Touraine, 1997) within a wide range of sociocultural possibilities that mark telematic change;
- To overcome digital exclusion, various contradictions and gaps, through the promotion of awareness and training in new sociocultural and productive activities;
- To strengthen the processes of protagonist anticipation and participation through a social and educational practice that promotes the collective construction in the long-term in cooperation, dialogue, and sustained emotional empathy.

These are great challenges for social thinkers, sociologists, political scientists, philosophers, educators, anthropologists, systems analysts, economists, etc., who should explore, deepen, combine, and reinterpret the understanding of the historical, philosophical, sociopolitical, anthropological, economic, educational, and cultural contents, what was done by the Frankfurt School, towards a recovery and reprocessing of new theories which global change calls for.

This critical proposal would exceed the "official and hidden stories" within a new hypersociology which studies and reviews socially established "collective expectations", (Bourdieu, 1991), through informational embodiment, which increasingly penetrate through a cyberinfrastructure all human activities. At the same time, beliefs and concepts, values and attitudes, historically dragged forth, would be resemantified, some of which concerning life and the world, science and technology in general, are still in force.

If the knowledge society is characterized by the centrality of the settings of the intangibles, invisible technologies (or thought strategies in our minds or *mindware*, without which any hardware and software of the ICT could not operate), it is necessary to configure alternatives of a meaningful and egalitarian nature to develop in individuals, groups, and organizations a greater productivity and reflexivity (Giddens, 1997) of a cosmopolitan (but not hegemonic-conqueror) profile and with an inclusive logic that overcomes what is sectarian and exclusive as shown by the global marketplace.

## The Shift to an Alternative Sociotechnological Educational Paradigm

The metaphor that is presented to define the framework of thought and action for the shift to an alternative sociotechnological educational paradigm refers to the configurations of creative (conceptual and methodological) synthesis, to many comparable to a rhizome. "A rhizome as a subterranean stem is absolutely different from roots and radicles. Bulbs and tubers are rhizomes [...] The rhizome itself assumes very diverse forms, ramified s urface extension in all directions to concretion into bulbs and tubers [...] the rhizome connects any point to any other point and [...] this is very different from the tree or root, which plots a point, fixes an order".

The "imagining" of the rhizome is evident in a paradigmatic way in the language/s where there are connections between semiotic chains and/or technological networks, such as organizations of power depending on the circumstances related to the arts, sciences, technology, and social contexts. A semiotic chain is like a tuber that accumulates very different acts, not just linguistic-communicational ones, but also perceptive, mimetic, social, and cognitive ones. There is no language in itself, nor linguistic truths, but rather a particular set of dialects, argots, jargon, and specialized language as "a power takeover by a dominant language within a political multiplicity" (Deleuze).

The shift towards an alternative social, technological, and educational paradigm is based on a rhizomatic concept of sustainable development, which despite its unpredictability, wouldcombine new energy sources, greater effectiveness in the selection and use of resources, the production and sustainable consumption, within an environmental and ethical dimension of life. This dimension would not only respond to "global-fundamentalist-mercantile- neoliberal" trends which have been carried over since the mid-twentieth century, as profit-seeking –it´s only goal-without assuming social responsibility of any organization or enterprise.

In this way, education should be devised as a space of equality and social mobility with equity, as a social right that overcomes sociocultural segregation. A new educational paradigm for an alternative knowledge society should include, among others, the following points:

1. the establishment and restatement of images of the world that recognize and uphold education as a privileged social right so as to achieve social and political equality and equity, within a planetary multi/interculturalism, which emphasizes respect for individual and collective, political, economic, educational-cultural, and ecological rightsin dignity for all human beings;
2. the training of leaders in accordance with the complexity of the structure of life today, specialists in very different and varied professions within democratic frameworks as a means to organize societies in a fair, ethical and dignified way;
3. understanding that science and technology are nothing more than social processes and products that allow the apprehension of reality through non-neutral human activity, which is why we should be aware of the, wanted or unwanted, consequences that their development generates. The scientific-technological activity which is ethically committed to life would transform the logic of sociotechnological capitalist

change- subject to the principle of a greater accumulation and concentration of capital- towards a new principle of satisfaction of human needs with a humanist vocation.

The dimensions of education within the new sociotechnological educational paradigm proposed are those that relate primarily with the political-cultural and socioeconomic spheres, namely:

a) Political-cultural, given by a legitimization of power for the formation of innovative frameworks.

   Considering education as a social right amplifies and reformulates the competency development pedagogical model, which reduces the educational responsibility to helping individuals join the job market, with their respective professional success or failure, regardless of the social location and share of power of individuals and groups, in other words, ignoring the existence of an unequal and exclusive sociohistorical context that predetermines them.

b) Socioeconomic, to form a skilled and creative labor force.

   The need to train a workforce that will promote the development of science and technology, aimed at transforming and improving products and processes in their design and distribution, makes education responsible for synthesizing and projecting scientific-technological progress, in higher education institutions and universities, laboratories and research centers to train the suitable specialists.

## What Is the Alternative?

Science and technology with their protagonists must articulate bridges between the scientific-technological knowledge and everyday life, to integrate ideas and build opportunities for sociocultural development towards a comprehensive development of individuals and, especially, lead to an understanding of the complex relationship between the world of major global informational flows and this everyday life.

While the information society accentuates the technological aspect of ICT, the specificity of an alternative model of development of "a" knowledge society (not only would there be several, but also different or alternative ones) is the action of knowledge in one's own knowledge, or deepening of knowledge within knowledge, as the principal engine of productivity and creativity leading to a sustained and self-sustainable development by creativity and social interaction, which in the twenty-first century are telematic.

So, what is the profile of the knowledge society as an alternative option and what would be the role of ICT in it?

In the alternative knowledge society, ICT promote and speed up communication, transform and increase productivity, and overcome a local vision of reality within the global context. For the structuring and dynamics of this "social alternative", the contributions of socioconstructivism and social connectivism (Siemmens, 2004) are proposed aimed at the training of a full citizenship. This involves:

- On the one hand, an attitudinal and procedural training for technical mastery and handling of each technology which will enable the search, selection, analysis, understanding,and re-creation of the enormous and fast amount of information accessed through ICT, with reflective values and realistic and critical attitudes. Giving a value to the media, mediators, and technological mediations in everyday life means recognizing them not only as resources for consumption or leisure, but also as potential environments for expression and communication.
- On the other hand, the practice of solidarity, and participation through technological mediations within the groups and communities. It is about viewing technology and ICT from a *substantive* perspective, with a humanizing and humanizador sense for local appropriationof technologies and the re-creation of information, towards understanding and respect for different cultural values -involved in the production of knowledge-, which overcome practices of linear transfer.

ICT and their networks can contribute to shaping and development of individuals and communities, in other words, the entire citizenry, who learn together, in order to pass from the stage of transmitted information and individualistic learning to the production and social use of knowledge shared through collaborative or group learning.

Within this context it is thought that an *alternative knowledge society* would answer to the irreversible changes introduced in human productivity in all areas of knowledge within a framework of a different "human ecology and sociocultural mapping". It involves overcoming the hegemonic project of ICT, in form, content, and mission, to make way for different projects of various formats of virtual interaction, where spaces, worlds, multiple contexts, and so on, are recreated, with individual designs and the generation of opportunities for equitable and relevant interaction.

Giving another meaning to the production, distribution, and social use of information in an alternative knowledge society is a controversial issue due to the resemantification of technology and ICT, in other words, regard them as mental tools that enhance ideas, and not only artifacts. It means recognizing that they enclose various capitals: economic (because they are assets), social (involving networks of socioelectronic relationships), and cultural (with general and specialized knowledge), which is what establishes a real difference in terms of producing a cultural *change*.

We will have to give a radically new direction to ICT, so that they can be useful to people and not vice versa (Dertouzos, 2002). This is a fundamental change in order to exploit the Web, the Internet, and new devices, as we try to see beyond their instrumental implementation and also overcome the feeling of ambivalence and confusion in users and specialists in terms of their potential. These are fully justified doubts, since this new and exciting technology, help us "be inbetter conditions" or feel, very often, a growing frustration? Without an absolutely new and resignifying approach to infotelematics, confusion will worsen the current state of devices and the information revolution will remain unfinished (Dertouzos, 2002).

The approach in cuestion is called (Dertouzos, 2002) "human-centered computers": computer and telematic systems must focus on the needs and abilities of individuals and groups, instead of bowing to their incomprehensible mechanical details. It is not about only making more "intelligent" or more "user friendly" computers and networks -because their potential is unpredictable, besides being huge-, nor only overcoming gaps in order to reach more people with great coverage, but to promote systems focused on genuine human needs.

It would seem that the challenge is to "finish the unfinished revolution" (Dertouzos, 2002). If information technology is ubiquitous and intersects life without being noticed, the question is: will we be in better conditions? Or will there only be an increase in efficiency and productivity? If ICT save time, what will be done with all the time saved? Will be work harder and in a uniform way? Will computers help us to be more humane? Or will humanity drown in greater and faster amounts of information? What are the benefits? Will there be a qualitatively new social change, a new social order?

Proposing the construction of a solidarity in action and design aims at least to think of a (evolutionary?, revolutionary?) reformulation of the creation (historical-sociocultural re-creation?) of knowledge, which requires exploring the possibilities of overcoming the infointoxication given by the current overwhelming excess of information in all areas of knowledge and practice.

## Ways of Knowledge

The knowledge society proposed as an alternative option requires acknowledging endless unknowns and being open to legitimize other ways of knowing or producing knowledge, namely:

1. Changing the view of science with a mathematical basis for a holistic and comprehensive interdisciplinary vision, where the hermeneutic approach is the guide for the investigation ofknowledge. Knowing would be like being in possession of truth, and the truth is a process with actions to reveal. The alternative science would rely on a systemic ontology where the center of knowledge lies in the interrelationships of the phenomena it explains. The dialectical understanding of the object and subject is caused in the sociohistorical context to arrive at provisional theoretical practical interpretations while investigating. The ontological principles, the metacommunication, and self-reference allow the critically reflective spirit to be transmitted in the processes of mass communication to disseminate the constant questioning and analysis of the phenomena being studied.
2. The continuing recursive evolution maintains the relationship of what is produced and who produces it, without seeking in reality an absolute or finalexplanation of what was produced. The postmodernistas criticize the previous modernist paradigm and reject all objective and absolute control of science in the production of knowledge, while leaving open the interdisciplinary road as an alternative mechanism for socio-historical-constructivist research, not only for scientific and technological development, but for the comprehensin of the phenomena, the advances of human understanding, and the self-sustaining development within the social structures.
3. The recognition of the influence of everyday knowledge in interpretations and actions of lay individuals or experts. It is the knowledge that is acquired in daily experience, consisting of weak or erroneous conceptions, unrelated, superficial, not

systematic, and uncritical knowledge. Although it changes its content and scope depending on the times and the belonging to different social levels, its centrality is recognizable.

4. Considering *technologicalknowledge* with its own existence and to a great extent, its tacit nature, overcomes the long accepted scientificist conceptualization of the position of "technology = applied science" -still in discussion- so as to recognize the non scientific components of technological knowledge as a system of thought and specific action independent from science. There are also differences with the technical know-how, which is random, rectified, and procedural, while scientific knowledge is formal and universal.

   Technological thought is different then basically from the scientific in the technological ideas that are captured in the "design" –later implemented by techniques- to produce hard devices (machinery and equipment) and soft processual systems (instructional systems such as telematics). The technological knowledge incorporates the dimensions of direct observation and the systematic experience work under various conditions and/or circumstances at first hand, as well as carefully designed systematic actions (though not scientific) and the use of experiential methods. Moreover, it enhances the understanding of good faith by empirical scrutiny procedures and, above all, intuition and imagination (implicit modes of an individual which are not derived from a scientific understanding), about what could be the more appropriate design, the procedure, or application to carry out or complete a technological task.
5. The phenomenological methodology (or "ethnomethodology") addresses and makes explicit the truth of the primary experience of the social world. The aprehesion of the social world as a natural world through hermeneutics builds relationships that structure objective practices and representations of the same. In particular, the primary practical knowledge of the familiar world and tacitly assumed presumptions shape the social world as an obvious (Bourdieu, 1972). The social practice is perceived as pure creativity from the dialectical relationship and synthesis between the subject and object where there is no rupture between "practical" knowledge and "scientific" knowledge of social phenomena. Subjectivism and objectivism are two polar ways of knowing through practices with creativity and spontaneity. For the first position, it is the result of free creativity subjects practice with technology, while for the second alternative, it is the necessary outcome of the various objective conditionings of models, structures, etc.., underlying technology.
6. The centrality of -factual and virtual- networks of knowledge within the complex and contradictory characteristics of the systems of knowledge production in general, and in particular, science and technology, linked to the social environment, require organizational designs and research programs that are flexible and adaptable to unpredictable changes.

However, some also insist (Bourdieu, Chamboredon and Passeron, 2002) on the need of a break from the immediate and "familiar" representations of social life as a condition for genuine social science, which, considering the sociological tradition from Marx to Durkheim, upholds the constitution of the social phenomenon as an objective reality that transcends the will of the subject. It helps to understand, thus, that the pedagogical discourse, in all its forms, is permeated with subjectivity; it does not lose sight of the social practices which, by definition, are inscribed within a social space identified as a greater political context.

In this way, the attention in favor of an epistemological rupture from the representations of common sense does not involve bringing the sociological explanation to the field of objectivism, typical of a certain simple empiricism and of "ethical neutrality". It involves the *juxtaposition* of the fictitious and arbitrary opposition of subjectivists and objectivists (Bourdieu, Chamboredon and Passeron, 2002). It resorts to intermediating, articulated, and mediating concepts between the subjective and the objective, as "alignment", "attitude", or "*ethos*", and considers the way of knowing from a system of relations that encompasses the measurable regularities of the objective conditions relations, and the singular relations that subjects maintain in their contextualized existence.

The contributions set forth are central within a sociological analysis of education mediated by technology. The rupture represented by this analysis is directed toward the proposal of a society in ongoing review of its parts and its dynamics, which means we must carry out an evaluative and critical analysis of what is "artifactual" and informational. Therefore, any attempt to consider education in general, and the one mediated by technology in particular from a sociological point of view, leads to a practice of a sociology of education that builds knowledge in a situated, shared, and distributed way.

It may be worthwhile to recall a diagnosis (Marcuse, 1968) where alienation via media that massified and stupified was denounced, which stimulated consumerism, which converted a potentially free man into a "one-dimensional man" incapable of critical thinking and countercultural attitudes. To overcome this, the individual should understand the mechanism and rigorous management of the technological-cultural hybridization which penetrates all the phenomena of daily life.

Consequently, the social and educational events that are presented in the converging interaction of knowledge mediated by ubiquitous technology need to be "epistemologically monitored" (Bachelard, 1979). These are times of practising a "sociological imagination" (Wright Mills, 1977) to re-create alternatives, in our case, of models of knowledge society which could otherwise be adapted to the current technological realities.

This reconstruction, which is replicated in a proposal of alternative knowledge society, involves reviewing the conceptual and methodological bases, as well as the organizational and operational, in our case, of distance education mediated by technology. It is necessary here to appeal to the symbolic sciences-since they argue that social life creates rules and representations, symbolic processes and products of situated, shared, and distributed interaction -and the critical sciences –which require the contrast, demystification, and deconstruction of social facts, including information flows.

In connection with what is *conceptual* and *methodological*, we should consider mediators and mediations where ICT are the basis of the information society and digital culture. In terms of what is *organizational and operational*, we should consider the sociocultural agents and agencies of the mass media and ICT in general, manifested in online distance education programs and materials in particular, since they are the ones that pilot the network society and society of flows on a daily basis.

Arguing, as do Bourdieu, Chamboredon and Passeron (2002) –perhaps in a mechanical way- that education issues are not independent of the processes of reproduction of the social order, involves placing these phenomena within a technological space, today of ICT. For this reason, the sociology of education should assume the specific role of science considered as a bridge in the relations between the cultural reproduction and social change (Bourdieu, 1978). The break with spontaneous performances that would suggest the explanation of the educational fact mediated by ICT represents a socio-historical-epistemological starting point suitable to support the stated discourse. Therefore, its effects in the realm of politics are inevitable.

This context of sociological reflection of the digital and global environments, of the twenty-first century, deserves to be discussed and criticized, that is, it should not be subject to the ideas of an established order.

In other words, so domination does not continue legitimizing the undisputed aspects of their positions, it is necessary to legitimize the conflict as an opportunity or space of mature confrontation between various positions, where everyone can talk and understand, learn and grow ... and deploy reflexivity, which represents the sociological task by definition (Bourdieu, 1990).

We believe in a potential and real, intelligent use (Fainholc, 2004) of new technologies to generate alternative sociocultural environments, and thus, digital learning that possesses a new *meaning* for individuals and groups, which are self-regulators of the training process –by a mediated pedagogical discursive work- commensurate with the needs and dynamics of contemporary life. This is a timely and urgent debate to take into account; leaving it aside would cost each society or social group dearly; it would mean straying from the current cultural-historic times that call for more intelligence, lucidity, and reciprocity among people and regions.

## Distance Education, a Producer of Culture and Knowledge

To understand the contribution that the sociology of education makes to the modality of distance education, it is necessary to visualize not only the rooting of the production and use of knowledge within society. "The men of a culture, through their way of knowledge, produce theculture that in turn produces its way of knowing. Culture generates the knowledge that re-creates culture. Knowledge depends on many sociocultural conditions and conditions the change of these conditions" (Morin, Watzlawick and Krieg, 1994).

Considering to what extent knowledge is produced by a culture depends on recognizing what culture it is inscribed within. The field of educational technology, in which electronic modality of distance education is inscribed, requires a careful resignification of its founding assumptions, not only because of their theoretical and practical implications, but so as to not lose sight of the cultural perspective of what is proposed. Some assumptions:

a) It is necessary to strengthen the frameworks of diversity in order to overcome ethnocentrism and promote participation and interactivity, tailored to the needs of settings and actors in specific projects and materials;
b) To structure technological-educational mediations for the production of knowledge and culture, as the search for relationships of understanding on the part of individuals who learn, preferably in a collaborative, close or remote way in networks;

c) To bring about the linking between theory-practice and practice-theory in action-research (search, confrontation, and recreation) of processes and products, to deepen the knowledge society through contextualized programs of production of knowledge and culture.

The goal is to devise the socioeducationaldistance practice with ICT of technological and cultural knowledge production as an open space, ofcritical reflection and investigation of any proposal mediated by training projects and materials (formal, non-formal and informal) increasingly articulated with ICT.

Among the most outstanding bases, applicable to strategic project planning, telematic products, collaborative virtual simulations, and others, the following criteria are listed, useful triggers for a prospective.

A. Practical pedagogy of communicative, reconstructive, and critical ethics, of respect for multicultural diversity for the solidary coexistence of the citizenry.
B. Appropriation of technological resources to human scale, promoting equity, equal participation, and personal and collective self-mastery.
C. Resignification of uncertainty to overcome various fragmentations and expansion of reflection and lucidity along with other forms of theoretical and practical thinking.
D. Epistemological demystification in interactive and interconnective navigation to strengthen critical reading and understanding of the respect for diversity in hermeneutical wagers.
E. Construction of the "glocal telematic"through meaningful mediations-negotiations and valuable for sociocognitive development in the everyday practice of the citizenry.
F. Development of autonomous morality and rational and mature self-regulation in metatechnical educational contexts.

The design of new settings for the social sciences and therefore for future training in the format of the electronic distance education (pure or blended) defies scenes and actors with movements to anticipate future problem-solving situations, still unimaginable. Within this framework, the planning of settings should:

1. Define their reach: setting the time frame and magnitude of the analysis, with which products, pointing to which geographic areas, technologies, etc..; conducting good diagnosis of the present situation, which involves *practices of analysis*; determine the most important interest groups in order to identify their current roles, interests and positions of power, for example, presenting a fact and imagining the consequences in five years times...
2. Recognize trends: trying to establish which will be the political, economic, social, cultural and legal course that will affect the issues identified in determining the scope; identify key uncertainties. This involves:
    - *Practices of simulation* of contexts and actors: imagining oneself as the protagonist of a process, where he/she is the only one able to give a solution to the situation.

- *Practices of prospection*: given a current fact, imagining its consequences within a year, prioritizing views.
- *Practices of inventiveness or creativity*: to formulate projects or anticipate paths of action. In other words: given a program, imagining situations of interaction we are not accustomed to.

This is a particularly interesting sociological production for the study the phenomena of distance education in the technological culture of the twenty-first century, whose very complexity requires overcoming obstacles in the shape of assumptions, carried over from earlier times, disguised by interests that want to remain hidden, without appealing to the task of searching for an explanation with some scientific prediction or prospective.

## WHAT DO WE EDUCATE FOR?

The problems posed by and posed to education are analyzed and discussed by all societies today. What do we educate for? Openness and access to information followed by the intelligent and reflective use of ICT should serve to eradicate ignorance, marginalization, and exclusion. Ignorance and freedom are mutually exclusive concepts, since those who ignore their options are unable to choose between them. Democratic participation is given and is the door to knowledge when knowledge is accessible and democratic.

However, the question that lies at the base, is the essence of the above-mentioned, and underlies the educational phenomenon is not always asked: what is the fundamental goal of the training of individuals and groups with ICT in electronic education programs?

So, *what do we educate for*? For every man and woman to become more of a person, in other words, enhance the ability to transmit and re-create to the new generations what is specific in human experience, drawing from every human being the best or most valuable things that characterize them as a person, that is, the moral and cultural subject is rescued.

We educate so that the destiny of the human being is amplified in the various electronic educational proposals, by strengthening *critical thinking* and to decide what to accept and believe, because information and ideas are evaluated in a self-regulated way. We arrive at, thus, an interpretation, analysis, inference, and explanation of the evidence, in its concepts, methodologies, and contexts on which judgements are based. In other words, it involves thinking about the validity of the understanding possessed and we re-think the world.

Critical thinking simultaneously makes use of critical *reasoning* and *methodological reflection*. The first is aimed at the analysis and evaluation of arguments or their reflective formulation. The second points to understandingand evaluating the purposes, assumptions, and procedures used in the search for truth or knowledge.

Being human involves the critical-reflective and methodological practice of thinking: Today technology helps enhance these activities if we are aware of this, plus access to connectivity and an orientation guide. In this way, the incorporation of ICT means going beyond the quest for efficiency, ease of use, having fun, and increasing labor productivity in the information society and digital culture.

The issue is to analyse whether these technologies can "do more" to improve humanity and contribute to, among other factors, shaping "better" people through their interaction.

There are several historically considered dimensions that involve "being human" (Dertouzos, 2002): the use of "reason" or rational thought, which is behind science and technology; the use of "feeling", which promotes the arts and humanities; the use of "faith", which helps explain the inexplicable; and the use of physical "action" or the acts that are carried out.

Thus, what is rational in the human being would benefit, because it forms the raw material of sciences and technologies, and thus allows greater access to information and better communication, among other features. The physical action would also benefit, because through the electronic automation of equipment and devices, there can be a more effective control (with all the risks that this entails), which is why a forecasting and planning of the future action is recommended.

With regard to feelings, one may communicate emotions in a virtual way (we laugh and cry when faced with a good story or movie that comes across the network) and one may enhance sensory perception by generating more brilliant colors and sounds, from a distance. Today, this is enhanced with the three-dimensional simulation avatars, which in a more or less superficial way, made possible by the "tyranny of shapes"- may cause emotions or make people feel more deeply.

Many argue that we face a cognitive-sociocultural and moral revolution which rethinks not only the dimensions of sociopolitical life, but also the configuration of new subjectivities within a life of fractal (or rhizomatic) edges, with epistemological, ethical, and cultural implications which are not fully identified and studied: let us only consider the unknown impacts of the virtual reality of Second Life, biotechnology, nanotechnology, new materials, etc.., inecology, intersubjectivity…

New technologies reformulate all frameworks and approaches of thought, feeling and action, of conceptual categorization, methodological procedures, and perceptual and emotional resignification, which lead to rethinking of the ways to understand human life, in the shaping of apersonality and in their social relationships.

## DESIGNING THE FUTURE

It means creating and anticipating today a range of futures as factual and electronic contexts or environments in a strategic way for decision-making and being prepared to deal with possible contingencies. By planning settings –an alternative method to better understand the future and, accordingly, more effectively adapt to changes-, a series of effective projections are obtained to master critical situations criss-crossed by different logics.

For Latin America, cultural environments appear in a mix of diverse hybridizations represented by the orality of popular culture (music, stories, jokes, and gossip, among others); the literate culture, which is still the most valued, although it presents reductionism; the audiovisual with radio, television, films; and the digital mass media (especially music in MP3 fomat, informal communication in chats and blogs, and multiplayer games for the youngest), all these formats subsumed in the language of the Internet.

When it comes to shaping an alternative knowledge society for emerging countries and complement, supplement, and counteract the "official" knowledge society, produced and widespread by the central countries, it is believed that the proposals of distance education, today with ICT, contribute to a strategic political setting of the no longer so distant future, which could: 1) overcome exclusion and/or supplement the supply of conventional education systems, alreadyanachronistic in relation to the cultural mutations presented by societies, and 2) deepen democratization as regards majorities, noting everyday subcultures, by offering opportunities to appropriate knowledge through new mediations in terms of media, languages, and narratives.

It helps, thus, to not ignore that, in certain sociocultural conditions, the possession of knowledge, a scientific discovery, the use of information, the invention of an idea, may become decisive acts, as innovative or transformers of sociohistorical praxis. It would involve recognizing that knowledge allows us to access and gives power. Therefore, just as an example, today genetic knowledge and nuclear knowledge reveal and involve power over life and death, respectively, as never before in the history of humanity.

Knowledge is linked to and conditioned, determined, and produced by all of the parties that structure culture, social organization, historical practice, as it also conditions, determines, and produces the same, which shows, in a fascinating way, the adventure ofthe current scientific-technological knowledge today.

While, on one hand, it is necessary to battle the social inequalities of infoexclusion, on the other hand, the commodification of higher education concerns us, namely in those high sectors which access sophisticated and elitist virtual postgraduate degrees.

ICTs are training tools, media, and spaces, and also powerful socioeconomic and cultural, individual and collective accelerators. Hence the need for universal access and use, namely as a door and product of an open knowledge or without restrictions or barriers for anyone with a corresponding digital, critical, committed and responsible literacy.

Although access and sensible use are overriding themes, there are previous questions such as: What are ICT for?; what role could ICT play with their open and unrestricted access to knowledge production in alternative knowledge societies, in other words more free, democratic, and egalitarian? (III Online Congress of the Observatory for CyberSociety, 2006). We should also consider what different ways of building knowledge are caused by technological mediation, to avoid simplifications by opposing – like Umberto Eco´s "apocalyptic and integrated"- what is harmful in the saturation of superficiality of the alienating image of ICT and the Internet, to the highest reflective concentration enabled by print materials without rescuing the empowerment of other sociocognitive activities given by the visual representation, remote dialogue, interactivity, and collaborative online production, which establish new ways of knowing through technology and ICT.

Higher education institutions play a central role in knowledge societies, in their functions of production, dissemination, research, and application of knowledge. Universities no longer respond to single models and their educational offer has been diversified to the extent that knowledge was specialized and deepened (in polytechnical schools, schools of engineering, business and management schools, research laboratories, among others ).

However, many times the public and private budgetary constraints have valued unconventional electronic modalities, with remote schools. Thus, appear the risks of a "commodification" of these services as markets for the sale of careers and higher education degrees (the so-called "mcdonaldization" of knowledge). Therefore, for the construction of knowledge societies, in the same way as it is necessary to promote digital equity, we will also have to deconstruct improvised and marketing-centered tendencies that eventually undermine the original mission of producing socially useful knowledge and raising the human condition through education in general, and higher education with ICT in particular.

## SOME CATEGORIES TO HELP US CONSIDER TOMORROW'S EDUCATION IN AN ALTERNATIVE KNOWLEDGE SOCIETY

Notwithstanding the promises of social equality through various utopias of our time: free trade intotal globalization and Internet´s cybersociety (Bunge, 2004), it seems to be these omens have not become a reality.An unbridled rise in consumerism has contributed to a disposable and liquid lifestyle (Bauman, 2006), while the computer utopia is leading people, as well as countries to a cultural uniformity by equalising connectivity (being connected to the Internet).

The growing inequality both between nations and among individuals and groups, with the consequent deterioration of living standards of the vast majority of humanity, faces enormous global problems, which, far from being solved, are compounded, namely (Bunge, 2004):

1. The increasingly intense and global economic dominance of hegemonic transnational corporations with the weakening of local economies and the power of ordinary people.
2. The political marginalization of the majorities disappointed with the traditional political parties, with a consequent weakening of ethical values and democratic ideals and the emergence of (violent) totalitarianism worldwide.
3. The growing environmental degradation, due to the absence of national and international regulations on central issues such as degradation of ecosystems, accelerating climate change, depletion of non-renewable natural resources (including energy), extinction of forests, use of pesticides and fertilizers, desertification, loss of biodiversity and cultural diversity without the type decision-making that would revert the situations described.
4. The continuous increase of armament and wars in certain areas; unemployment and emergence of new diseases.
5. The cultural disciplining provides ways of thinking, values, and aspirations of uniform distribution through advertising and "supermarketing", which shape the global hybrid culture.

While the idea and practice of interaction with the Internet has proved, through various empirical research, that it contributes to globally divide the "connected wealthy people" from the "disconnected poor people",as well as to segregate men and women, among other social differences; it also globalizes and spreads the cultural democracy –of both authentic and counterfeit goods- with popular access and use, the telematic revolution, at the same time, has been one of the forces that has caused the rise in global inequity. If this happens in the northern countries of the world, you may have an idea of how pronounced it is in the south, in LatinAmerica and Africa.

Incorporating the categories of analysis of *contradiction*, *codetermination*, *critical-reproduction*, *change*, *work*, and *praxis*, is still not common in the analysis of distance education programs and even less so from a sociological perspective of distance education. However, they are central to think and anticipate designs of an education mediated by technologies in the future; at the same time, other crucial categories should be articulated when it comes to conducting this kind of prospective. These would be:

1. *Education for sustainability, the survival of the speciesand full universalization of human rights*, by making citizens into promoters and active drivers of change in history, culture, and society.
2. *Inter/transdisciplinarity* for the epistemological consideration in the construction of knowledge, by including the categories of transculturality, interculturality and transversality,complexity and holism.
3. *Dialogue* within a reflective practice, considering the categories of analysis (Hegel´s phenomenology) of determination, contradiction, necessity, and possibility.
4. *An emerging citizenry in the global context*, which involves addressing the design of a socio-political-educational project for the participation and difference.
5. *Planetarization*, which means that education is for the world (or *ecopedagogy*); it involves overcoming the defense of private interests and values in the short term, and the realization that solidarity and global protection of biological and cultural diversity-through solidary sociopoliticalactions- constitute a prerequisite for a genuine training of individuals and groups.
6. *Sustainability*, although coming from the economic and ecological field, it is permanently installed in the of sociological and philosophical field education, considering a "sustainable education for survival of the planet".
7. *Virtuality*, for a distance learning with convincing scientific and inquisitive power, with the combination and intelligent use of a telematic rationality (information technology associated with telecommunications).
8. *Globalization* articulated with the local culture, which modifies politics, economy, culture, history, and thus education. The global and the local merge into a new reality: the glocal, where the role decentralized in small entities, in municipal governments, and the regime of collaboration of the network configurations is central to a relevant training practice.
9. Including new knowledge bases, actions, rules, or attitudes that suggest an autonomous and mature *interactiveprofessionalism*, for decision-making within a culture of cooperation, aid, and support, with critical reflection about the purpose and value of what we educate for, what is taught, and how it is taught in the virtual training proposals.

Will we be able to maintain this proposal ethical outline based on producing shared knowledge enabled by ICT within a collaborative sociocultural and non-competitive project? Or, rather, are we witnessing the (re)birth of an (old) new model of cooperative knowledge that can aspire to break the hegemony of a market predator based on taking advantage of the existing barriers in the horizontal expansion of knowledge?

"Those who do not investigate reality can not aspire to repair it. Those who do not plan on the basis of sound knowledge become slaves of the plans of others. And those who do not swim against the tide are dragged into the anonymous ocean."

We are dealing with socioformative challenges of great commitment: persevering, investing, and inscribing the educational efforts in general and those which are online in particular, in the sociopolitical field of teaching and learning to ask questions. The question, the only search trigger, characterizes the human species, unlike the answers, which although they shape the profiles of individuals and objects in the long or short term, they are fragile and temporary. The question involves engaging in analyzing and experimenting. This is central and is the most important mark in the various social organizations in order to understand and articulate technologies and ICT in an appropriate manner to specific settings and actors. We aim, thus, at the materialization of lifelong learning, as a synergistic, open, and utopian concept, for the entire citizenry who will be responsible for (re) building a knowledge society.

# INDEX

## A

## B



## C

## F

## I

## N

## O



## P

## Q



## R

## S

## T



## U

## V



## W



## X



## Y